Atlas of World Architecture

DESIGN MEDIA PUBLISHING LIMITED

©2010 by Design Media Publishing Limited
This edition published in July 2011

Design Media Publishing Limited
20/F Manulife Tower
169 Electric Rd, North Point
Hong Kong
Tel: 00852-28672587
Fax: 00852-25050411
E-mail: Kevinchoy@designmediahk.com
www.designmediahk.com

Editing: "Atlas of World Architecture" Team
Proofreading: Maggie Wang
Design/Layout: Yang Wu

ISBN 978-988-19739-7-9

Printed in China

Preface

Buildings are now on the drawing board and they are nothing like the places we may recall from our childhood. New materials and new technologies are reshaping the way we build. At the same time, many architects and designers are also drawing upon ancient materials and building techniques but interpret them in modern ways. With the advanced development of economy and diversity of social life as well as increased sensitivity to the environment, architecture design is far from the primitive forms and styles; it is on the way to be comfortable, economical and rustically beautiful.

The book *Atlas of World Architecture*, with 250 projects selected, is a detailed and comprehensive portrayal of the best and latest architecture projects from six continents of more than fifty countries. Designers can be inspired a lot to search a balance between the overwhelmingly globalised trend and the increasingly personalised feature.

It offers readers a visual feast with the collection of world's most classic architecture projects and is categorised into ten parts, including Cultural, Commercial, Hospital, Educational, Corporate, Residential, Hotel, Transportation, Recreational and Complex architecture. Each project is illustrated with real photos, plans and a text. In addition, each geographic region is distinguished by a different colour-code. We firmly believe and hope it will serve as a source of pleasure and inspiration to all its readers.

Featured with its timeliness, globalisation, regionalisation, and professionalisation, it will help readers from all over the world to find inspiration and approach new materials and the cultural heritage.

Location of the selected projects of *Atlas of World Architecture*

1. Canada	8. Norway	15. Spain
2. USA	9. Finland	16. France
3. Mexico	10. UK	17. The Netherlands
4. Colombia	11. Denmark	18. Luxembourg
5. Chile	12. Germany	19. Switzerland
6. Brazil	13. Poland	20. Italy
7. Iceland	14. Portugal	21. Austria

Contents

Daytime view

The Belleville Public Library and John M Parrott Art Gallery

The new Belleville Public Library not only provides resources for research and recreation; it is also a cultural and community destination. At 38,000 sf, the building includes a library, art galleries, meeting rooms, and a café as well as a significant outdoor public space. A large plaza frames the rotunda building, welcoming people from Campbell and Pinnacle Streets.

Interpretative and flexible spaces are at the heart of the architectural design of the building's programmatic elements. A rectangular element houses the galleries, library stacks, lounges and study spaces while the circular element – the rotunda – is the public hub of the library and plaza that includes the entrance, gift shop and street café. The third floor gallery entered from the rotunda connects the building activities vertically and increases the diversity of the building programme. The library provides both quiet spaces for contemplation and study as well as dynamic light–filled open spaces for other social activities.

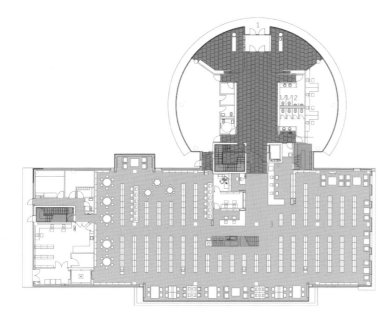

1. entrance
2. WC
3. reading room

Night view

Entrance

Reading room

Completion Date: 2006

Architect: Zeidler Partnership Architects

Hilton Baltimore Convention Centre Hotel

The hotel is poised to play a key role in the continued success of the Pratt Street and Inner Harbour Entertainment and Convention Centre District. To take advantage of this unique position, the design team aimed to create and enhance the pedestrian experience that flows from the convention centre to Camden Yards. Civic spaces and defined urban edges are critical components to defining the area, which long lacked cohesive commercial activity and animation.

The hotel's exterior skin was designed to embody Baltimore's complex personality, hinting both backward and forward. Red brick façades wrap the building's lower floors and establish visual connection with the historic brick warehouse across the street that serves as a backdrop to the Ballpark at Camden Yards and with the traditional row houses that line the residential neighbourhoods to the west. If brick serves as a nod to the past, the metal cladding makes a more overt nod to the future, calling to mind Baltimore's industrial bulwark while offering a modern edge that relates to the sleek high-rises bordering the site.

The interior continues the sense of openness and visibility that drives the public spaces. Arranged to limit barriers between interior and exterior, the lobby and public areas provide constant but unobtrusive visual interest and activity.

Details

General view

Interior   Lobby   Entrance

1. Eutaw Street
2. Paca Street
3. Howard Street

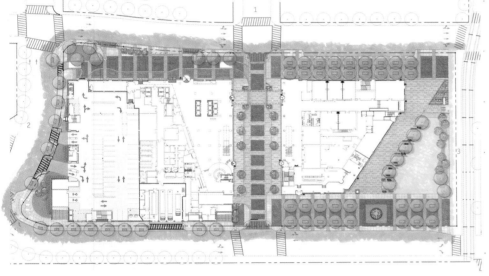

Landscape   Passageway

Photo: RTKL/David Whitcomb

Hotel

Completion Date: 2008

Architect: RTKL Associates Inc./Mckissack & Mckissack; Interiors: Daroff Design
Landscape Architects: Mahan Rykiel Associates Inc.
Lighting Design: Brandston Partnership Inc.

Experimental Media and Performing Arts Centre

The building incorporates a wide variety of venues designed to the highest professional standards, which accommodate both the traditional performing arts and new, experimental media. Also provided are artist–in–residence studios, audiovisual production and postproduction suites, audience amenities and student and support facilities.

By taking advantage of the slope of the hillside site, the design solves one of the persistent challenges of performing arts projects: concealing the windowless mass of a very large hall and fly tower. This use of the topography also creates vistas over Troy towards the Hudson River, as seen from the campus approach and from major visitor spaces within the building.

The entire north façade of the building is a glass curtain wall, providing transparency between the EMPAC interior and the city of Troy. The glass wall allows daylight to flood the atrium, augmented by a halo skylight around the top of the concert hall that washes the cedar hull with the changing light of the day. By night, the wood hull is lit up from within the building and creates an iconic external identity that can be seen from distance.

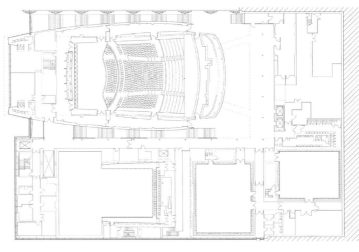

Photo: Aaron Esto, Paul Rivera

Cultural

Completion Date: 2008

Architect: Grimshaw Architects

General view

Evans House

Here is a residential building designed by Bittoni Design Studio (architects Mark Bittoni, Ross Jeffries and Salomé Reeves). This project is actually a redesign of a private residence located in the Crestwood Hills, near Los Angeles. This house has a special site, located on the hill with a panoramic view all around. Inside the house there is also a luxurious interior, spacious rooms, large windows, polished floors, comfortable beds, swimming pool and kitchen and adequate dining room. It is correct to say that this house is a real dream.

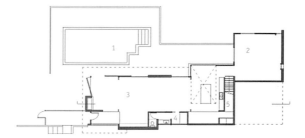

1. entrance
2. kitchen
3. living room
4. toilet
5. staircase

Exterior

Living room

Kitchen

Outdoor view and kitchen

Photo: Bittoni Design Studio

Completion Date: 2009

Architect: Bittoni Design Studio

20th Street Offices

Environmental sensitivity went into all aspects of the design and construction of the 20th Street Offices. The initial concept began with an open linear tube–like form sitting atop a series of moment frames. This concept allowed the occupiable space to be lifted above the at–grade parking, maximising opportunities for open green space, natural ventilation and daylight. With the open ends oriented to the east and west, the natural flow of air coming off the Pacific Ocean circulates through the tube, maximising fresh air and minimising the need for mechanical systems. The building envelope of the tube element consists of custom–designed diamond–patterned cladding, fabricated out of sheet metal. This cladding combined with recycled content insulation of high R–values, minimises heat gain and puts less stress on the mechanical systems as well.

Broken up into different multifunctional spaces the building allows occupants, visitors and clients to congregate for discussions and events, hold visual presentations, share a meal, watch a film or even hold a yoga class on the green roof. The 20th Street Offices strives to create a lifestyle, an office culture and a connection to the community synonymous with its environmentally conscious informed design. The building functions as a laboratory and gallery to explore ideas, test products, promote green initiatives and market "building responsibly" to its clients and the surrounding community.

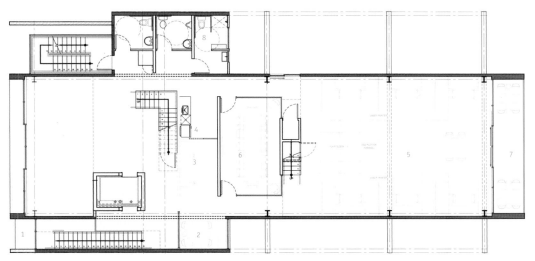

1. entrance below
2. reception
3. manager office
4. kitchen
5. work studio
6. conference room
7. balcony
8. restroom

Photo: Belzberg Architects

Completion Date: 2009

Architect: Belzberg Architects

Façade

Arizona State University Walter Cronkite School of Journalism & Mass Communication

Located in downtown Phoenix, the new six-storey, 22,500-square-metre building has become an integral part of the fabric of ASU's energising downtown campus and a harbinger of Phoenix's redevelopment. As truth and honesty are guiding principles to journalism, so are they to the design of the building. The architecture is specifically expressive of function and materiality. The design is based on an economical 30-foot-square exposed structural concrete column grid with post-tensioned concrete floor slabs. The exterior is clad with glass, masonry and multi-coloured metal panels – the pattern of the panels is inspired by U.S. broadcast frequency spectrum allocations (the Radio Spectrum). The composition is kinetic and dynamic – symbolic of journalism and media's role in our society. The building's massing incorporates appropriate sun screens on each of the four façades; their specific architectural treatment reduces the heat loads and is one of many of the LEED Silver building's sustainable strategies. Burnished concrete block walls, ground and polished concrete floors and warm wood ceilings further express the forthright and direct nature of news delivery.

The Cronkite School occupies all of the second and third floors and a portion of the fourth and sixth floors. The airy, multi-tiered First Amendment Forum is the heart of the school. By day, students gather spontaneously between classes, and in the evenings, the grand hall transforms into a public forum where students and industry leaders discuss the most critical issues facing today's news media.

Front view

Night view

Presentation hall

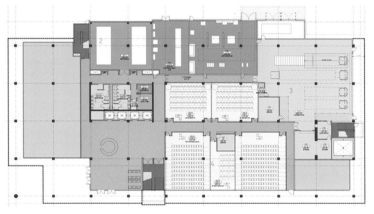

1. lobby
2. service centre
3. presentation hall
4. classroom

Service centre

Photo: Bill Timmerman

Architect: Ehrlich Architects (www.ehrlicharchitects.com)

Exterior view

Northern Arizona University

The building forms a long arc oriented to the south to capture the winter sun in a glass–enclosed three–storey gallery that serves as a thermal buffer space for the offices behind. Louvres and blinds shade the gallery from the hot summer sun, yet allow sun penetration to warm the building in the winter. The south façade of the building is expressed in brick, wood, glass and aluminium. Sustainable strategies integrated into the building include:
a long and thin shape to maximise daylight and minimise electric lighting needs;
concrete structural frame stores heat in the winter and cool in the summer to reduce energy required for heating and air–conditioning;
low–pressure under–floor air distribution reduces fan sizes and energy requirements;
nearby field of photovoltaic panels (donated by APS) produces 160 kilowatts and produces more than 20% of the building's electricity;
triple–glazed windows on the building's north side minimise unwanted energy loss and gain;
automated shade controls regulate solar gain to maintain a comfortable gallery environment.

The combined impact of all these strategies is to reduce the energy consumption by 89% compared to a typical building. Ninety percent of construction waste materials were recycled, and 30 percent of the materials used in construction were made from recycled materials, including insulation made from recycled denim jeans. Water conservation measures include the use of indigenous landscaping, low–pressure faucets, waterless urinals and dual–flush toilets.

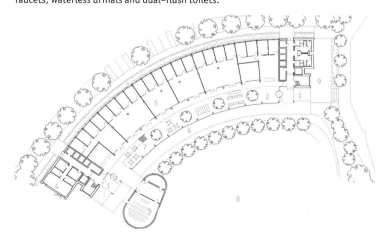

1. entrance
2. atrium
3. conference pod
4. plant
5. offices
6. terrace
7. café
8. detention basin
9. entrance plaza

Exterior view

Photo: Timothey Hursley

Educational

Completion Date: 2008

Exterior view

Passageway

Architect: Hopkins Architects with Burns Wald and Executive Architects

21

Exterior view of north façade

Taubman Museum of Art

Located at one of Roanoke's most visible and historic downtown intersections, the new Museum is the first major purpose–built museum ever constructed in the city. The building, with forms and materials chosen to pay homage to the famed Blue Ridge and Appalachian Mountain surroundings, quadrupled the size of the Art Museum's previous facilities at Centre in the Square. The building features flexible exhibition galleries for the Art Museum's important permanent collection of 19th and early 20th century American art, contemporary art and regional crafts; education facilities with a library, studio and study Centre; a multi–purpose auditorium; a café; a book and gift shop; a black–box theatre; and outdoor terraces providing unique vistas of the city.

The finish on undulating, stainless steel roof forms reflects the rich variety of colour found in the sky and the seasonal landscape. Inspired by mountain streams, translucent glass surfaces emerge from the building's mass to create canopies of softly–diffused light over the public spaces and gallery level. As it rises to support the stainless steel roof, a layered pattern of angular exterior walls is surfaced in shingled patinated zinc to give an earthen and aged quality to the façade.

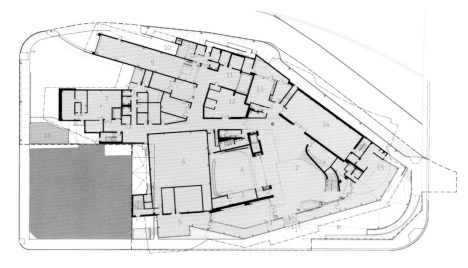

1. Salem Avenue entrance
2. museum lobby
3. museum shop
4. auditorium
5. theatre foyer
6. theatre
7. mechanical
8. museum services
9. art handling
10. loading dock
11. protective services
12. catering kitchen
13. e & o studio
14. art venture gallery
15. museum café
16. electrical equipment

Exterior view from Salem Avenue

Atrium view from gallery level

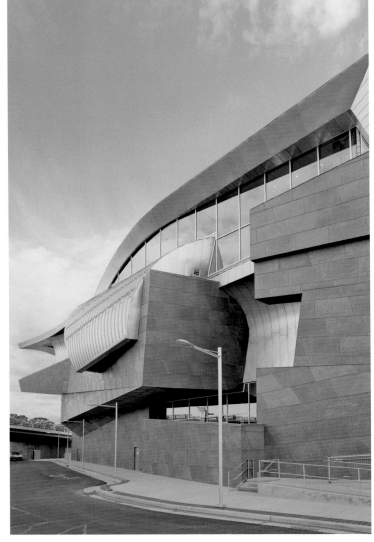

Exterior view from Norfolk Avenue

Photo: Timothy Hursley

Completion Date: 2007

Architect: Randall Stout Architects, Inc.

Cultural

41 Cooper Square - The New Academic Building for The Cooper Union

41 Cooper Square, the New Academic Building for The Cooper Union, aspires to manifest the character, culture and vibrancy of both the 150-year-old institution and of the city in which it was founded. 41 Cooper Square aspires to reflect the institution's stated goal to create an iconic building – one that reflects its values and aspirations as a centre for advanced and innovative education in Art, Architecture and Engineering.

In the spirit of the institution's dedication to free, open and accessible education, the building itself is symbolically open to the city. Visual transparencies and accessible public spaces connect the institution to the physical, social and cultural fabric of its urban context. At street level, the transparent façade invites the neighborhood to observe and to take part in the intensity of activity contained within. Many of the public functions – an exhibition gallery, board room and a two-hundred-seat auditorium – are easily accessible on one level below grade.

The building reverberates with light, shadow and transparency via a high performance exterior double skin whose semi-transparent layer of perforated stainless steel wraps the building's glazed envelope to provide critical interior environmental control, while also allowing for transparencies to reveal the creative activity occurring within. Responding to its urban context, the sculpted façade establishes a distinctive identity for Cooper Square. The building's corner entrance lifts up to draw people into the lobby in a deferential gesture towards the institution's historic Foundation Building. The façade registers the iconic, curving profile of the central atrium as a glazed figure that appears to be carved out of the Third Avenue façade, connecting the creative and social heart of the building to the street.

Built to LEED Gold standards and likely to achieve a Platinum rating, 41 Cooper Square will be the first LEED-certified academic laboratory building in New York City.

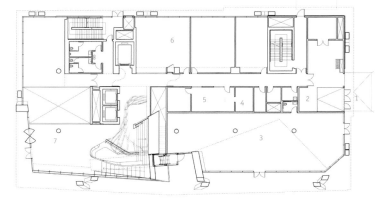

1. entrance
2. loading bay
3. retail
4. storge
5. office
6. classroom
7. main lobby

Street view

View from distance

Night view

Stairwell and roof

Photo: Iwan Baan

Completion Date: 2009

Architect: Morphosis Architects

View from west; manufacturing building at night

322 A Street Office and Manufacturing Facility

The building is clearly split to reflect the two parts of the programme: a single-storey metal fabrication workshop and two levels of office area. The office building is elevated to create a covered parking area underneath, raise the occupied spaces above the 100-year flood plane, and assure that the presence at the street intersection is given due prominence. The lower-level offices house the metal fabrication administration connected through a bridge to a mezzanine in the shop. The second level is the headquarters of the real estate development company. The building is book-ended by two high spaces: a lobby atrium that functions as exhibition space for company products and a common space oriented towards the river and the city.

The material palette consists of two primary materials: zinc flat locks panels are used to highlight people spaces, and pre-manufactured, field-assembled corrugated metal panels are used for the workshop. Glass curtain wall assemblies present the multi-storey gathering areas to the public and provide near and distant views to the occupants.

The office floor plan is only 60 feet (18 metres) wide. Offices, located on the perimeter, and all conference rooms are enclosed by client-made translucent shoji screens or transparent glass walls fabricated with painted steel angles and exposed fasteners. The desks, tables and credenzas within were all produced by the client's shop and continue the integration of design and manufacturing to showcase metalwork as a craft.

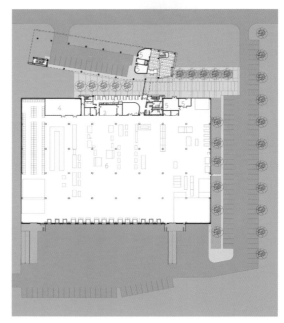

1. lobby
2. lunchroom
3. take-off
4. storage
5. mechanical
6. manufacturing
7. parking

View from west towards office building common area and terrace

View of connecting corridor between office and manufacturing building

EJDESETA

First floor conference room

Photo: Woodruff/Brown Architectural Photography

Corporate

Completion Date: 2005

Architect: KlingStubbins

A generously-sized, colourful urban oasis

Lausd William J. Clinton Middle School

Located just south of downtown Los Angeles in an isolated pocket of light manufacturing and vacant buildings with minimal community life, this middle school links two city blocks and provides a safe learning haven for more than 1,500 students. Within a tight budget, a clear and simple design was employed to allow for quality materials including corrugated steel and concrete masonry.

The 150,000-square-foot campus (plus 65,000 square feet of structured parking, canopies and bridges) includes a three-acre academic quad and, across the street, a 6-acre athletic quad. The two-storey academic building houses administration, library, lecture space and shared classrooms on the first floor, with individual classrooms on the upper level. Each side of the U-shaped plan, colour-coded in blue, green or yellow, forms a community of about 500 students; each individual classroom within its cluster is painted a different shade of the principal colour.

The two quads are joined by a pedestrian bridge over a wide, busy street that links classrooms with a gymnasium, playing fields, a track, and faculty parking for 142 cars. All shade canopies are tilted at an optimal angle to the sun, to enhance the performance of photovoltaics.

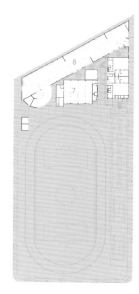

1. main administration
2. library
3. multi-purpose
4. general classroom
5. art room
6. kitchen
7. gym
8. parking

The site design treats the school in an urban way

Durable, low–maintenance materials were used throughout the design

Coloured corrugated steel and concrete masonry

Large open–air canopies

Photo: Tom Bonner

Architect: Ehrlich Architects (www.ehrlicharchitects.com)

Completion Date: 2007

Educational

View of the Margot and Bill Winspear Opera

Bill Winspear Opera House

The Margot and Bill Winspear Opera House is engineered specifically for performances of opera and musical theatre with its stages equipped for performances of ballet and other forms of dance. The opera house's principal entrance features the 60–foot Annette and Harold Simmons Signature Glass Façade that wraps three quarters of the way around the building, creating a transparency between the opera house and the surrounding Performance Park. The transparent façade provides dramatic views of the Margaret McDermott Performance Hall, which will be clad in vibrant red glass panels. From within the Winspear Opera House, the Simmons Glass Façade provides a sweeping view of the skyscrapers of downtown Dallas that line the northern edge of the Performance Park.

Radiating from the Winspear Opera House on all sides, the sky canopy will provide shade over three acres of the Sammons Park, creating new outdoor spaces for visitors to gather and relax. The glass solar canopy's louvres will be arranged at fixed angles following the path of the sun, calculated to provide optimal shade for the outdoor spaces throughout the day, as well as preventing direct sunlight from hitting the Simmons Glass Façade during the warmest months of summer.

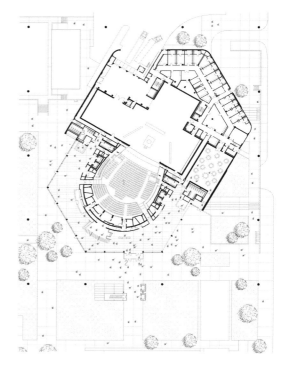

1. theatre
2. entrance
3. restroom

Front view

Exterior view

Stair and lobby

Photo: Iwan Baan, Tim Hursley

Cultural

Completion Date: 2009

Architect: Foster + Partners

Chandelier

Public gallery flanked by social lounges and student entrance

Hassayampa Academic Village, Arizona State University

Located at the southeast corner of Arizona State University's Tempe campus, The Hassayampa Academic Village interlaces 1,900 beds with classroom, computing, dining and retail components. The buildings are organised as a series of four-storey courtyard buildings sharing a public gallery space with a seven-storey tower. The towers flank the primary east-west and north-south connections to campus and serve as thresholds to the gallery spaces with their entrance to the residential buildings. Each of these buildings is composed of four floors of forty student communities sharing a social lounge with the adjoining floor. Together, the four floors of student suites gain a shared identity through the colour of their respective courtyard elevations, thereby promoting an individual identity for each building within the life of the academic village.

The project is designed to respect the demands of the climate and environment through its orientation, building envelope, mechanical systems and harnessing of breezes. Devices such as canopies will shade outdoor public spaces, which in turn temper the environment around the buildings. Coupled with material selection and efficiencies of the building, these strategies to reduce heat gain have achieved an LEED Silver rating for the complex.

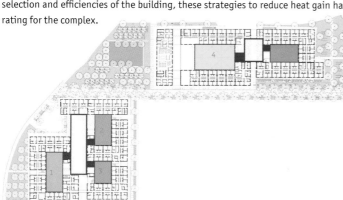

1. Chuparosa Court
2. Arroyo Court
3. Jojoba Court
4. Verbana Court
5. Acourtia Court

View of Sky Lounge outdoor terrace and the Hassayampa Academic Village

Public gallery flanked by social lounges and student entrance

Arroyo Courtyard looking towards social lounge

Photo: Farshid Assassi, Anton Grassl/Esto

Completion Date: 2007

Architect: Machado and Silvetti Associates with Gould Evans, LLC.

Front with pool (west)

ViLLA NM

ViLLA NM is not a regular house; it is not meant for everyday living. It is a house for summers, for weekends, for stolen time. This is a house that you share with your immediate family, with your most intimate friends. The house is compact as vacation homes often are: like the dacha and lake-side cabin of Russia and Scandinavia, the house offers a simple, private, family-and-nature orientated retreat from urban life.

The conceptual model for Villa NM is a box with a blob-like moment in the middle; a twist in both plan and section that causes a simple shoebox to bifurcate into two separate, split-level volumes. One side clings to the northern slope of the hill; the other detaches itself from the ground, leaving room underneath for a covered parking space.

All the internal spaces maximise the potential for wraparound views. The kitchen and dining area on the ground floor are connected by a ramp to the living space above, the 1.5-metre (5 feet) height change allowing for a sweeping outlook over the surrounding woodland and meadows. A similar ramp connects the living area to the master and the children's bedrooms on the first floor. Facilities such as the bathroom, kitchen and fireplace are clustered in the vertical axis of the house, leaving the outer walls free. Large glazed windows feature in all but the most private rooms.

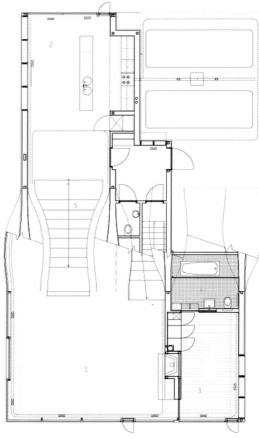

Ground floor plan
1. living
2. kitchen
3. bedroom
4. bathroom
5. stairs

Distance view

Entrance

Interior with furniture

Photo: Christian Richters

Completion Date: 2007

Architect: UNStudio

Residential

Green Circle Shopping Centre

The Green Circle Shopping Centre located in Springfield, Missouri, is one of the most sustainably developed retail spaces in the United States. Slated to achieve an LEED Platinum rating, the highest rating possible, the 23,000-square-foot centre incorporates recycled materials, utilises sources of renewable energy, and maximises energy efficiency.

Site location was treated with great sensitivity. The conventional shopping centre would clear the site of trees and maximise parking and retail space. As a sustainable alternative, Green Circle preserved over forty existing trees on site and in doing so provided building tenants and customers with green space for recreation and visual relief.

A geothermal system with forty wells located under the parking lot utilises the earth's heat energy for heating and cooling 100% of the spaces. Paired with both an ERV (Energy and Heat Recovery Ventilators) and heavily insulated walls and floors, the geothermal system provides a 50% improvement in efficiency and decreased utility demands when compared with the baseline case of a typical shopping centre. Increased efficiency translates to lower electrical bills for the tenants and less air pollution for the environment. Lighting controls, efficient light fixtures, photovoltaic panels and extensive daylighting by the strategic placement of windows play a large part as well. The roof and the south façade have photovoltaic panels producing several kilowatts of electrical energy for building use. Interior spaces are capable of having almost no artificial lighting during daylight hours. Furthermore, all of the glass used for daylighting is high performance which minimises solar heat gain where necessary and transmits a high percentage of visible light.

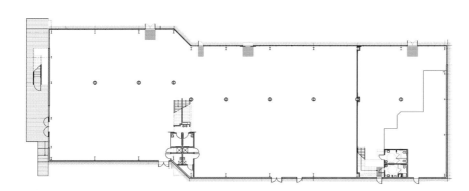

Aerial perspective © Bob Linder

Aerial perspective with roof details © Bob Linder

Exterior corner details © Bob Linder

Exteiror stairs © Sinclair

Interior © Bob Linder

Photo: Bob Linder, Mike Sinclair

Commercial

Completion Date: 2008

Architect: Hufft Projects, LLC / Matthew Hufft

Exterior night view ©Travis Fullerton

Virginia Museum of Fine Arts

The design of the new $151 million building, plaza and sculpture garden opens up the Virginia Museum of Fine Arts (VMFA) to the city. The E. Claiborne and Lora Robins Sculpture Garden combined with the Mary Morton Parsons Plaza act as a square onto the Boulevard, and under a hill at the end of the gardens a new 600 car parking deck completes the redevelopment of the campus which also includes three other historic buildings.

The new 15,330-square–metre McGlothlin Wing provides extensive new space for the museum's collections and study centre. The museum reports that this expansion makes them one of the ten largest encyclopaedic museums in the United States.

VMFA announces itself to Richmond with the atrium's twelve-metre-high window facing the Boulevard. Natural light floods into the heart of the museum and a wall of glass opens the atrium, café and restaurant onto the pools, fountain and sculpture garden. Five bridges connect the new to the original museum, across all floors of the building. It adds fifty percent additional exhibition space to the existing building. There is 139 square metres of changing exhibition space for major touring exhibitions. The building also includes the Art Education Centre, the Freeman library, a gift shop, state-of-the-art object and painting conservation facilities, a 150-seat lecture hall, the "Best" café with garden terrace and pool, and a restaurant overlooking the Sculpture Garden.

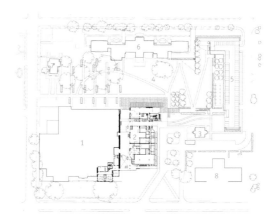

1. existing museum
2. James W and Frances G. Mcglothlin Wing
3. Robinson Farm House
4. E. Claiborne and Lora Robins Sculpture Garden
5. parking deck
6. Vmfa Centre for Education and Outreach
7. Confederate Chapel
8. United Daughters of the Confederacy

Exterior ©Travis Fullerton

East window ©Travis Fullerton

The atrium bridges ©Tippy Tippens

Photo: Travis Fullerton, Tippy Tippens

Architect: Rick Mather Architects

Cultural

Completion Date: 2010

Social Condenser for Superior

The Social Condenser project is located at the base of the Superstition Mountain Range in the Town of Superior, Arizona which was founded in 1882 and has strong ties to mining of copper, silver and gold.

The project is uniquely positioned between historic Main Street and Queen Creek. The site consists of two parcels, the project parcel to the north and an open landscaped parcel to be developed into future outdoor dining and music pavilion, and is bisected by an access path from the upper street level and a lower wooden footbridge that spans across the creek.

The project is a renovation and expansion of an existing two-storey block building and addition of an exterior dining terrace. The lower level is developed into kitchen, mechanical and storage spaces and the upper level is designed as an open gathering space. The south-facing wall of the upper level of the existing building is removed to expose the volume within. The remaining form is rendered to closely match the shadow tones of the surrounding hills and acts as both backdrop and anchor for the new addition.

The project was informed by the concept of the "public house". Classically an obscured, introverted diagram, the Social Condenser conversely aims to balance concealment with exuberant exposure of the internal activities to the streetscape, the pedestrian walking path and the adjacent landscaped parcel.

The project is envisioned to be the living room of the community; a place to congregate, socialise, view work of provincial artists and enjoy the breathtaking landscape vistas that envelop the region.

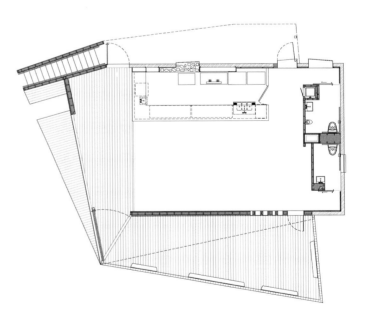

Photo: Bill Timmerman, Timmerman Photography, Inc., Phoenix, Arizona, USA

Recreational

Completion Date: 2007

Architect: Blank Studio

Building

Sustainable Residence – 3716 Springfield

The residence at 3716 Springfield in Kansas City is an environmentally conscious, modern home performing completely "off-the-grid". Being the first LEED platinum home in the Kansas City Metropolitan area, the building serves as an example of sustainable practice and living for buyers considering a life in the city. The combination of the passive glazing with the louvres for shading and active systems integrated with the roof plane flush to the siding calls out visually the environmental building standards. Also, the residence is dedicated to teaching the community and provides tours for all interested parties in order to effectively encourage the neighbourhood to become knowledgeable in sustainable architecture.

A broad south exposure was purposely sought after to support the passive solar effort. Additionally, operable windows along the lower south glazing and roof-top skylight allow for stack ventilation throughout the interior. The entire site was planted with drought-resistant landscaping and the south was intentionally left open to encourage the homeowner to plant a native garden. The hardscape surrounding the exterior of the home use pervious concrete which permits rainwater to seep through and into the water table.

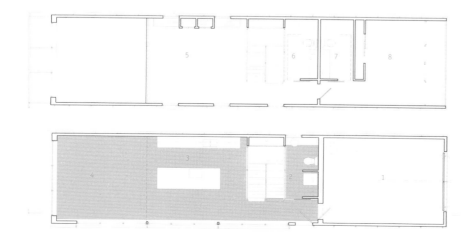

1. garage
2. bath
3. kitchen
4. living room
5. flex space
6. bath
7. master bath
8. master bedroom

East view

Kitchen and dining space

Bath on the ground floor

Photo: Courtesy of Studio 804, Inc.

Architect: Studio 804, Inc.

Residential

Completion Date: 2009

Two additions in relation to the existing structure

Cohen Levine Residence

Reconsidering the expression "the whole is greater than the sum of its parts", a series of modern interventions were introduced to a traditional home. Responding to a number of paradigm shifts in the clients' lives, each project was contemplated as an independent entity yet considerate of the assemblage as a whole.

Initially, the entrance sequence was rethought, moving the front door out of the living room and creating an intimate yet articulated space. A flat roof stitches together the new and old entrance while introducing the modern idiom to the traditional fabric. The living room was expanded into the side porch, adding volume and light to the tired dark environment.

The largest intervention is a new building equalling the footprint of the existing home. Capped with a butterfly roof, the solution was a direct response to not overwhelm the small scaled colonial house. Inside, light shafts link the open-plan living, dining and cooking space to the first floor and inverted roof above. Cabinetry elements were inserted into the various living spaces to provide storage and act as a bridge between the interior spaces.

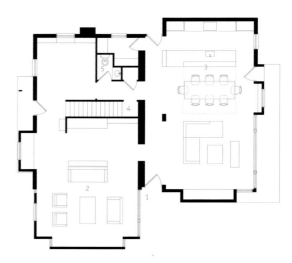

1. entrance
2. living room
3. kitchen
4. stairs
5. bath

Living room of the side addition

Dining area, looking up to underside of butterfly roof

View of back elevation

Photo: Paul Warchol Photography

Completion Date: 2010

Architect: David Jameson Architect

Spertus Institute of Jewish Studies

Acclaimed as the finest cultural addition to Chicago after Millennium Park, the Spertus Institute of Jewish Studies is one of the city's most celebrated and discussed new projects.

The façade is an innovative, 21st–century approach to the use of glass and the expression of identity. Folding glass planes on the façade give drama and presence to this ten–storey building located in a city of skyscrapers. The folds also scale and modulate the Spertus façade and relate it to the mostly brick and stone neighbouring buildings in the Michigan Boulevard Historic District.

The project includes an asymmetrical, fan–shaped auditorium with seating for 400 people, and full projection, lighting and sound mixing capabilities. The balcony is uniquely multi–tiered so that smaller groups can attain a level of intimacy with the onstage performance even when the auditorium is partially filled. The back of the auditorium has a faceted form, revealed within the main lobby of the building, that gives a dynamic expression to the activities inside.

Moving up into the building, visitors follow a sequence of light–filled spaces which connect and overlap Spertus's mixed–use programme of exhibition galleries, library, auditorium, college classrooms and administrative offices. A great hall at the top floor looks back across Grant Park to the skyline and the lake, connecting both the institution and visitors back to city and nature.

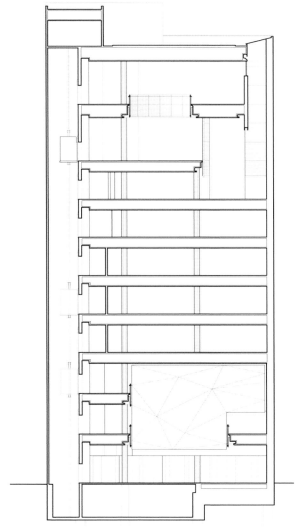

Photo: William Zbaren

Completion Date: 2008

Architect: Krueck+Sexton Architects

General view

Crockett Residence

It was decided to locate the living level on the upper floor to capture views and allow privacy without curtains. Within the lower level, a flex space of sorts was created which could act as a family room, a room for mother–in–law, or be closed off to act as a separate (legal) rental unit.

The surrounding area is an eclectic mix of charming craftsman homes and apartment buildings. Early on the decision was made to go with surface (though mostly covered) parking rather than a garage to both allow more space for the home and avoid the "garage door dominated" front façade look. This also speaks to the clients, lifestyle as they commute more on bicycles than they do in cars.

The final design was realised through the creation of three simple elements: a horizontal volume, a vertical volume and a folded plane. The private programme elements (bedrooms & bathrooms) were located in the two volumes while the public areas were contained within the interstitial spaces created when the three elements were combined. The entrance and stairs occur in the space between the folded plane and the metal clad volume; the living level within the upper fold of the Minaret plane. In both cases, the simple massing allows the spaces to seem as if they flow out from the home to connect with the neighbourhood, adding energy and size.

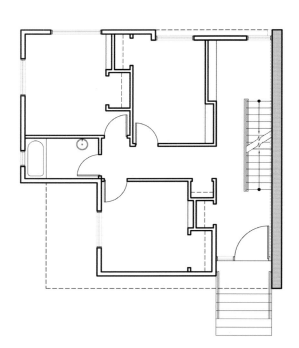

Night view

Roof

Interior

Photo: Pb Elemental Architecture

Completion Date: 2008

Architect: Pb Elemental Architecture, Dave Biddle, Chris Pardo

Building in the evening

Strauchaus

This home rests on the edge of a wooded area. The diagramming process analysed the programme and needs of the two owners in effort to resolve a cohesive experiential sequencing of spaces, suggest massing arrangements and uncover elevation compositions. The abstraction of the programme is made in effort to make the two paths: the movement, and the connections become an extension of the landscape.

As the building takes form, the graphic maps and modeled paths begin to prescribe how the structure relates to the surrounding context. A patterning of thin floor–to–ceiling windows connects the structure to the neighbouring forestry by continuing the event of a body passing through the forest.

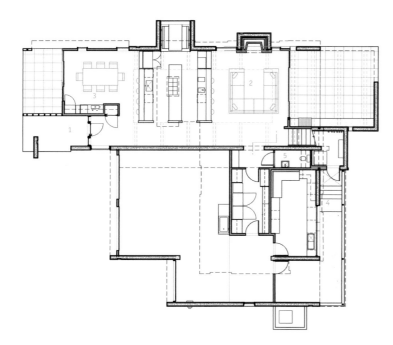

1. entrance
2. living room
3. kitchen
4. stairs
5. bath

Patio in the evening

Hallway

Front side in the evening

Photo: Peter Jahnke

Architect: PIQUE llc.

Residential

Completion Date: 2008

Mt. Crested Butte Residence

This is a special house built in a ski resort community by two brother carpenters who happen to own a truckload of redwood siding. The house was designed to be attractive to two families who might want to be in a resort at 3,100–metre elevation. From the front door one could ski down to the ski lift, take the lift and ski back down to the house. A central shaft that runs vertically through the house supports the house. In the interior the central shaft is a fireplace for each of the house's three floors. The house is designed with two garages on each side of the entrance. One enters the house on a split–level. A half level up has two master bedroom suites separated by the central shaft with a fireplace and whirlpool in it. A half level down from the entrance is the community family areas, living, kitchen, etc. The lowest level is a children's playroom/dormitory. The undulating roof reflects the mountaintop behind the house. Local people refer to the house as the "snow clam".

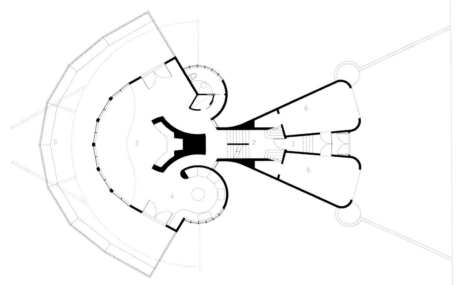

1. outer entrance
2. inner entrance
3. great room
4. kitchen
5. deck
6. garage

Photo: The Studio of Robert Oshatz

Completion Date: 2008

Architect: Robert Oshatz

Driveway

Whitten House

This residence sits on a remote site composed of Sage & Juniper trees in Central Oregon. Conceived as two simple cubes in the landscape, one box for sleeping and one for living, the structure offers two distinct means of interaction with the landscape. The larger sleeping box is low & burrowed into earth, while the living box floats above, hovering just at treetop level. East & South orientations are exploited for views as well as passive solar orientation of the home.

Exterior materials were chosen for durability and fire resistance. All rainwater will be harvested & stored for landscaping or fire fighting purposes. The future pool will provide an additional margin of wildfire safety as a usable body of water on the remote site.

Evacuated tube solar water heaters will efficiently provide most of the heating for the home through in–floor radiant tubing. The building's narrow profile and extensive glazing combined with the region's low humidity allow for passive cooling of the home.

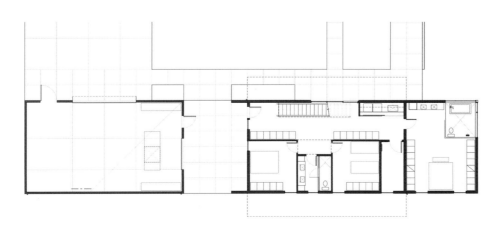

Back view

Living room

Library

Photo: Peter Jahnke

Residential

Completion Date: 2009

Design: PIQUE llc.

Weiss Residence

Located on a sloping site in hills of West Linn, the Weiss Residence provides an exclamation mark in the streetscape. It's strikingly rigid geometric forms and unusual detailing which accentuate its shape make for an intriguing composition.

The 179-square-metre building is spread over three floors giving the house a vertical emphasis and making the east and west elevations somewhat tower-like, yet the building is by no means menacing from the street. The entrance to the home is made onto the middle level after descending a short concrete driveway, while the upper floor is almost absorbed as the eaves slope downward to form the diamond shapes that can be seen on the side elevations. The building opens out to a large rectangular deck through sliding doors. The deck is intended to act in the same way as a traditional porch would help to merge the lives of the home's occupants with the rest of the neighbourhood, which helps to soften the building from the street. The deck is also used to roof the garage and reduces the scale of the building by extending out towards the sidewalk. The façade is further broken down by the planter box, adorned with small shrubs which help to reduce the scale of the building.

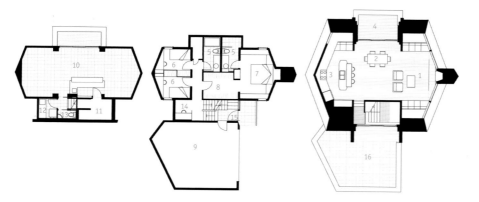

1. living
2. dining
3. kitchen
4. deck
5. bathroom
6. bedroom
7. master bedroom
8. closet
9. garage
10. reception room
11. wine cellar
12. laundry
13. powder room
14. computer alcove
15. entrance
16. stairs

Photo: Meredith Brower

Architect: Robert Harvey Oshatz

Completion Date: 2007

Residential

Aerial view of Ford Assembly Building and San Francisco Bay

Ford Assembly Building

This waterfront project rejuvenated the formerly abandoned and dilapidated Ford Assembly Building. The historical factory was transformed into a vibrant centre of 21st-century building uses, including entertainment, dining, office, and a visitor centre. Today it has a lively mix of public/private uses and accommodates a range of commercial tenants with offices, Research & Development facilities, light industrial, retail functions, and the NPS Visitor Centre celebrating WWII's "Rosie the Riveter". The project also incorporates significant sustainability features.

The designers' vision for the rebirth of this magnificent edifice was to retain yet enhance the architectural aspects of the original building's awe-inspiring shell, continuous bands of steel sash windows and floods of daylight, while maintaining its original waterfront relationship. This goal to renew the building was driven by an impetus to salvage and restore features inherent to the building's architectural spirit. "Intervention elements" of our century: lighting, furnishings, free standing buildings within the building, rooms, stairs, ramps, platforms, walls, etc, placed and designed to work with existing 1930's industrial architectural features are most apparent in the results for the Boilerhouse Restaurant/Café, SunPower Corporation and Mountain Hardwear projects. Low-water usage landscaping was designed on the building's west side to reflect the more public and formal façade. Lighting internally and externally was a way to highlight the building, particularly at night. The red-lit stack of the Boilerhouse, itself an icon of the project, is especially arresting at night.

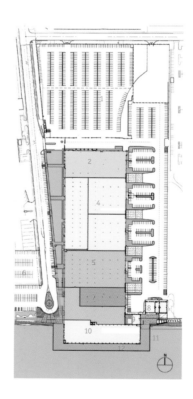

1. parking
2. Mountain Hardwear
3. loading dock
4. other tenants
5. SunPower Corporation
6. electric vehicle parking
7. Vetrazzo
8. Rosie the Riveter Visitor Centre
9. Boilerhouse Restaurant
10. the craneway pavilion
11. San Francisco Bay
12. sf bay trail

Boilerhouse Restaurant interior

Craneway interior

Photo: Left Side Images of the Spread by Steve Proehl; Others by Billy Hustace

Complex

Completion Date: 2009

Architect: Marcy Wong Donn Logan Architects

Craneway and Boilerhouse exterior

West façade elevation – entrance approach to Recreation Building

Orange Memorial Park Recreation Centre

Orange Memorial Park is the most important public recreation venue for the citizens of South San Francisco and is the context for the new recreation building which is encircled by soccer, picnic, basketball and other outdoor amenities. The building's most significant element is an airy, light-filled Activity Pavilion for cultural, recreational, celebratory, and educational activities. The architects chose wood flooring and an exposed wood truss roof to add warmth and grace to this important room.

The recreation building is conceived as a focal point of the park and an icon for the community. Towards that goal, a juxtaposition of two distinct rectangular masses was created – one large, light and largely transparent, housing the Activity Pavilion, with large areas of glass in concert with red and yellow cedar, and another mass that is by contrast a smaller, nearly solid box of basalt stone. The interior use of cedar specifically in the Activity Pavilion creates a dynamic and inviting environment for a central meeting place for the community. Moreover, the horizontality of the building is accentuated by the roof of the Pavilion whose paired glu-lam wood trusses span the room; these trusses cantilever beyond the enclosed footprint to provide covered outdoor patio areas.

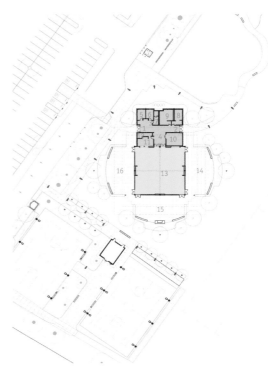

1. main entrance
2. entrance from fields
3. reception counter
4. foyer
5. office
6. office
7. utility room
8. men's restroom
9. women's restroom
10. storage
11. kitchen
12. pantry
13. multi-purpose activity pavilion
14. east patio
15. south patio
16. west patio

East façade elevation – view from fields at dusk

Photo: Sharon Risedorph

Recreational

Completion Date: 2008

Architect: Marcy Wong Donn Logan Architects

Detailed exterior cedar and glass façade of multi–purpose pavilion on west, south and east sides

Interior of multi–purpose pavilion

Library and Media Centre of the University of Guadalajara

This building is a pioneer in the implementation of standardised norms for accessibility for people with disabilities; it has a set of ramps and aisles specially designed to make it 100% accessible. It will have a collection of 120,000 books, DVDs, and videos in a total surface of 5,346 square metres, making it the biggest public library in the western region of Mexico and the second one after the recently opened Central Library Jose Vasconcelos in Mexico.

The programme was met within a very narrow margin, and the goal was of course to have first of all a very functional building. The building is organised into three different prisms, each built with different materials in order to make each volume's programme recognisable. The reading volume is built with red brick and is mainly opened to the north so the interior receives the best illumination for reading without any direct sunlight. The volume that contains the books is built in concrete and completely closed to the exterior, so this volume is read from outside as a closed, protected box. The media centre is allocated inside a metallic volume; this volume makes use of the latest technology in metal cladding and isolation.

General view

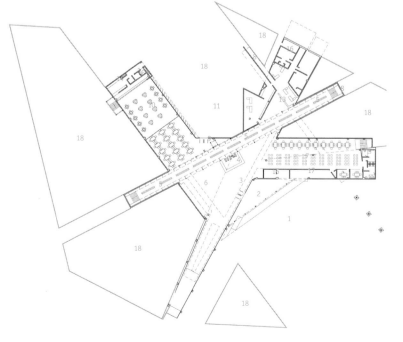

1. plaza
2. entrance
3. main lobby
4. front desk
5. book shelves
6. casual reading area
7. reading area
8. ramps and stairs
9. cubicles
10. snack area
11. reading plaza
12. toilets
13. administration
14. kitchen
15. copy centre
16. service
17. lockers
18. green areas

Main façade from plaza

Media volume

Photo: Heriberto Hernandez Ochoa

Educational

Completion Date: 2007

Architect: Laboratorio en Arquitectura Progresiva S. C.

It is an almost 100–metre–long building, with a series of vertical strips used for ventilation by tip–up windows

A.M. Celaya

The A.M. newspaper in the state of Guanajuato, Mexico, is subsidiary to one of the main national journals of Grupo Reforma. Its local contents are produced in Leon where it is printed, and from where it is distributed throughout the state, once it has received the news generated in Celaya. Therefore, printed without any industrial facilities, the A.M. Celaya had been operating in a rented unit with no urban presence whatsoever. So, in order to create an appropriate projection according to the social importance and financial viability of the newspaper, the owners destined an outstandingly located terrain. This was a long and slim land, facing one of the main avenues in the city, to be used for three purposes: the newspaper headquarters, shopping units and an additional rental business block in the upper level.

This is how the architectural programme comes out, bringing a triple–height cube as main volume for the newspaper brand image. The central stairway is set here, communicating the main entrance to the public attention areas as well as meeting rooms, whereas on the first floor comes the editors and directors office, as well as the newspaper offices. On the other end of the building is the main entrance for the rental business units, having underneath the shop units, all of them with direct access from the street.

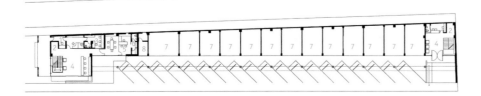

1. security
2. lifts
3. classified section
4. lobby
5. sala de juntas
6. files
7. local commercial
8. services

The programme comes out of a triple–height cube as main volume for the newspaper brand image

The long and slim terrain, facing one of the main avenues in the city, dictated the programme

The volumetric statement is the triple–height lobby hall with a big granite plate that holds the newspaper's logo

The stairs lead to the first floor where the editors and directors office, as well as the newspaper offices come

Photo: Mito Covarrubias

Corporate

Completion Date: 2008

Architect: Ricardo Agraz

Manantiales de Espejo Apartment Building

The building is located in a regeneration zone of Mexico City that is growing in popularity, housing forty-seven apartments, fifty-five square metres each. The building has a green rooftop that stands in contrast with the grey surroundings of the area. The structure is "U" shaped, with all the apartments having views both on the inside and outside façades. The windows on the outside are designed as a reference to barcodes used to tag commercial products. The inside windows bring light and movement together. The architecture of the building reflects the site, located next to a speedy avenue that connects the northern side of the city and surrounded by small streets with low circulation and speed, with a very dynamic expression in façades which contrasts the regular form of the plan. In the lower level there is the parking. The next six levels are apartments and the upper level is the roof garden. The materials used are mostly concrete for the main core of the building and steel for the circulations, making the building look both strong and modern in contrast to the building and houses in the immediate surroundings that are much older.

1. main bedroom
2. bedroom
3. living room
4. dining room
5. kitchen
6. utility
7. toilet
8. WC
9. study
10. balcony
11. lift
12. corridor

Photo: Gustavo Slovik

Residential

Completion Date: 2008

Architect: SLVK: Gustavo Slovik, Daniel Dickter, Emanuel Teohua

Omegablock, Colegio Anglo Colombiano (Omega Block, Anglo Colombiano College)

The Omega Block Building is located in the Anglo Colombiano School in the Bogota, capital of Colombia. This building is the summary of three buildings in progression, which are adapted to the morphology of the triangular area disposed for its development.

The three volumes are combined with low to high mass or vice versa. Greater Volume houses general classrooms, specialised classrooms medium volume music and art rooms and smaller volume of media. The master volume is structured through the subtraction of the mass, the average volume level through the envelope, and the smaller volume is a sieve or perforated in the mass sequence. The dominant materiality of the project, large format brick and slender pre-stressed concrete elements (beige in colour), binds the outside spaces with that of the large internal atrium space. Further tonal and material compliment is found in the vibrant green special divisions (doors and divisions), with smooth Formica finish.

A grand staircase, or tiered seating, ensures a fluid connection between the base plane (ground floor) with level above, while offering a congregational space. With this element, the scale of the building changes, and the use of the atrium space is re-interpreted.

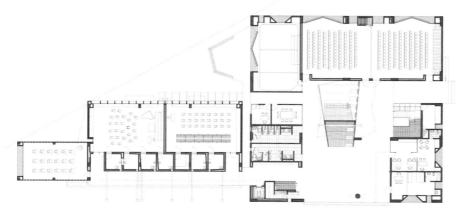

General view

Main hall

Educational

Exterior

Details

Completion Date: 2009

Architect: Daniel Bonilla

69

Front View

Museum of Memory and Human Rights

The Museum is conceptually organised in two moments: the Exposition Beam and the Base. The first, elevated, housing the history, the information, and the act of living memory, is open on both ends, like someone who lets life pass naturally. The other, the Base, in a first step deep as a mine, where the study, the production, the invention, the seminars, the knowledge of the land and the territory are located; in another step is the necessary support by the administration sectors. The Beam is a specific museographical space and the Base is a museological one, a place of study and support.

Along both sides of the Exposition Beam are the circulations, bathrooms and support systems, lightened by the translucency of the perforated copper plates and the second external skin, made of transparent glass, thus creating a totally controlled inner environment. On a second effect, the light also penetrates all the exposition space through the semi–opaque glass walls.

Exterior

Exterior

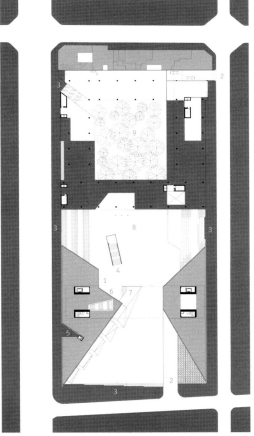

1. museum access
2. parking access
3. pedestrian access to the square
4. memorial alfredo jaar
5. lift access
6. subway connection
7. parlatorio
8. square memory
9. garden desires

Interior

Interior stairs

Photo: Cristobal Palma

Completion Date: 2009

Architect: Estudio America

Façade

Benavides Drugstore and Warehouse

An architecture of simple lines, contrast of transparencies and closed walls answers to two complementary functions: the buildings (distribution centre and offices) and the usability (services in the pharmaceutical area, incorporated with technologies of the last generation in the production and passive ventilation systems for the buildings).

The lot is located in a new expansion of an industrial park, made by the firm Kalos in the north of Monterrey (international airport highway). The new pharmaceutical complex is the gateway to the urbanisation, on one side the great park, on the other the central axis with green spaces.

The architecture of the complex is simple and outright. A vertical and diagonal texture of relief lines on a big closed white volume produces a game of light and shadows while giving movement to the façades. It contrasts with the administrative building, which is designed like a cube of blue glossy glass, subdivided by aluminium blades, giving the building a decisive character of transparency, both during day and night. The second skin is suspended from and offset to the volume of the administrative building, above a multiuse water pond. The water pond permits the thermal control of the building through evaporation produced during the hot months and the effect of transparencies, reflex, light and shadows.

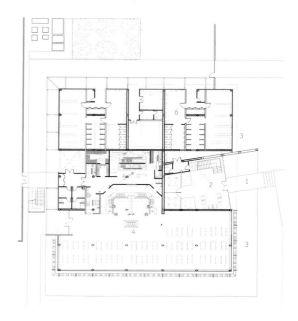

1. access
2. hall
3. water
4. cantina
5. kitchen
6. bathroom

Main façade

Factory hall

Photo: Guillermo Hevia

Architect: GH+A Arquitectos

Commercial

Completion Date: 2009

Far view

ALSACIA

The volumes level the architecture to the lines of the perimeter, while fitting itself to the urban context and the counterfort of the cordillera, using a roundly colour scheme of red and black. The project defines itself by the use of simple lines, extreme colours and pure volumetry.

The use of the buildings (distribution and classification of auto parts) and its complexities define the architecture to a big, closed volume which terraces itself to follow the urban boundaries. The contrast between the red and black, draws attention to accent the simplicity of the volumes, transforming the architectural ensemble to a unique icon of the access to the ENEA business site. The main building contrasts with its black metal to the administrative building and the service areas due to its morphology and materiality. The second volume is made out of insight concrete, glass and steel. The suspended roof crosses the volume, bearing itself on both sides on metal columns of double height, generating covered and protected areas. An access atrium, preceded by a water pond (obey the function of chilling the main façade by evaporation) and the square in the subsequent façade assigned for social activities, contains the big stairs which cross the diagonal, dynamising the space and giving access to the educational and staff rooms.

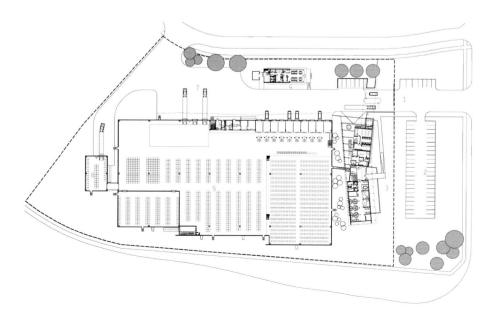

1. access
2. parking
3. offices and services
4. cafeteria
5. distribution centre
6. storage for dangerous elements
7. truck operation patio

Sunset view

Stairs

Corridor

Bridge

Photo: Cristián Barahona, Guillermo Hevia H., Guillermo Hevia García

Corporate

Completion Date: 2008

Architect: GH+A Arquitectos

Entrance

SESC

The library evidently has a great influence of the modern architecture from São Paulo. It is possible to perceive the influences from Vilanova Artigas and Paulo Mendes da Rocha. The influence of Artigas' building, the FAU–USP building, is also visible, almost as a tribute from the alumni to the building in which they studied architecture.

This construction is composed by a great entrance atrium surrounded by a concrete beam one storey high. This beam, which has the role of structure and sealing to the superior portion, organises a long footbridge which gives access to the library's general collection. Therefore, this structure not only serves as sealing, but it also shelters the collection and creates the footbridge for visitors. Under the concrete beam, the glass sealing produces a contrast between the weight of the concrete on the superior portion versus the transparency and lightness of the inferior sealing. It is at this tension point that the visitor is invited to enter the library.

Part of the library is suspended over SESC's great central water mirror, and the access is made through a footbridge which symbolises the passage to a study place. When over the water mirror, it is possible to have very interesting views that may change during the day as daylight itself changes.

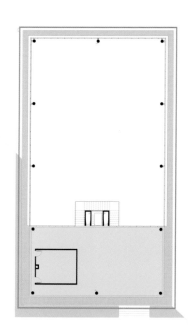

General view

Details

Interior

Interior

Front building

Laranjeiras House

This is a lovely beach house. Ultra wide openings and imperceptibly transition between indoors and outdoors that make this place very comfortable. Minimalism softened through wood surfaces and stone walls make the house design's modern but not cold. Six bedrooms with balconies are located on first floor creating great places for rest and catch sunrise views. Ground floor have kitchen and maids quarters at the one wing and dining room, living areas, bar and games room at the other.

Elements of the colonial architecture of the historic city of Paraty were incorporated into the modern design of the House of Laranjeiras. The ceramic tiles and the use of rustic material offering great thermal isolation, remit back directly to the large old houses of the neighbouring city.

Likewise, ecological concerns were incorporated into the architecture through the use of these materials (both the ceramic and wood were recycled) and an integration with the surroundings, a beautiful beach in the state of Rio de Janeiro.

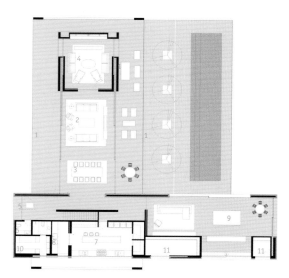

1. terrace
2. living room
3. dinning room
4. TV room
5. main entrance
6. bath
7. kitchem
8. laundry
9. cardroom
10. bedroom
11. storage

Swimming pool in the yard

Photo: Nelson Kon

Completion Date: 2008

Pool and deck

Architect: Studio MK27

Living space

Front façade

House 53

The House 53 volumetry was defined following São Paulo city building laws and the site's peculiar shape, which is just over ten metres in front and approximately thirty metres in length. According to the legislation one can build in the neighbourhood up to a two-floor building, settled upon the site's lateral limits. A third floor is allowed as long as the lateral setbacks are respected.

The house was conceived as a wood-and-mortar monolithic block with another concrete and glass volume upon it. Due to the ground's small front and volumetry, the box's two edges had to make the most of light's entrance, which explains the large windows. It was also desirable that these windows would make it possible to darken the internal environment whenever needed.

The house's interior volume, which comprises the living room on the ground floor and the bedrooms on the first floor, is a glass box with wooden brises that open as folding doors. The rooms' front and back façades were designed to be completely closed or opened.

1. living room
2. bedroom
3. lounge room

Deck at night

Photo: Rômulo Fialdini

Residential

Front

Dining room

Completion Date: 2009

Architect: Studio MK27

Star Place

The city of Kaohsiung is the second largest city on the island of Taiwan and has a population of some 1.5 million. Its geographical position along the Taiwan Strait has allowed it, over time, to become a maritime hub. After the Second World War, the city grew rapidly, transforming itself from an undeveloped fishing village into a booming, heavily industrialised port city. Today, like other places in this position, Kaohsiung is in the process of re-envisioning the industrial identity that has brought it so far. For a city such as Kaohsiung, which takes a secondary role on the world stage in comparison to global cities such as Hong Kong or Beijing, this question of reassessing the identity can be problematic to address. The kind of urban environment that is produced by rapid industrialisation does not provide a platform that is conducive to effortless regeneration. Moreover, the absence of symbolic markers such as those found in leading cultural or administrative cities makes it difficult to identify obvious starting points for the desired regeneration.

What seems to be happening in Kaohsiung is that the city has sought to find a focus for its urban renewal in the residential experience, that is to say, in what the city means in the everyday life of its citizens. The overall goal is to enhance the attractiveness and the comfort level of the city as a place to live. In order to fulfill the goal of establishing a sustainable urban environment, the planning focus has been directed towards strengthening both the natural aspects of the city and its public infrastructure. The SHE concept (safe, healthy, ecological) is the driver behind the development plans, which include cleaning up the river and creating parks and wetland regions.

Within this context, Star Place fulfills a role in the lively and resident-orientated urban landscape that is more on the urban than on the natural scale of the spectrum. As a shopping centre, the project typifies a contemporary public-private form of architectural space. In summary, while the project does not find itself directly within the scope of the nature-enhancing urban regeneration schemes, we still feel that there is a link with the overall improvement goals of Kaohsiung, because thoroughly urban facilities with mass-appeal also form a contributing factor to the livability of a city. Moreover, the project is completely in synch with a resident-orientated approach to urbanism, in which the experience of everyday space by the citizen is the central consideration.

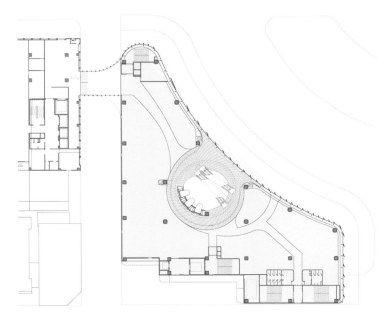

Photo: Christian Richters

Completion Date: 2009

Architect: UN Studio

Exterior view

Kerry Plaza, Futian, Shenzhen

Located on the southern part of the Futian CBD between the Exhibition Centre and Civic Centre, this comprehensive development houses a six-star flagship Shangri-la Hotel complex and the Futian Kerry Plaza.

The Futian Kerry Plaza calls for a pair of connected towers. The two 23-storey office towers soar up to 99.8 metres high. Symmetry is forgone for a more tectonic interplay between two rectangles. The two towers are connected on grade with a podium containing the hotel lobby and retail facilities. The entrance is framed with an iconic portal and matching canopy in the form of sweeping curves.

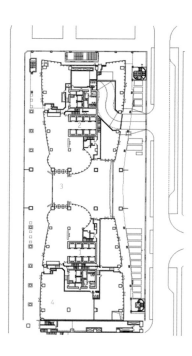

1. office areas
2. office areas
3. central passage way
4. activity space

Exterior view

Photo: Daniel Wong (iMAGE 28)

Exterior view

Entrance way

Complex

Completion Date: 2007

Architect: Wong & Tung International Ltd.

Full view

Nokia China Campus

Nokia China Campus in Beijing is China's first LEED – NC (Leadership in Energy and Environmental Design – New Construction) Gold certified building. The facility includes a research and development laboratory, office space, canteen, auditorium, formal and informal meeting areas, gymnasium and bike shed.

From concept to detailed design, ARUP was aware of the sustainability issues and the building boasts energy–efficient features such as a temperature–controlled cavity between the panes of the glass façade which balances the sun's natural heat and the building air–conditioning so the intense summer and winter climates of Beijing do not affect the internal climate. The building also incorporates water conservation techniques, methods to reduce air pollution and improved air ventilation. Thirty design techniques altogether result in 37% of water saving and up to 20% energy saving. Ninety-seven percent of the interior is afforded views from the glass façades, and skylights and a large communal atrium provide natural light and ventilation throughout the building.

This six–storey facility is the realisation of an integrated multidisciplinary design services. The building is the product of cutting–edge engineering design services – ARUP employed Computational Fluid Dynamics, thermal and energy modelling, structural optimisation and building sustainability tool kit to design the energy efficient building.

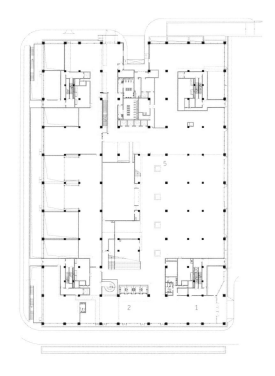

1. hall
2. reception
3. stairs
4. WC
5. dining

Exterior façade

Interior hall

Structural details

Photo: Jerry Lee, M Moser, Ben McMillan

Corporate

Completion Date: 2007

Architect: ARUP

87

Exterior view

Bird's-eye view

Zhongguancun Christian Church

With its free curved shape, the building forms a solitaire in the park–like open space between Zhongguancun Cultural Tower and the "City of Books". On the upper floors it houses China's largest Christian church, while on the ground floor commercial spaces are situated. The shape of the church body does not only allow for a sightline to the south media façade of the Cultural Tower but also emphasises its special function in contrast to the surrounding commercially used buildings. The rod system of the façade forms a homogeneous skin, which however lets in sufficient daylight.

The entrance to the main church hall faces northeast and opens up to the street as well as to Zhongguancun Cultural Tower. A cross, clearly identifying the building as a Christian church, develops from the façade rod system. Through a large portal, worshippers mount a stairway to enter the main church hall on the first floor. With its alternation of open and massive wall sections, the façade rod system creates a special lighting atmosphere inside the church hall, matching the ecclesiastical function of the space. The entrance for clergy and church employees is placed on the northwest side and gives access to a side chapel as well as to stairways and a lift to all the floors of the church building. The parish offices and community spaces are on the second and third floors of the south and west wings. Some of the upper–floor spaces open onto a roof terrace – a substitute for a churchyard – that offers parishioners an attractive outdoor space.

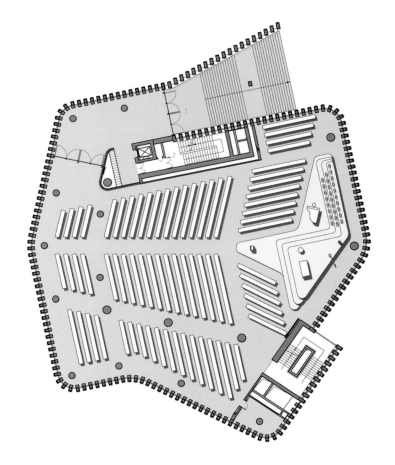

1. entrance
2. stairs

Interior view

Interior view

Night view

Shanghai-Pudong Museum

Opposite the historically grown city centre of Shanghai a new "Manhattan" comes into being on the other side of the river: the district Shanghai-Pudong with the highest office – and hotel building at present in China. The Shanghai-Pudong Museum is one of the most important urban projects in this new district. It is supposed to document and archive the district's history and development comprehensively. At the same time modern multifunctional and open exhibition spaces are created to inform the public with a permanent exhibition and special exhibitions about selected topics.

Three elements form the building complex: the square-shaped horizontally orientated glass body with exhibition halls, a much broader, four-metre-high base with surrounding stairs, which accommodates the archives, and a bar-shaped building on the eastern side for the administration. The base as one of the main architectural features of the museum lifts the main building with the exhibition halls above the level of the surrounding streets and emphasises the central importance of the complex. Simplicity and reduction of the materials dominate the clear cube. The façade of the upper, closed part of the main building not only serves as weather protection but also as a communication surface. It is made of two parallel façade-layers. The outer layer consists of glass and the inner one of room-high closed wall panels. These elements can be rotated along their longitudinal axis and can be opened or closed, according to the particular requirements of the exhibition concept, so that views from the inside to the outside and vice versa are generated.

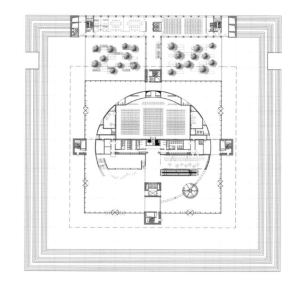

General view

Front view

Night view

Interior view

Photo: Christian Gahl, Berlin

Completion Date: 2005

Architect: Gmp – Von Gerkan, Marg and Partners Architects

Night view

SOHO Shangdu

The faceted façades of the two 32–level towers and smaller landmark building onto Dongqiaolu are clad in a random pattern of grey glass and aluminum panels. The dynamic qualities of the pattern readily allowed the proportion of glass orientating to the south and west to be reduced, thus lowering the heat gain to units in those directions. Inscribed within the faced facets are a large–scale geometrical parametric network of lines which at night create continuous light–lines and the project's distinctive nocturnal image. The façade pattern was directly generated on the same principles and visual image of the traditional Chinese ice–ray pattern, a decorative motif used primarily for joinery and paving, which is parametric in its geometric properties.

The organisation of the retail was designed on the principle of a vertical hutong with a series of internal streets and passages which vary in their position, width, height from floor to floor, thus generating differentiated circulation patterns which in turn, create the potential for localised and specialist retail zones.

Two large internal courtyards, which spiral vertically and link all the floors provide a navigational and activity focus to the retail area's "east" and "west–ends", facilitating a range of events from fashion parades, commercial launches to concerts and talks activities.

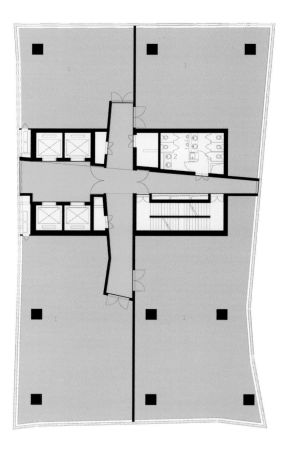

1. office area
2. WC

Outside view

Outside view

Hall

Interior view

Photo: Lab Architecture

Architect: Lab Architecture

Completion Date: 2007

Complex

Bird's-eye view

Jishou University Research and Education Building and Huang Yongyu Museum

The project is concerned mainly with two important issues relating to site: the first is the relationship between the architecture and surrounding environment, and the second is how to establish a relationship between local architectural tradition and local culture.

The building sits on development–ready levelled land that once was part of the hillside on the university campus. The Research Education Building and the Museum form a wedge–shaped composite section that juts into the land. The building mass, multiple roofs and integrated windows blur the vertical and horizontal forms of the walls and roofs, which in turn, contribute to rebuilding and reestablishing the physical presence of the site.

Respect for cultural tradition of architecture evolves into two types in Jishou: protection of the typical traditional architecture in old town; copy of the traditional residence regardless of the difference in structure, material, function, and size. Conceiving maintaining a modern, new architectural logic as precondition, they try to introduce the style of traditional residential building into the building, so as to build relationship between new structure and local building visually. Therefore, in concept, this building is a "mountain" as well as a "village".

Entrance plaza

Part of the elevation of the academic building

Entrance hall of gallery

Photo: Shu He

Completion Date: 2006

Architect: Atelier Feichang Jianzhu

Ninetree Village

A small valley, bordered by a dense bamboo forest, forms the site for this luxury housing development, situated near the Qian Tang River in Hangzhou, southeastern China. The particular charm and beauty of the place are the determining factors. Twelve individual volumes are arranged in a chessboard pattern to create the maximum amount of open space for each building. Through planting new vegetation, each apartment building is set in its own clearing in the forest. The buildings adapt to the topography, creating a flowing landscape through a slight turning of the blocks.

The grounds will be accessed from the southern entrance via a network of lanes. All buildings are linked to an underground car park, enabling the site to be free from vehicles above ground. Within the development there are six types of building differing in size and floor plan depending on the location, view and light conditions.

The individual apartment buildings contain five generously proportioned apartments, each accommodating a full floor of approximately 450 square metres. The floor plan concept creates a flowing interior space defined by solid elements which accommodate auxiliary functions.

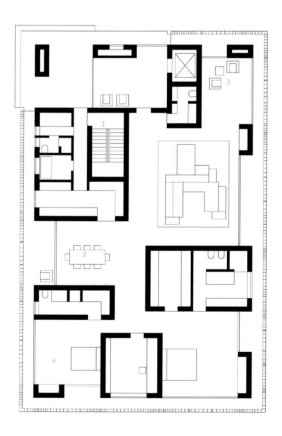

1. stairs
2. dining
3. living room
4. bedroom

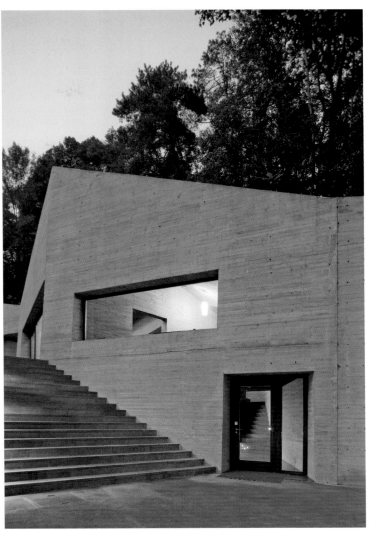

Photo: Christian Richters, Shu He

Residential

Architect: David Chipperfield Architects

Completion Date: 2008

Liberal Art Department, Dongguan Institute of Technology

The ground floor of the Liberal Art Department building is plugged in the hill, thus the building is melted in the terrain. The ground floor's two sides are opened to the outside and own the nice scenery, while the other part of the building get the daylight from the L-shaped courtyard. The roof of the ground floor become an open platform in rolling hills, while the elevated square building stands above the platform. The platform, courtyard and corridors together create a centralism of outdoor public square. In the main direction of walking, strong feeling of block building have clearly been faded away, which reduced the building's pressure to the environment. When eyesight crosses the elevated building and falls on the behind hills, people may recall the original image of this area.

General view

Southeast elevation

Inner court of the first floor

Inner court of the first floor

Entrance

Photo: Deshaus Studio

Completion Date: 2004

Architect: Deshaus Studio

SIEEB (Sino–Italian Ecological and Energy Efficient Building)

Sino–Italian Ecological and Energy Efficient Building (SIEEB) is realised in the Tsinghua University Campus in Beijing. It is a 20,000-square-metre building, forty metres high and it will host a Sino–Italian education, training and research centre for environment protection and energy conservation.

The envelope components as well as the control systems and the other technologies are the expression of the most updated Italian production, within the framework of a design philosophy in which proven components are integrated in innovative systems.

The SIEEB building shape derives from the analysis of the site and of the specific climatic conditions of Beijing. Located in a dense urban context, surrounded by some high-rise buildings, the building optimises the need for solar energy in winter and for solar protection in summer.

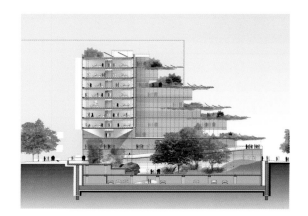

Gas engines are the core of the energy system of the building. They are coupled to electric generators to produce most of the electricity required. The engines' waste heat is used for heating in winter, for cooling – by means of absorbtion chillers in summer and for hot water production all year round.

Photo: Daniele Domenicali, Alessandro Digaetano, MCA Archivi

Educational

Completion Date: 2006

Architect: Mario Cucinella Architects

South façade

Ordos Protestant Church

Located on top of a hill of Ordos, planned as a green open space for the city, the project takes its inspiration from the topography of the land. The surrounding landscape offers a strong contrast of colours and depth, creating a rich changing background from day time to night time for the church's settlement. It sets framed views of the church in a characterised landscape of excavated rocks proper to a city like Ordos, in Inner Mongolia.

The scheme, named "Dove of Peace", gives its metaphor and poetry to the church by re–interpreting a contemporary and abstract silhouette of the bird caring a branch of Olive in its beak. The Church has a concrete structure and uses white crepi finish for its façades. Its dynamic shape follows the adjacent curved road that crosses the site. The dialogue between the outside and the inside space is emphasised by the play of shadows and light that creates complexity and depth in the reading of the space. Its elements are thought to reflect harmony and tranquility in this place for prays and celebration.

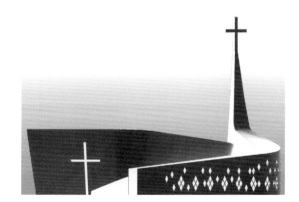

North façade

Birdeyeview

Interior

Photo: Beijing Sunlay Architectural Design Co., Ltd.

Architect: Beijing Sunlay Architectural Design Co., Ltd.

Cultural

Completion Date: 2009

Liangzhu Museum

The museum houses a collection of archaeological findings from the Liangzhu culture, also known as the Jade culture (~3000 BC). It forms the northern point of the Liangzhu Cultural Village, a newly created park town near Hangzhou. The building is set on a lake and connected via bridges to the park.

The sculptural quality of the building ensemble reveals itself gradually as the visitor approaches the museum through the park landscape. The museum is composed of four bar-formed volumes made of Iranian travertine stone, equal in width (eighteen metres) but differing in height. Each volume contains an interior courtyard. These landscaped spaces serve as a link between the exhibition halls and invite the visitor to linger and relax. Despite the linearity of the exhibition halls, they enable a variety of individual tour routes through the museum. To the south of the museum is an island with an exhibition area, linked to the main museum building via a bridge. The edge areas of the surrounding landscape, planted with dense woods, allow only a few directed views into the park.

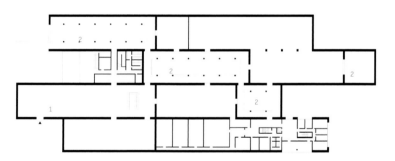

1. entrance
2. courtyard

Photo: David Chipperfield Architects

Cultural

Architect: David Chipperfield Architects

Completion Date: 2007

Tianjin Bridge Culture Museum

The Bridge Culture Museum is located at the centre of the QiaoYuan Park, Tianjin. Because of it special location, on the central axis facing to the main entrance, and because it is supposed to be the landmark of the Bridge Park, this area is designed as a leisure and exhibition space in order to meet people's needs of "pleasurable show space".

The origin of the design concept is "operable bridge". Steel bridge, folded surface, variable structural columns, U-shaped enclosed space and extended platform, all create a "Building for Strolling". This building is "accessible and passable". It brings people exciting and surprised experiences because of the conversion between interior and exterior spaces. The steel bridge between the buildings leads people to the exhibition space, which is all green; the bottom of the building is multidimensional surface, which is accessible for people to go through; the sixteen structural columns have been treated in different ways to distract people's sight; the Z-shaped building, U-shaped enclosed space, the coffee break deck and the combination of the interior and exterior spaces, merged the building together with the site. One can find attraction of the building through their own experience to it. The "accessible and passable" Bridge Culture Museum is interactive for people, both interior and exterior.

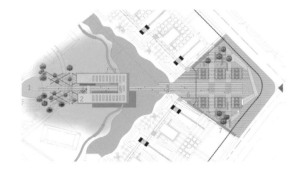

1. performance plaza
2. rooftop viewing terrace
3. green roof
4. water terrace
5. "Bridge Culture" steel plate
6. iron gate and fence
7. main entrance plaza

Architect: Sunlay Architecture Design Co., Ltd., Zhang Hua, Fan Li

Photo: Shu He

Completion Date: 2007

Cultural

Beijing Nexus Centre

The Nexus Centre is a structure of sophisticated form and superb function. Its column–free and unusually large 2,200-square-metre floor plate allows ultimate freedom for tenants to fully customise their space and maximise efficiency according to individual needs.Located on a long, linear site, the dual–tower complex slopes from south to north from its 551–foot apex in order to limit shadow casting on its northern residential neighbours. The eastern façade fronts the heavily–trafficked ring road and gives retailers prominence along the base. The western façade, by contrast, overlooks the serene setting of an urban park. On the south, the building curves in relation to its corner site, opening up to a large landscaped plaza that segregates vehicular and pedestrian traffic while creating an inviting amenity for tenants.

The design of the complex uses a combination of stainless steel and granite to define distinct fenestration that visually breaks down the overall mass into more slender elements. Expansive floor-to-ceiling glass is applied throughout in order to bring natural light deep into the office floors. Extensive vertical shading devices on the east and west façades control heat gain, and operable windows on all floors promote the introduction of fresh air throughout the work environments.

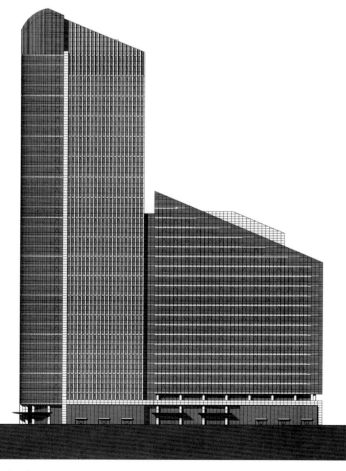

East elevation

Photo: Doug Snower, Doug Snower Photography

Corporate

Completion Date: 2008

Architect: Goettsch Partners

UF Soft R & D Centre, Beijing, China

For the UF Soft R & D Centre, the architecture began the architectural design by studying the way computer programmers work and live. In order to create a healthier working environment, they borrowed the basic fabric of the old Beijing – the courtyard houses, which offer their residents the proximity of the nature – to mix indoor and outdoor spaces. To further reinforce the integration of the architecture and the landscape, the complex was limited to only three storeys and shallow depth that allows better natural ventilation and daylight. The end result is a mat building that could extend horizontally or a fine-grained fabric urban design that is the antithesis of treating buildings as objects. In the plan, the complex consists of three inter-connected buildings. Two major courtyards are situated in between the buildings with various smaller courts and terraces on different levels.

Besides the concern of health, making team working more spontaneous is another important aim of the design. The diverse public spaces indoor and outdoor have been proven to encourage people to interact, to communicate, and to socialise. While there are a number of materials and construction methods employed in the project, glass blocks embedded in the concrete masonry units is the main technological innovation, which gives the building a solid and transparent appearance at the same time.

1. R & D Centre I
2. R & D Centre I, Phase 2
3. entrance & exit

View of courtyard from bridge

Night view of courtyard

View of courtyard

Inside of wall

Photo: Shu He

Completion Date: 2007

Architect: Jia Lianna, Chen Long, Liu Yang

Corporate

View from far away

Raffles City Beijing

Raffles City Beijing is located at Dongzhimen with convenient access to the Subway, west to the East Second Ring Road and Southwest to the Airport Express Way. This building complex includes retails, offices, clubhouse, studio apartments, parking space and supporting facilities. The design concept is to create a unique impressive architecture in city centre with multiple function choices, clear and flexible functional spaces and smooth internal traffic.

Different buildings have been illustrated by different surface texture, for example, the surface of the podium is pixel–like glass pattern; the curtain wall of the office building is composed of aluminium frame and 1.4-metre-wide and full–height double glazing; the façade of the studio apartment is illustrated by panel curtain wall and French window system; the roof of the club employs coloured aluminium, to show the connecting of the pieces.

Around the buildings, the gardens are linearly distributed, with the plants and flowers connected to the open spaces with the buildings. The two gardening entrance can not only guides costumers but also emphasise the retail atmosphere. There is a courtyard on the roof of the podium, and the landscape of the courtyard creates a screen which separats the office building away. The central of the courtyard is also the glass roof of the atrium, whose diamond surface forms a special view of the yard.

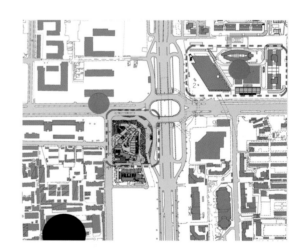

1. entrance
2. main part of the project
3. green plants and landscape

Full view

Entrance with light

Photo: Sunlay Architecture Design Co., Ltd.

Complex

Completion Date: 2008

Architect: Sunlay Architecture Design Co., Ltd.

Details

Escalator

View from southwest

2010 Shanghai EXPO – Shanghai Corporate Pavilion

In 2010, we have gone through a long period of rapid technological advancement and the amount of infrastructure in a building has dramatically increased to the point that technologies are today's basic building blocks. For Shanghai Corporate Pavilion at the World Expo, the architect would like to manifest this observation in their design: the interior spaces of the Shanghai Corporate Pavilion, which are shaped as a series of free, flowing forms, will be enclosed not only by walls of the static kind but also a dense, cubic volume of infrastructural network, including LED lights and mist–making system, which are capable of changing the appearance of the building from one moment to another as programmed through computer.

However, the design is not embracing technology for the technology's sake. Rather, they like to convey visually the spirit of the Shanghai Corporate Pavilion, the dream of a brighter future, through sophisticated technologies. Technology is about the enrichment of imagination and symbolic of the industry and industrialism of Shanghai. Also through technology, they like to address the pressing issue of energy and sustainability. A part of the architectural infrastructure is designated for the solar energy harvesting and rain water collecting, and the external façade will be made of recycled polycarbonate (PC) plastic.

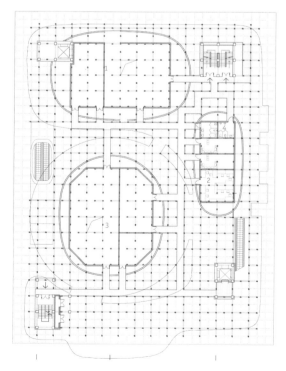

1. power distribution room
2. air condition room
3. office
4. WC

West elevation

View from northwest

Queuing area

Photo: Shu He

Completion Date: 2010

Architect: Atelier Feichang Jianzhu

Qingcuiyuan Club House

Qingcuiyuan Club House is located on the west bank of Wenyu River, Chaoyang District, which has excellent condition of graceful natural landscape. The design concept is not only to create a unique building, but also to integrate it into this attractive landscape environment.

Qingcuiyuan Club House shows two topics, Collision and Blend, the collision of different cultures and styles, the blend of time and space. It is telling a story which is ancient and modern. It is describing an aesthetics encounter between east and west.

The architectural design scheme considers "axis and symmetry" which are emphasised by classical architectural language, and "fluxion and consistency" which are sought by modern architectural language. Red brick walls and transparent glazing are employed to create coagulated building mass and flowing spaces. Inside courtyard with comfortable scale is the continuation of greening, water scene and original natural landscape.

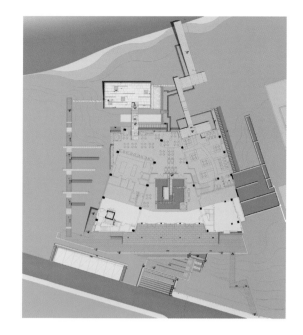

Façade and entrance

Interior landscape

Corridor

Photo: Shu He

Completion Date: 2008

Architect: Sunlay Architecture Design Co., Ltd.

Night view

General view

Bridge School

Located at a remote village, Fujian Province in China, the project not only provides a physical function—a school + a bridge, but also presents a spiritual centre. The main concept of the design is to enliven an old community (the village) and to sustain a traditional culture (the castles and lifestyle) through a contemporary language which does not compete with the traditional, but presents and communicates with the traditional with respect. It is done by combining few different functions into one space – a bridge which connects two old castles across the creek, a school which also symbolically connects past, current with future, a playground (for the kids) and the stage (for the villagers).

A light–weight structure traverses a small creek in a single, supple bound, essentially, it is an intelligent contemporary take on the archetype of the inhabited bridge. Supported on concrete piers (which also have the function of a small shop), the simple steel structure acts like a giant box girder that's been slightly dislocated, so the building subtly twists, rises and falls as it spans the creek. Inside are a pair of almost identical wedge–shaped classrooms, each tapering towards the mid point of the structure (which holds a small public library). Although it's possible to use the building as a bridge, a narrow crossing suspended underneath the steel structure and anchored by tensile wires offers an alternative and more direct route.

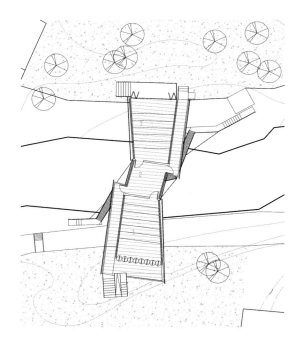

1. classroom
2. library

Photo: 5 Plus Design

Architect: 5 Plus Design

Completion Date: 2007

Complex

View from sea

One Island East, TaiKoo Place

Design Concept
One Island East is the latest office development at TaiKoo Place, Quarry Bay, Hong Kong. It comprises fifty-nine office floors with a typical floor plate of 2,300 square metres, providing a total office area of 140,000 square metres. With a height of 308 metres, One Island East becomes the landmark of the district and the centre piece of this office campus.

Form / Façade of the Building
The basic form of the building is a square plan with central core. The four corners are rounded. Two corners facing north and south "open up" at the top floors to address the Harbour view. At the base, the two corners facing east and west "open up" to address the open space.

The edges of the four façades "sail" beyond, creating a "floating" effect, and giving lightness to the building. Lighting feature is incorporated into the edge of the four façade to enhance the floating effect. Architectural fins are introduced in a staggered pattern to add texture and scale to the façade.

Landscape Forecourt
Without a podium structure, the tower sits freely in front of a large landscaped open space to the east. The canopy at the porte cohere is specially designed as a piece of sculpture.

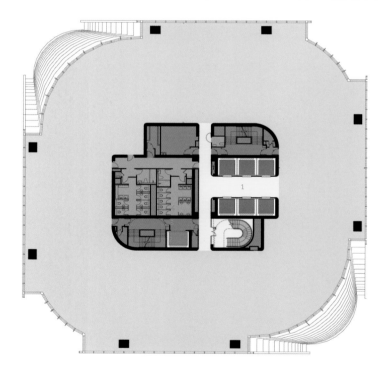

1. passenger lift lobby
2. service lift
3. service lift lobby
4. WC

Footbridge to OIE

Escalators at ground floor

Typical Lavatory

Office lift lobby

Main entrance

Exterior

Photo: Wong & Ouyang (HK) Limited

Completion Date: 2008

Architect: Wong & Ouyang (HK) Limited

Perspective

Hong Kong Polytechnic University – Hong Kong Community College (West Kowloon Campus)

Innovation and Communal Spaces
Due to the limited land resources, the Hong Kong Community College (West Kowloon Campus) aims at experiencing the transformation of the campus communal space design, which is usually, provided in the form of garden on lower floors, into major sky decks similar to high-rise landscape gardens. With associating activities like canteen and student union facilities, campus atmosphere is provided to the sky communal decks. They form the nodal points in the upper campus, which are also proudly visible in the architectural form of the building. The two sky decks are provided to create a sense of community and a place for students' gatherings.

Material and Form
The twin towers and the connecting structures are carefully articulated. Solidity and transparency are the key architectural manipulation for such articulation. "Red-brick" tile is adopted for the solid twin towers while aluminium cladding with glass wall are employed for the transparent connecting bridge structures. This layering put a great emphasis on the connection between the two towers. The twin tower design can minimise the plan depth of each tower and so facilitate the penetration of natural ventilation and lighting into the tower campus.

Sustainability
The building design encourages embrace of natural environment and use of environmentally friendly materials. Innovative building technologies are used in the design with close collaboration with academics from the Hong Kong Polytechnic University in order for the building to achieve energy efficiency and a healthy community. Besides, the lower floors accommodate most mass teaching spaces to facilitate effective pedestrian circulation.

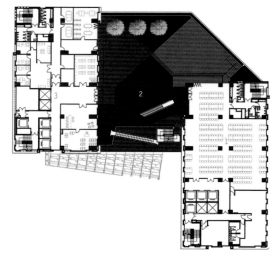

3F Podium Garden
1. canteen
2. podium garden
3. student union centre

East elevation

Stairs

Interior view

Completion Date: 2008

Architect: AD+RG Architecture Design and Research Group Ltd.
In Collaboration with AGC Design Ltd and Wang Weijen Architecture

Photo: Wong Wingfai, Tang Kafai

Hong Kong Polytechnic University – Hong Kong Community College (Hung Hom Bay Campus)

The form composes of various teaching blocks stacked spirally in the air, which are separated with sky gardens at different levels. The various blocks have different degree of opacity. The opacity controls the degrees of direct sunlight casting into the interior of the building with different degree of intensity. The interface of the low block and high block is spatially separated with a top sky-lighted atrium. It serves as a focal point to link up various facilities together and orientates the internal space and circulation.

The mass teaching facilities are arranged on the lower floors. They are shared and connected effectively with the escalators and lifts system. Main staircases are always provided next to the escalators and also link up all sky gardens together. It helps to bring the outdoor atmosphere to the interior.

Sky garden is one of the major design features. From the appearance of the building, a spiral-chain of sky gardens could be perceived and the conspicuous feature is distinctive from the surroundings. The sky gardens are conducive to students' discussions on projects and casual gathering for socialising. Among the intense urban fabric, the sky gardens provide good locations for viewing towards Hung Hom district and the relatively open Hung Hom Station and Coliseum areas. The choice of bamboo in the sky gardens suffices to let sun light shining into the interiors and some large trees are also planted to form a lively and pleasant atmosphere.

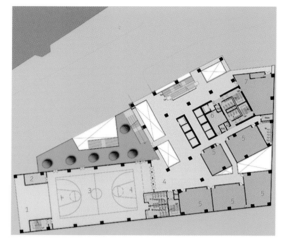

1. stage and backstage area
2. store room
3. multi-purposes hall
4. building line above
5. classroom
6. AHU
7. lecture theatre

Distant view

East elevation

Main entrance

Sky gardens

Natural daylight to library

Photo: Wong Wingfai, Tang Kafai

Architect: AD+RG Architecture Design and Research Group Ltd.
In Collaboration with AGC Design Ltd and Wang Weijen Architecture

Completion Date: 2007

Educational

Panoramic view

Kaohsiung Metro Station

Kaohsiung city decided a construction of the subway, and designated Shin Takamatsu to design a new subway station. The design range was the concourse (total floor area: 10,000 square metres) and the entrance. The station is located under an intersection in the central Kaohsiung city. Concretely, four main entrances on four corners and eight sub-entrances along the road are architecture on the ground. Therefore, through urban point of view, these designs influence the landscape of the city. As the result of researching the characteristics of the site with basic recognition, Shin Takamatsu found a historical fact that this intersection was the place where the Taiwan democracy movement began. The confusing design task because of the simplicity of functional request was rapidly solved by the symbolic information. An idea, which settles the four entrances located on four corners as an architectural synthesis and gives each entrance the form of joining hands while unifying them was generated in one sitting. At the presentation for the concept, these forms were named "Form of Prayer". Kaohsiung city gladly accepted it. An idea that the emitted laser beams from the top of the four entrances meet above the central intersection was proposed at the presentation.

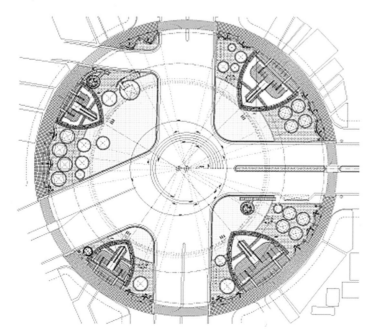

Exit

Station exit

Interior

Transportation

Photo: no credit

Architect: Shin Takamatsu +Shin Takamatsu Architect and Associates Co., Ltd.

Completion Date: 2008

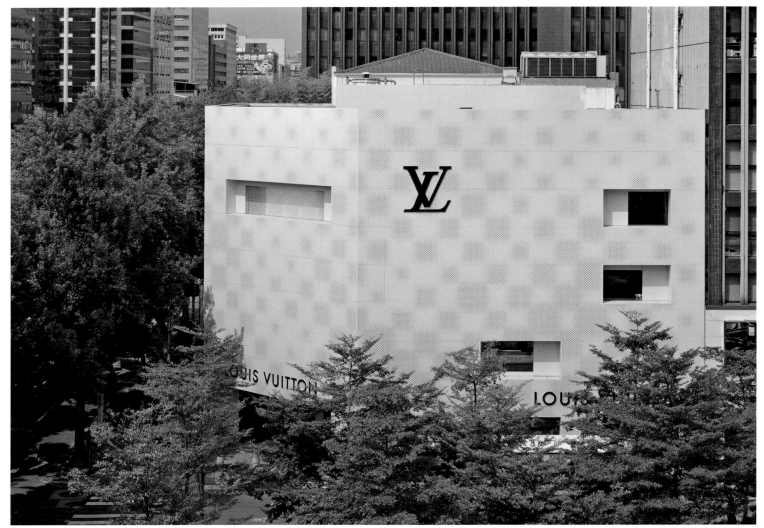

Panoramic view

LV Taipei

Since Taipei is in the subtropical zone, the city is filled with lots of trees. The designers tried to use the landscape of trees for the motif of the façade. Tree does never relate to the brand image of Louis Vuitton, however they thought it was important. The main material of the façade is perforated stone. The designers used half-artificial stone, and made square holes with water jet machine. Then they filled up holes with synthetic resins. The pattern of the hole was based on Louis Vuitton's checker flag pattern called DAMIER pattern. Even though DAMIER pattern usually is homogeneous, the designers made each square in different sizes. There are more than thirty sizes. The smallest is seven millimetres, and the biggest is thirty-five millimetres. Using such difference of sizes, they made another pattern in bigger scale which is also the checker flag pattern. The bigger pattern is not homogeneous. The size of each square is different. Using such difference of sizes, they made one more pattern which is the silhouette of trees. What the designers really wanted to do is to weaken the symbolised image of the brand. Usually symbol does not relate to the context, which the designers really do not like. They want to make something linked to the surroundings delicately. If the designers can refine the commercial façade architecturally, this is one way to do it.

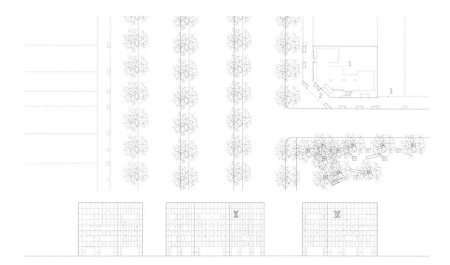

1. retail space
2. entrance
3. arcade

Entrance

Exterior façade

Lobby

Photo: Daichi Ano

Completion Date: 2006

Architect: Kumiko Inui

Night view

Xi Gallery

Located in Yeonsan–dong, Pusan, this building was constructed for the purpose of promoting "Xi", a brand of apartments. In addition to the standard type of an apartment unit exhibition space, an even larger share of the floor area is allocated as a variable cultural space for the locals, which as a result creates a brand–new building typology: a Housing Cultural Centre. As economic forces and cultural activities seem to form complex interrelationships causing our private and public spheres to merge and invade each other, this building comes as a product of these current phenomena. The focus of the designers' investigation is to create a fluid space that can respond to the "continuously new" situations arising from the dynamic flux of economy and culture, and in the organisation of the movement system to correspond to such a space. This new movement organisation is necessary to maintain the existing individuality of the spaces, but at the same time be able to expand/unify them in diverse manners to suit future possible needs.

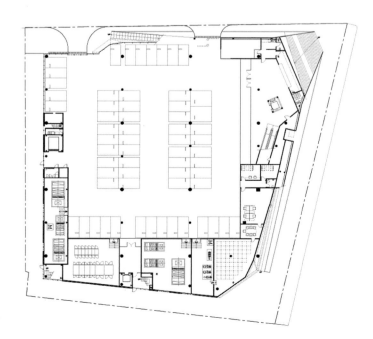

Building front

Hall

Interior

Photo: Yong–Kwan Kim

Completion Date: 2007

Architect: Mass Studies

133

Building in normal environment

Model House

The Model House for I'Park City is a showroom to exhibit the residential urban and façade design for an eighty-eight–building development in Suwon. The principal design intention was to curate the visitor experience by elaborating on an implicit circulation strategy. The route of the visitor, from the approach to the building and throughout the tour within, is treated as an ongoing exhibition.

The building is therefore configured as a clear illustration of this strategy, which becomes the central feature both within the interior space and as a generator of the façade design. The resultant crossing of the circulation ribbon produces various viewpoints of the exhibited content, in this case, the façades of the show–units. In parallel, the same path oscillates between a focus on the interior exhibited content and the adjacent larger site and landscape, which is the location of the future development. The circulation route underscores the importance of the "coming home experience" which is the organisational driver of the entire I'Park City Urban development, and the core of the overall site branding strategy.

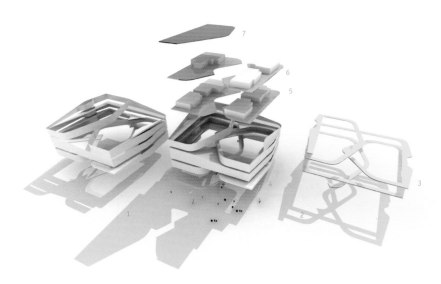

1. skin
2. volume
3. exhibition ribbon
4. entrance level
5. level 1
6. level 2
7. roof terrace observatory

Façade details

Interior

Photo: Christian Richters

Residential

Building front

Completion Date: 2009

Architect: UNStudio

Daytime view from the street

Myeongdong Theatre

Due to the soaring land price in Myeongdong and increasing propensity to consume, the former Myeongdong National Theatre building was under threat of being torn down and replaced by a high-rise commercial building. However, the exterior wall was preserved thanks to the campaign for preserving the building and the purchase by Ministry of Culture, Sports and Tourism. The new cultural interface of the newborn Myeongdong Theatre holds the memories of the past and the vital energy of the district and has become an artistic beacon. The exterior wall, which keeps the memory of Myeongdong, was preserved and a vessel of regeneration (auditorium mass) was created for the culture of Myeongdong streets in the past, present and the future. The energy of the streets was brought inside the building and filled between the wall of the past and the auditorium mass.

For an urban space open to people, the auditorium mass was lifted above a floor to create a large lobby. The natural lighting pouring down through the skylight, which has been installed between the hall and the auditorium mass, runs along down the mass and reaches the lobby, making the narrow space into one enriched by light. As for the auditorium, the balconies of two floors are surrounded in a three-dimensional way and compose a friendly performance hall in the shape of a horseshoe.

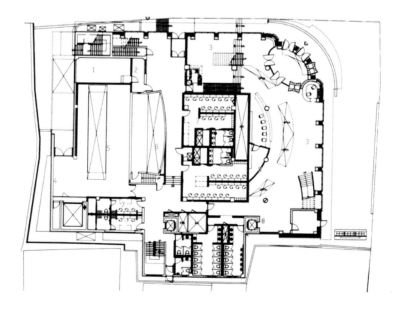

1. disaster preventing room
2. guard room
3. lobby
4. space for loading and unloading
5. under stage
6. orchestra pit
7. make-up room
8. office

Roof

2F Hall with showcase for preserved past wall

Auditorium

Completion Date: 2009

Photo: Park Young-chae

Architect: Myung-Gi Sohn, Jong-R. Hahn

Daytime view

Sungkyunkwan University's Samsung Library

A resource centre where people can retrieve information systematically is an essential goal that the designers bear in mind for this information centre. The theme named the "Digital Library" has been the most basic concept to apply in this design. The Sungkyunkwan University's Samsung Library has an image of a ginkgo leaf, which is the symbol of Sungkyunkwan University as well as an image of an opened book. The Digital Library which has been embodied with transparent and metallic materials is set to reorganise the context of the campus as a hub of information exchange in the heart of the campus.

The centre is a multi-functional facility providing conventions and resting areas. The inner round-shaped void creates a hall, allowing sunlight to flow inside. Group study rooms are freely dispersed near the hall, creating dynamic rhythms. Besides, free community zones are a new type of multi-functional place, and are far different from the quiet and closed typical studying rooms. The Sungkyunkwan University Samsung Library represents a new type of library that is appropriate for the digital era where students can study while socialising with friends, surfing the internet, listening to music and drinking coffee.

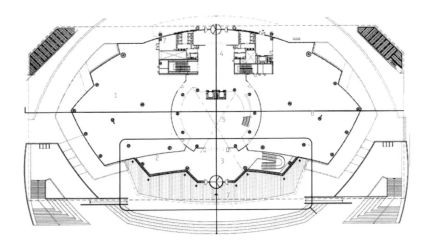

1. search room
2. exhibition hall
3. lobby
4. hall
5. upper open
6. free reading room
7. data keeping room

Rear entrance

Completion Date: 2009

Architect: Samoo Architects & Engineers

Lobby

Meeting room

Canadian Diplomatic Complex

The design of the Canadian Embassy in Seoul creates a dialogue between Korean and Canadian cultures, expressing common links and in particular a shared reverence for nature. This unique site shares a "place" with a 520–year–old tree, a living symbol of nature, called Hakjasu or "scholar" tree in the historic Jeong–dong district near Deoksoo Palace.

The composition pulls back and suspends the two main building masses creating an entrance plaza and gathering place with this tree at its focal point. The building base ties together these two main blocks. This undulating mass is wrapped with a continuous wooden screen composed of western red cedar. Its soft curves frame the public space around the tree adding to the rich composition of textures and materials at the entrance to the building. The wood will age to resemble the undulating walls surrounding Deoksoo Palace.

The historic Jeong–dong context plays an important part in the building materials and organisation of the embassy. Jeong–dong is built of stone, brick and wood in varying hues ranging from grey to red. Embassy materials have been chosen carefully to harmonise with these colours and textures and to extend the pedestrian walk that meanders along the undulating Deoksoog Palace wall.

A protection plan for the 520–year–old tree was critical. The massing was designed for minimum impact on the tree rootball. Using an existing urban site, directing drainage into landscaped areas, coordinating with local materials, minimising parking through a high–density automated system, providing open space, reducing light pollution by screening and curtain wall design, maximising energy efficiency, commissioning – these were all measures taken to promote sustainability.

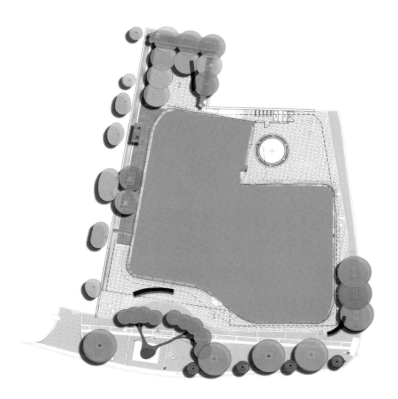

1. reflective pool
2. garden
3. main public entrance
4. 520-year-old tree

Photo: Kim Yong Kwan

Corporate

Completion Date: 2007

Architect: Zeidler Partnership Architects

General view

Post Tower

The Post Tower, situated in one of the most critical and highly visible sites in the historic central business district of Seoul, is the south gate of Myeongdong. Three major roads and their intersections form a triangle within the city that defines the district.

The 72,000–square–metre building presents a symmetrical face and dramatic silhouette to the primarily axial approach from Namdaemun. The building is developed with a primarily stone wall to convey solidity and permanence to the place and accented with a detailed stainless steel window system to provide shadow, richness and sparkle. A super scaled gentle arch that provides a generous and welcoming entrance for the project defines the lobby and main postal hall. The building is sited to the east of the site to maximise the public space in front of the project and create a memorable urban place that accepts the many pedestrian movements through and across the site.

Programmatically the first three floors contain the public postal spaces and the office lobbies. The next six floors contain postal sorting operations on large floor plates to minimise vertical movements. As the tower breaks into two individual towers, the central postal authorities occupy the south tower and the north tower is speculative office space to generate income for the owner. The tenth floor becomes the community centre for the project and contains dining, meeting and lounge spaces for the users all centred on a large exterior terrace.

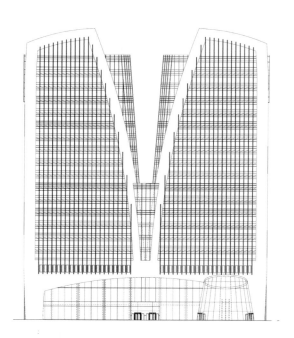

Elevation

Night view

Entrance

Hall

Commercial

Photo: Young-Kwan Kim

Completion Date: 2009

Architect: DeStefano and Partners, Ltd.

General view

Kumho Culture Complex – Kring

The designers' intention is to construct an architectural building to create codes for companies and consumers to facilitate communication, then embed an identity in that architecture. "Urban Sculpture for Branding" is the concept applied in Kring compound culture space to realise brand identity for the client. The way to create this building was different from the conventional method. It was about creating an urban sculpture, and then composing a compound space in it.

Uh–Ul–Lim, phonetic pronunciation of Korean word means "harmony", and the brand image of Kumho E&C was transformed as brand identity through the architectural shaping process. Through the architectural interpretation process, the phenomenon of harmony was connected and emphasised to the city and society with undulation, and the notion of undulation was deepened. The designers wanted to gather various elements of nature, life, and city harmoniously and the essence of harmony to rush out to the city creating echo and undulations, and that became the brand scenario of the project. Projecting images to the city and sucking up the energy of the city at the same time, gigantic container for echo was born, which leads to the concept of "Dream" as well. The designers wanted this to be the monument of the city day and night, specifically, a lighting sculpture when it is dark. Moreover, it becomes a pure white space when entered into, and contains all and any types of cultural programme. The pure white space which achieves spatial surrealism is acting as a stage for performance. Just like a stage changes itself to conform to the types and story of a play, this becomes a compound space to fit itself to diverse needs.

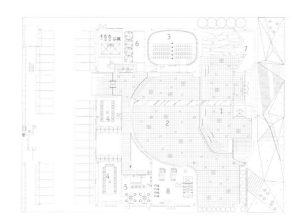

1. atrium
2. exhibition
3. cinema
4. meeting room
5. office
6. toilet
7. storage
8. machinery

Front view

Entrance

Hall

Reception

Photo: Unsangdong Architects

Completion Date: 2008

Architect: Unsangdong Architects

View from the street

Shin–Marunouchi Towers

Hopkins Architects have designed and built a landmark office, retail and restaurant development in Tokyo's most prestigious location for Mitsubishi Estate Group.

Hopkins Architects worked alongside architects, Mitsubishi Jisho Sekkei, to create a structure divided into three sections – two towers on a podium base. The six–storey podium incorporates retail and restaurants. The building's West façade looks onto one of Tokyo's most exclusive shopping streets. Conran, Prada and Hermes all have shops in the area. The offices are aimed at leading international businesses.

The commission required a mixed–use complex with large shop, luxury boutiques, restaurants, and offices for international business tenants; linked below ground level to the Tokyo Plaza metro station. The urban and intrinsic value of the project is revealed by the lightness of the volumetric relationships, the meticulous care taken over the details, the Miesian classicism of the structure that uses relationships on both the urban and human scales. The steel and glass structure resolves the relationship between architecture and its context.

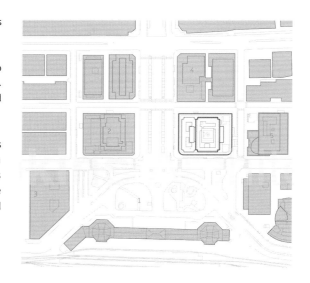

1. Tokyo Station
2. Marunouchi Building
3. Tokyo Central Post Office
4. Tokyo Marine Nichido Building
5. Industry Club of Japan/Mitsubishi Ufj Trust and Banking Building

General view

Façade corner

Corridor

Entrance

Photo: Ken'ichi Suzuki

Completion Date: 2007

Architect: Hopkins Architects

Towada City Hospital

Towada City is at the foot of the mountain Hakkoda–san in the Tohoku snowy district. It is distinguished by its fertile nature and the streets which are orderly marked off as the origin of the modern urban planning. In view of designing this hospital, the outward walls are coloured with the earth–colour and the balconies are with the colour of trunk of cherry blossoms to reflect the cherry blossoms at the government office quarter. The outward walls are designed with grid to match with the latticed streets in Towada City. The façade facing the streets uses of many glasses and extends back a long way with reflecting the trees lined in the streets and the streaming through the leaves of trees.

It aimed at making the building long–standing by adopting the PC structure and the quake–absorbing structure in the building frame, discontinuing the building frame burial of piping as much as possible, and adopting the simple partition.

Regarding the hospital rooms, the water–based facilities and water supply are placed along the outside wall. This design ensures that any future structural changes can be flexibly accommodated, that nurses can visually care for patients with greater ease, and that the window–side bed temperature during the winter season can be maintained at an adequate level.

Externals shining at night

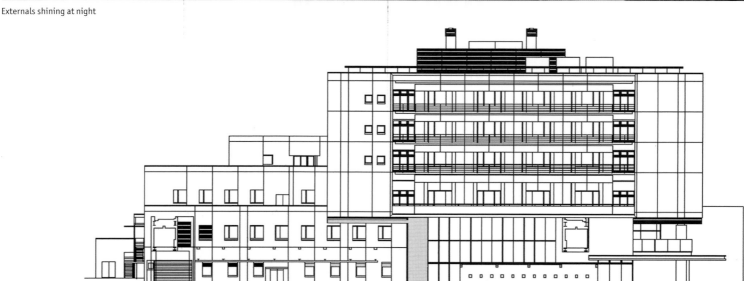

Externals considered in accordance with the streets at the government office quarter

Entrance hall that images nature

Entrance at night

Photo: Mitsuhiro Wada

Completion Date: 2007

Architect: Mikio Chikusa, Norihiro Sawa, Moriki Matsuguma/Showa-Sekkei, Inc

Exterior view

"Steel" House

Using 3.2–millimetre-thick corrugated steel plates, a house of monocoque construction which resembles a freight car was made, without having any beams or columns. The client, Professor Hirose, has been a devoted fan of railroads cars since childhood, and stores a few thousand models of trains in his home. He himself had wanted to live a kind of life in a freight-car environment. Fitting in to the L-shaped site, the house looks like a freight car stopping on a slope, curving into an "L" shape.

The basic idea of the architectural structure is to bend the steel plates to gain strength. By bending them, the detail of the bent parts tells us how soft the material of steel is. If the steel plates were used without being bent and the surface were to be painted, we would not be able to recognise that the material used is steel. There would only be the presence of a white abstract plane, the same as plaster boards or concrete. With such abstract detail, communication does not exist between the substance of steel and people. On the other hand, the detail created by bending the steel establishes communication between steel and us.

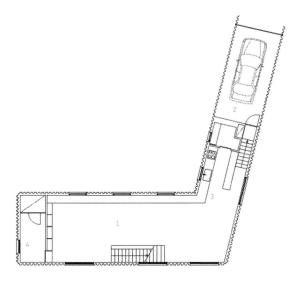

1. living and dining area
2. car parking
3. kitchen
4. wash room

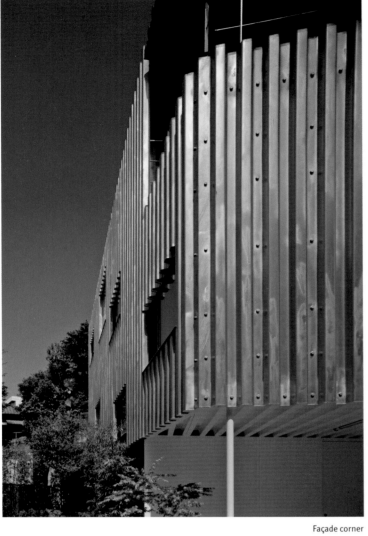

Façade corner

Stilts

Corridor

Common space

Photo: Mitsumasa Fujitsuka

Completion Date: 2007

Architect: Kengo Kuma & Associates

FUJITEC "Big Wing" Headquarters/Product Development Centre

This building was planned for the headquarters to take the hub of the enterprise and for the R & D to make use of the most advanced technology for the products development, in the site along the superhigh speed railway of Tokaido–shinkansen where a rural landscape is stretched around.

In order to strengthen and promote company's growth, the designers aimed to build a space that only showed the company's appeal, but also tried to create an atmosphere in which the employees could work together

The interior of the building is composed of the entrance hall with a working area to the north and a VIP area to the south. The two floors are open and connected, allowing for the working atmosphere to have a sense of continuity and togetherness. The atrium to the east serves multiple purposes besides being a way to move throughout the building, including as a meeting area and a space to take breaks. The atrium's two floors are open, further fostering a sense of workplace cohesion. Additionally, from the bridge that crosses to the lifts of the research tower, one can observe the latest research and development while seeing through the glass the green landscape that the Shinkansen tracks run through.

General view from west

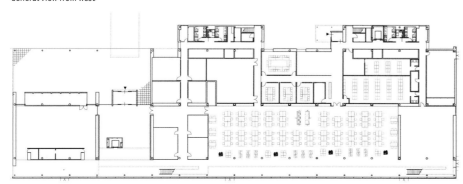

Conference room

Façade, night view

Atrium

Completion Date: 2007

Photo: Yoshiharu Matsumura, Yoshihisa Araki, Fujitec

Architect: Yoshihiro Matsuda, Hideaki Takagi/Showa Sekkei, Inc.

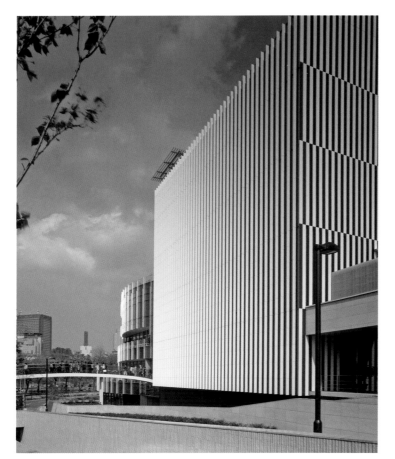

Front façade

Front façade

Suntory Museum of Art

A "Japanese–style room" in the city was to be the concept of the museum. A "Japanese–style room" is a comfortable space where people are able to relax on tatamis that are laid on the floor, and among the Japanese traditions, is the most relaxing and relieving environment.

People of the 20th century sought for a museum that was an exaggerated "urban monument", yet people of the 21st century are looking for a peaceful "Japanese–style room". In fact, as the Suntory Museum of Art worked on the theme "Beauty of Life" from an early stage of planning, there is no other museum which is suited to be a "Japanese–style room". This museum should reveal its natural self at the frontier of the global trend.

The "Japanese–style room" building should not be a pretentious bluff. The "Japanese–style room" is constructed by human–friendly materials cherished in our daily lives – for example white porcelain kind to the skin, paulownia which maintains humidity, and white oak used for barrels. A light adjusting device hinted from the design of the traditional Japanese window "Muso–Koshi" was placed on the frontage facing the greenery of the park. This device softens the scenery and light falling into the "Japanese–style room". Japanese people have used these kinds of devices to appreciate the four seasons and the passing time.

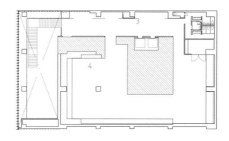

1. entrance
2. main entrance
3. lobby
4. gallery
5. gallery (void)
6. shop
7. café
8. member's salon
9. hall
10. deck
11. roji
12. ryuurei tearoom
13. small tearoom
14. mizuya
15. tearoom terrace

Terrace

Tea room

Gallery

Photo: Mitsumasa Fujitsuka

Completion Date: 2007

Architect: Kengo Kuma & Associates + Nikken Sekkei

Façade

Silent Office

The site is located at the side of an elevated highway near Haneda Airport, at the corner defined by the crossing of two roads. The neighbourhood townscape doesn't show any continuity. The architecture is composed of the closed space to catch silence. In a rectangular box is divided by two slits. The interval between those parts leads the air, the wind and the light into the office itself. To ensure an effective internal space, while respecting the legislative outline of the allowed building volume, the ceiling's height of the top floor is higher on the west side than the east one.

Not only to be functional, but aslo to give to the place some complexity, the inside and the outside spaces have been carefully thought out. The parking and the delivery areas are on the west side. The road side provides tree plantations, adding to the surroundings some green space.The ground floor is divided between the warehouse and working space for the personnel. The first floor is devoted to an other part of the warehouse function. The tenant office is on the last and second floor.

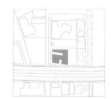

1. entrance
2. hall
3. lobby
4. office
5. storehouse
6. reception
7. storage
8. parking
9. space
10. utility
11. balcony
12. terrace

Terrace

Void

Office room

Photo: Takashi Yamaguchi & Associates

Coporate

Completion Date: 2008

Architect: Takashi Yamaguchi & Associates

External

Uwajima City Hospital

The Uwajima Municipal Hospital had opened in 1910 which has played the core of hospital in the outskirts of the district. It was reconstructed toward the new era of 100 years from now on. The total area of this project is 19,604.79 square metres, with a 11,233.09–square–metre building area. The roof slab occupies 50.38metres. The highest height is 50.98metres. The ground floor is in the underground, the tenth floor on the ground. The materials are PcaPC, steel structure and quake–absorbing structure. There are 435 beds in total.

The outward appearance is designed for representing the blue sky in Uwajima with lightening the size of the structure with a basic tone of a vertical stripe. And the interior appearance is designed rather for the well–ordered and calm hospitals. The colouring of the hospital is composed of being approachable to the regional people.

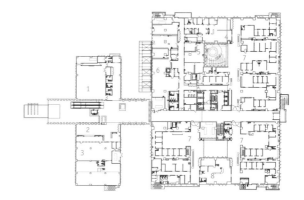

1. lecture hall
2. reception
3. office
4. dialysis
5. physiological examination
6. specimen lab
7. medical examination
8. central treatment

Night view of the front

Front view

Side view at night

Rehabilitation garden

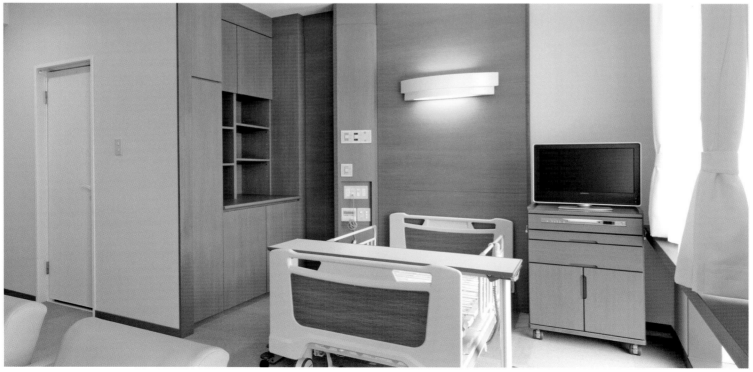

Special private room

Photo: SS-OSAKA

Completion Date: 2009

Architect: Mikio Chikusa

Bird's eye view

Namics Techno Core

Namics is a company that manufactures special paste for semiconductor boards. In the year of its 60th anniversary of founding, this innovative company has decided to rebuild its research centre. Riken Yamamamoto & Field Shop were invited to a design competition, and proposed an iconic, mushroom–shaped structure which appears to float in midair. Namics is a vigorous company which tries to constantly re-establish its corporate image by endeavouring in new projects. As Namics grew rapidly into a multinational corporation, its management sought a building which appropriately symbolises the company's momentum. Another design requirement was to "open up" the building to numerous visiting clients, and the interpretation of this requirement was that the building had to be legible and recognisable as possible.

They proposed an articulated three–layer structure with the ground floor and first floor pulled apart. The ground floor accommodates the research facilities, the middle first floor a floating garden, and the first floor a cafeteria and hoteling office. The research facilities on the first floor are arranged on a grid plan as requested by the client. The middle second floor, or the ground floor roof, is landscaped with a space for exhaust outlets coming from the research rooms and laboratories, which provide a relaxation area for the staff. On top of that there is the second floor mushroom structure. This building is sure to establish Namics' new image.

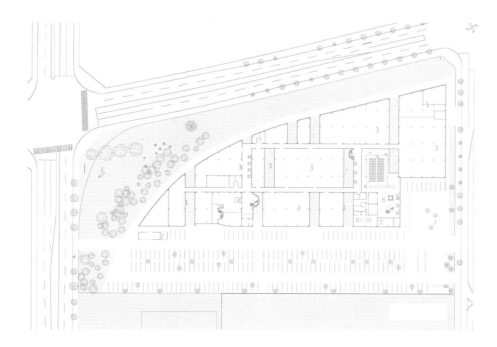

1. utilities room
2. waste and recycling area
3. laboratory
4. multi-function plaza
5. reception area
6. visitors room
7. general affairs office

External view

External view

General affairs office

Photo: Koichi Satake

Completion Date: 2008

Architect: Riken Yamamamoto & Field Shop

Front view

Flower Shop H

The designers tried to make small rooms without the presence of ceiling, which may make people feel as if they were in exterior space even though they are in interior space. Since it has a limit of height of the building, the designers divided a building into several small volumes. The smaller the footprint of each building is, the higher the impression of the ceiling is.

The context of the site consists of both the city and the park. Since the city and the park are completely different in various points, the designers were in two minds about choosing which context they take. If they design a pavilion, that does not fit in with the city. If they design just a building, that does not fit to the park. They did not want either of them. Thus, the designers decided to accept both of them. The division of the building made the proportion of each building vertical, which made the project resemble to the building around it. The designers love such way of respecting existing landscape. The project does not only copy the man-made context, but also respect the spaces like trees.

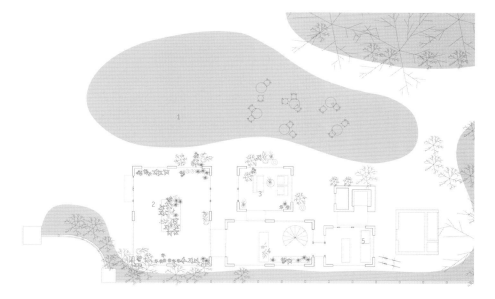

1. terrace
2. retail space
3. retail space
4. cashier
5. backyard

Lobby

Entrance

Entrance

Photo: Daichi Ano

Completion Date: 2005

Architect: Kumiko Inui

Daytime view

House in Yugawara

The south part of the slope, where used to be a tangerine farm, is the site. Flexible soil was found after the research and the pile work was necessary. The wooden bungalow was very light and the architects were able to have smaller number of stakes by making the groundwork positioning consolidate and distributed by blocks. With the post on the balanced groundwork, they made the box-shaped walls and the floor and roof.

The box, created as one of the groundwork, presents the softness in the continuous one-room spacing. Besides, the slope presents the multilevel floor, which gives the area some separation by the level. People who would live there can choose their own "space" as they like.

At the TEPCO comfortable Housing Contest, the prize was given especially for the understanding of the construction and consistency of the flatness plan. The project is particularly designed to fit the strange site of the area. The low cost of the construction of the project is also part of the consideration for the winning in this contest.

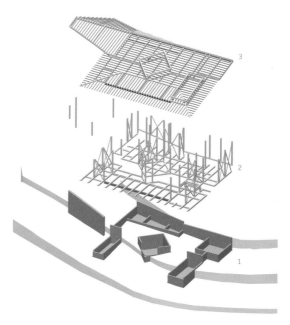

1. base
2. in-between column structure
3. roof

Side view

Terrace

Photo: Hiroshi Ueda

Completion Date: 2006

Architect: Kazuhiko Kishimoto / acaa

Front façade

Night view

Namba Hips

A client who has developed amusement businesses obtained a plot of a prime location fronting Midosuji, a main road in Osaka. The client planned to build a complex mainly containing amusement facilities and restaurants, and required many architects to submit their ideas in a long term. As the result of the comparison, he finally designated Shin Takamatsu. The idea which made the client decide was so clear. The lucid idea led a consistent architecture from the beginning to the completion. It is a separation from meanings. Takamatsu says without fearing the misunderstanding, this form of the architecture was developed as the theme which thoroughly hates the meaning. The architecture was designed by pursuing the form which ignores architectural urban scale and refered to nothing. The architect was sure that the only existence of unregistered glory can be the symbolic architecture in the city where there is super saturation with registered glory.

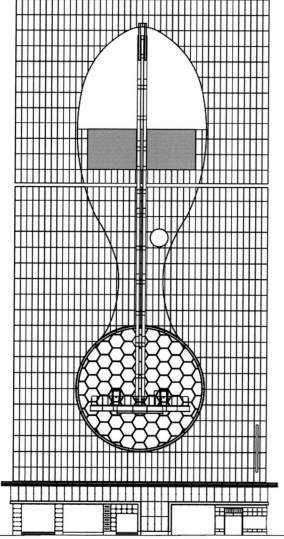

West elevation

Interior

Interior

Interior

Architect: Shin Takamatsu +Shin Takamatsu Architect and Associates Co., Ltd.

Photo: No credit

Completion Date: 2007

Recreational

Front view

Miyasaka Residence

The Miyasaka residence bridges the aesthetics of two disparate cultures (Western and Japanese), emblematic of neither, yet summoning echoes of both. Built to accommodate the busy lifestyle of the president of a major commercial building contractor, as well as providing a place of repose for his elderly parents; the house was conceived to appear as a radiant jewel in the midst of an urban garden oasis. From the beginning, the client expressed his wish for a "Western" style home, as well as his parents' desire for Japanese tradition.

The architect brought an approach to design that honours the use of natural materials. The architect's efforts to bring morning sunlight into the master suite and kitchen area, afternoon sunlight into the parent's suite, while preserving the existing landscape ultimately provided a genesis for the plan. Elevating the first storey allowed for the insertion of a continuous band of clerestory glazing between it and the canopy, thereby introducing an incredible amount of natural light to penetrate throughout the interior even during the heavy snow buildup of winter. This resulted in the entire first storey being held proud of the ground, providing the sensation of it appearing to float above its base, like a bird frozen in mid–flight.

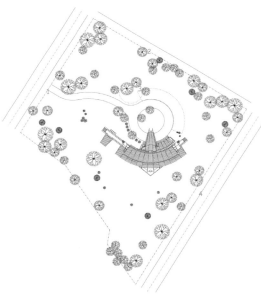

Site plan

1. entre gate
2. alley
3. future carport
4. street

Courtyard

Courtyard

Bedroom

Photo: Yoshihiko Tobari

Completion Date: 2008

Architect: Robert Oshatz

Façade

Akasaka Phoenix

The location of the site is around fifty metres far back from the heavily-trafficked main street, where we get the impression of quiet in a high-density city. The east side of the site faces "city air pocket" where is the open space of the complex facility, and it has a spacious atmosphere. For that reason, there is no concern about eye gaze from neighbours, and the internal space can get enough sunlight and natural ventilation. Since the site level is about six metres up from the road in front, the building has a high level of visibility. The designers have reinforced identity of the building by giving strong design impact on the east side, and tried to differentiate it from surrounding buildings.

It can be said that one of the characteristic design aspects of this building is louvres of the façade. Five louvres are made into a unit and each unit controls outside environment such as direct sunlight, eye gaze from outside and so on. In order to create comfortable indoor condition, the units consist of eight different patterns and each unit is arranged according to the function. For instance, upward horizontal louvre is used abundantly for shielding of direct sunlight.

Moreover, the louvres show various expressions according to the angle and direction of attachment. These variations give motion to the façade and create deep shade which gives dignity to a building. The louvres are coloured in vivid royal blue and a white and their expression change with the positions of eyes. The façade of Akasaka Phoenix is rich in diversity and creates a new city landscape.

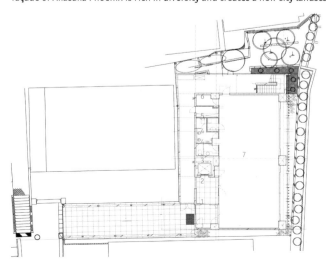

1. entrance
2. lift hall
3. lift
4. WC
5. staff kitchen
6. storage
7. office

Details

Different view

Windows

Interior

Photo: Takumi Ota

Completion Date: 2008

Architect: Atsushi Kitagawara

Façade

Rooftecture O–K

The Rooftecture projects, eight buildings designed by Osaka–based architect Shuhei Endo for the Japan–based used car dealership, O–RUSH, are whimsical structures with sweeping cantilevered roofs and continuous suspended steel sheets that minimise interior walls, leaving room to show off the glimmering cars inside.

In a similar use of suspended steel, Endo utilised a one–storey structural steel frame from an existing building and covered it with a new roof for the Kyoto O–RUSH building, Rooftecture O–K. Contact points within the building's frame stabilise the continuous suspended steel sheet roof that begins at ground level on one end, and waves upward to cover the two–storey showroom. The thickness of the steel sheets provides self–weighted stress, opposing gravity. The glazed façade opens the 2,000–plus–square–foot interior to natural daylighting.

The one–storey difference in elevation from the maintenance space to the two–storey showroom of the building is united with a continuous visual context under the sinuous metallic roof.

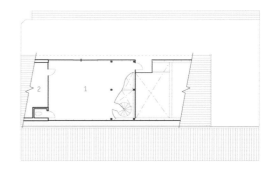

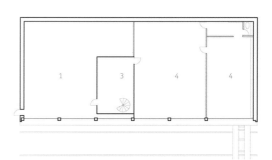

1. exhibition space
2. office
3. meeting space
4. workshop

General view

Workshop

Reception

Photo: Shuhei Endo

Completion Date: 2006

Architect: Shuhei Endo

Looking towards the elevation facing the scramble junction

The atrium becomes increasingly transparent at night as it is lit up

EX

The site of EX faces the front of a four-way crosswalk with heavy pedestrian traffic. The goal of the project was to design a core facility that could change the scenery of the Chiba station area that is suffering from economic decay. The solution to this problem was to design a building with a five-storey glass atrium in the front so the various activities inside would be seen from the outside. Then by having an atrium full of movement, the architects aimed to let the context and the atrium have a stronger connection to each other.

The main circulation for the building is gathered at the front atrium facing the existing shopping district. The atrium then is made with a transparent curtain wall so it visually opens up to the surrounding district. Besides, the escalator facing the atrium is cantilevered to make the space become open. The building's exterior is then clad with metal panels that vary in width to give the building a rhythm and avoids the monotonous surface.

The name of the building is "EX" which is a prefix meaning "out of". This is to emphasise on the designer's design concept: wide range of information and activities are sent out from this building, making the whole community a more attractive place.

Close-up of the exterior

The organic print on the building surface adds playfulness to the architecture

View from the main ground level entrance looking at the cantilevered floors

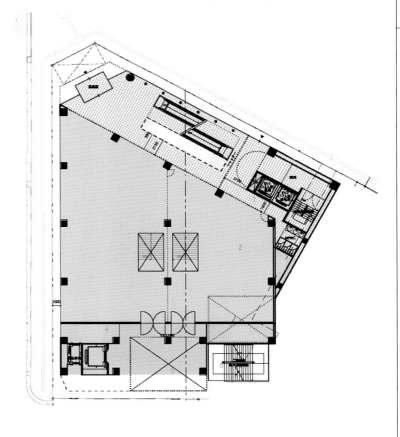

1. lift
2. tenant
3. WC
4. central monitor room
5. garbage place
6. escape staircase

Completion Date: 2008

Architect: SATOH Hirotaka Architects

Façade

Cat Building

This building stands in front of a street called the Cat Street. The Cat Street is a very narrow pedestrian walk, and under it a river lies which is made to a culvert. There are always many people walking around the shops and boutiques along the street. In front of the site, there are tall buildings standing along a major arterial road, and behind the site, there lies a hill with single–family houses at high density. This place is in a neighbourhood where urban city structure changes to a familiar human scale. The site is located at the corner of the Cat Street and can be seen in many angles from the street. This building is located on such an area, and is a commercial building mainly purposed for shops.

In this irregular shaped site, varieties of form regulations determine the outline shape of the building. Outside form of the building is designed as to visualise these regulation lines. It is rather clumsy and violent in shape, but like the innocent form of architecture standing in the dense city of Tokyo. Based on this form of the building, it became a theme to search for a tenants' space, in which co–responds to the dynamism of the dense city and the various aspects of activities inside.

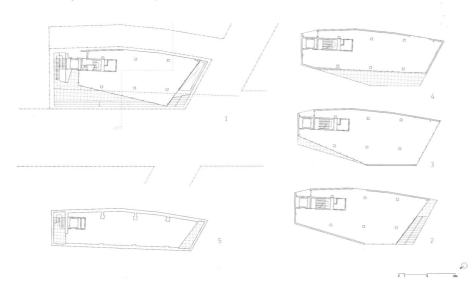

1. 1F plan
2. 2F plan
3. 3F plan
4. 4F plan
5. B1 plan

Interior

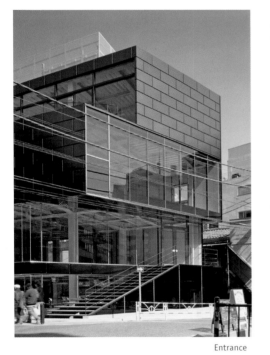

Entrance

Stairs

Side view

Details

Photo: Koichi Torimura

Completion Date: 2006

Architect: Taketo Shimohigoshi/A.A.E.

Iidabashi Subway Station

The significance of "INDUCTION DESIGN / ALGOrithmicDESIGN" project lies in the search for better solutions to given conditions. There were two types of conditions that "WEB FRAME" programme had to solve.
1. Restrictions on space & Conditions imposed by each component.
2. The intended volume and density of the space.

The first of them was an absolute condition allowing no margin for improvisation. The second condition – spatial requirements – became more flexible parameter. The issues here are different from those of conventional space frames. Simply because the degree of freedom is great, divergences can occur and lead in unpredictable directions.

Freedom can, of course, readily slip over into chaos. An important element of this concept is to give the appearance of chaos while in fact obeying certain regularities.

The coexistence of freedom and harmony! This sounds like a catchphrase put forth at some kind of meeting by people fully aware that such a thing will never come about in reality. This is not an empty slogan. Here we are (just) beginning to see signs that it can be realised.

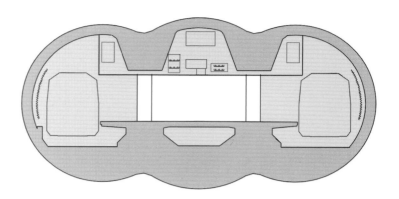

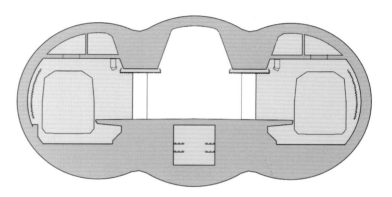

Exterior

Platform

The light of network structure

Passageway

Entrance

Photo: Makoto Sei Watanabe

Architect: Makoto Sei Watanabe, Architects' Office

View of the clubhouse from the golf course

Unimas Golf Resort Club

The Unimas Golf Resort Club house is part of the unimas master plan in Kota Samarahan, Kuching. The club house and golf course is the centre piece and communal heartland of a university township planned on the successful development of Universiti Malaysia Sarawak.

The facilities of the club house are located on three floors – with the guest arrival and main entrance at upper ground level. The second entrance point is for buggies located at the lower ground level. The upper ground floor houses the banquet hall with a capacity of fifty tables, i.e. 500 persons. Ancillary spaces to the banquet hall are provided in the form of VIP rooms and pre function spaces. The lobby and terrace that wrap around the building serves as both a viewing gallery and dining terrace. The kitchen and its supporting facilities are also located in this floor for easier operation and efficiency of use. The "open–plan" nature of the design means that all the facilities are visually linked with the exception of the services and amenities.

In order to liberate the upper floor plane for the members' viewing and f & b needs, the water courtyard and the amenities are located in the lower ground floor – the changing rooms and toilets are located here for proximity to the swimming pool level and the buggy parks. The second entrance is located at this level, with sixty buggy parks under cover nearby and other twenty-eight buggy parks outdoors. In keeping with the effort to maintain an open plan and maximum view advantage on the main floor, the roomed facilities such as offices, library and conference facilities are located in a mezzanine floor partially housed within the building's roof space.

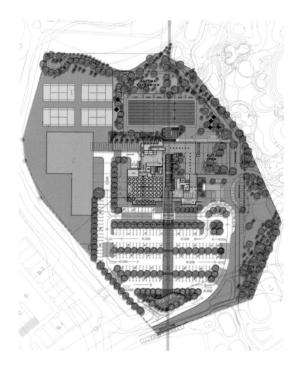

1. tennis court (future extension)
2. future extension
3. swimming pool
4. interior

The new clubhouse speaks of lightness and shade

Modern tropical style in a sombre palette and tidy lines

Resort–swimming pool

Façade

Yeoman's Bungalow

The house is entered from main staircase – an open structure where the timber–lined cantilevered flights of stairs double as a sculptural lookout. At the top of the stairs, one crosses the threshold into the first pavilion that is the conversation area, the kitchen and a dining room that overlooks at lap pool. From here, one crosses a water–court into the second pavilion further up the slope; which is the main living room with a large viewing deck. The spaces in these two pavilions are visually linked as one looks towards the lap pool.

Nestled uppermost in the hillside is the bedroom pavilion which contains the master bedroom suite, guest bedrooms and study. This longish block is flanked by a veranda, which can be turned into an informal living space when the guests slide open the glazed doors to the bedrooms. From this veranda and down a flight of stairs, one comes full–circle and arrives back at the first pavilion.

Ultimately, this is a house to be experienced – by standing in her rooms, by walking through her corridors and looking through her windows, because the architectural language is deliberately uncomplicated and its form is simple, acting merely as a foil to the more commanding presence of Mount Santubong.

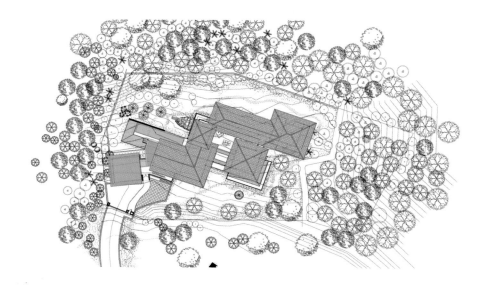

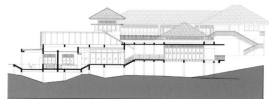

1. landscape
2. swimming pool
3. building

Savour the vistas

Night view

Stairs and countyard

Interior

Photo: Design Network Architects Sdn Bhd

Residential

Completion Date: 2009

Architect: Design Network Architects Sdn Bhd

Front view with pool

Enclosed Open House

The owners wanted a spacious, contemporary house that would be as open as possible but without compromising security and privacy at the same time. Surrounded by neighbours on four sides, the solution was a fully fenced compound with a spatial programme that internalised spaces such as pools and gardens, which are normally regarded as external to the envelope of the house. By zoning spaces such as the bedrooms and servants' quarters on alternative levels, i.e. upper storey and basement levels, the ground plane was freed from walls that would have been required if public and private programmes were interlaced on the same plane. The see–through volumes allow a continuous, uninterrupted forty–metre view, from the entrance foyer and pool, through the formal living area to the internal garden courtyard and formal dining area in the second volume. All these spaces are perceived to be within the built enclosure of the house.

The environmental transparencies at ground level and between courtyards are important in passively cooling the house. All the courtyards have different material finishes and therefore different heat gain and latency (water, grass, granite). As long as there are temperature differences between courtyards, the living, dining and pool house become conduits for breezes that move in between the courtyards, very much like how land and sea breezes are generated.

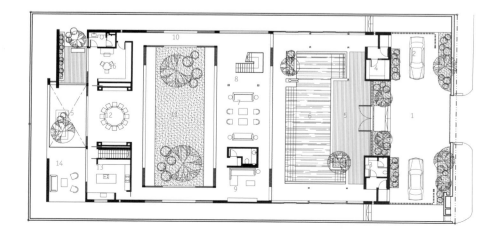

1. driveway
2. charporch
3. changing room
4. store
5. foyer
6. swimming pool
7. living
8. powder room
9. TV area
10. linkway
11. counrtyard
12. dining
13. kitchen
14. outdoor terrace
15. void to basement
16. study room

General view

Photo: Albert Lim

Entrance

Completion Date: 2009

Living room

Architect: Wallflower Architecture + Design

Profile

Studio M Hotel

A mere stone's throw away from the Singapore River, Studio M Hotel is in the heart of entertainment districts. Given its high visibility and the accompanying social vibrance of the site, the key idea was to design a trendy and memorable landmark worthy of gracing the historical river next to which it resides. The result is a building façade shaped like a boat sail, with the elevated deck being likened to a cruise deck. These features collectively paint an image of a ship moored by the riverside.

Rooms were designed as live-work-play spaces that cater to the needs of urban travellers. Conceptualised as a "box within a box", each 15 m2 room is compact yet luxurious, with double volume space for added depth and fully functional bathroom "pods" that can be easily reconfigured to create a diversity of room types. A staircase leads up to the furniture deck that either houses a bed or workstation, giving business travellers the added convenience of computer facilities during their stay.

Studio M Hotel's Urban Connector acts as an open space that links the hotel with outdoor areas like the landscape deck and Singapore River. The design concept of the park was to compliment the hotel and its public spaces, with lush greenery acting to buffer the stoic landscape while also reducing heat. Provision for adequate seating also encourages guests to relax in the park while breathing in the beautiful scenery.

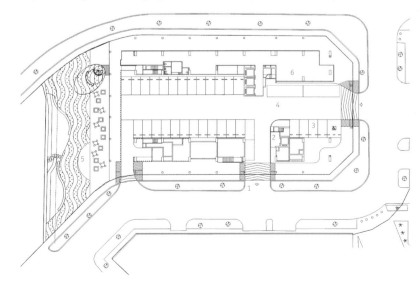

1. entrance
2. reception area
3. lobby
4. corridor
5. courtyard
6. lounge

Front

Profile

Detail

Bedroom

Photo: Derek Swalwell

Hotel

Completion Date: 2010

Architect: ONG&ONG Pte Ltd.

Multipurpose Building For Auroville Papers

This building houses a multipurpose hall and services for 60 workers (kitchen, laundry, lockers, bathrooms etc.) of the existing factory. The services are contained within closed rooms and the hall is left completely open on two sides for maximum cross ventilation and feeling of space at congregations. The hall is also marked by a curvilinear wall on one side and the linear block of services on the other. The roof is lifted from the building to provide a natural draft of air circulation in the room. A small bas–relief design on the ceiling animates the space otherwise left bare. Local natural smooth stones in shades of grey, yellow ochre and green are used in a pattern for the flooring of the main hall. Rough stone is used in bathrooms and the other service areas.

A natural root zone waste water recycling system treats the grey water from the toilets and the water is re–used for irrigation needs of the whole site. Leftover blue metal aggregate of the site with locally found boulders in conjunction with local species of the plants dot the green area around the building. Textured exterior wall paint in shades of orange adds to the tropical context.

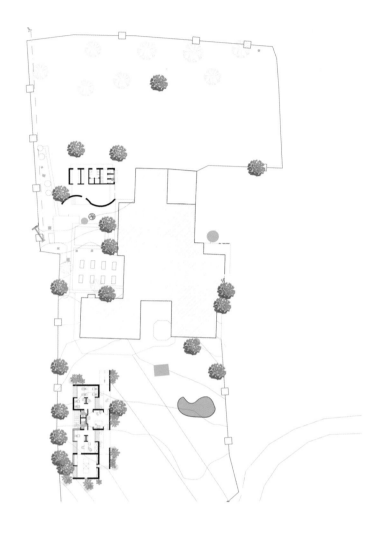

Architect: Sherilcastelino, C&M Architects

Completion Date: 2006

Photo: Pino Marchese

Complex

Entrance Canopy

Triose Food Court

Angled spaces projected towards different directions encapsulated in an organically folded concrete skin create a two–level building that houses a few retail shops, a food court, two restaurants, a large bar and an entertainment gaming area.

The entire frontage of the site along the main road overlooks large trees and a riverbed and hills. The axis of the building changes constantly from one side to the other allowing each space within to look out towards different views of the surrounding landscapes.

The concrete folded skin that forms most of the building creates large open frames towards the external views and the plans of the building also open out towards these large frames accentuating the beautiful natural surroundings to the inner spaces. A natural slope in the site towards the rear allowed an entire parking level to be created to facilitate the high traffic expected for the building with natural light and ventilation from the rear housing over 100 cars.

The building is created sculpturally from within & externally and is a unique manifestation of abstract volumes that are fluid in the interior and perceived as a dramatic juxtaposition of trapezoidal volumes on the site.

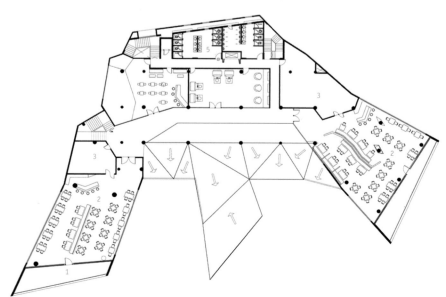

1. entrance
2. restaurant
3. kitchen
4. pub
5. WC

Landscape with the building

Water

Food Court

Photo: Vinesh Gandhi

Completion Date: 2008

Architect: Sanjay Puri, Mamata Shelar

77/32, Gurgaon

Located in Gurgaon, the office hub in the suburbs of New Delhi, the building moves away from the typical office typology, and provides an alternative with interweaving open social spaces and closed workspaces.

The design is envisaged with two types of informal spaces – one at the public level and the other at the individual office level. The ground floor is designed to be a recreational, informal meeting space which defines the entrance as well. A passive cooling strategy is adopted to create a modified environment which is non–air–conditioned. This is done through the creation of water bodies, and allows for built mass only on two sides and the remaining two sides are left open to allow for wind movement. A café is designed as a part of the recreation zone. Each individual office has been provided with a terrace garden which becomes its private, informal breakout zone.

To address the environmental issues that concern the contemporary office, orientation is optimised in the creation of built volumes. The East and West sun are blocked off with the help of solid stonewalls that act as a thermal buffer. The two long sides, north and south, are provided with glazing and punctures respectively. Each floor plate is designed to be fifteen metres wide to allow for daylight penetration. The use of post–tensioned beams allows for the creation of column–free spaces, which permits maximum flexibility within the office space.

Exterior view at night

Landscaped area

Informal breakout spaces

Entrance area

1. entrance
2. exit
3. food court
4. landscape garden
5. landscape court
6. reception
7. lift lobby

Exterior view

Centra Mall

Chandigarh is a city with a high degree of urbanisation and most of the commercial areas in Chandigarh are concentrated in specifically-designated sectors. Hence, there arises a need for developing other commercial centres within the city. The site for Centra Mall is located in the Industrial Sector on the most visible corner plot on the main sector road and there are excellent linkages from the airport, railway station and the residential and institutional areas of the city, thus making the site an extremely vital component of the city fabric.

The design intent for the mall has two predominant aspects viz. the socio-cultural aspect and the environmental strategy. Traditionally, malls have been approached with a Box-type morphology that excludes people and is not democratic in nature. Hence, the approach has been to reverse this morphology and open up the Box instead towards the site context and surroundings. The built form enclosure is straight-off the road and the design approach is directed towards providing a High Street nature to the mall which opens up. An atrium along the premium road access helps to attain the public disposition, whilst maintaining the mall typology. The retail shops and the entertainment block face the atrium and being wholly transparent, it allows visibility of all the shops from the road. State-of-the-art escalators and lifts allow for the vertical movement and build in pedestrian linkages inside the mall. The layout is extremely efficient with very low super area loading. There are two levels of basement with adequate parking and centralised building services.

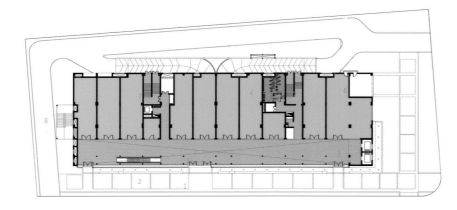

1. mall entrance
2. escalators
3. lift lobby
4. public toilets
5. atrium
6. cinema ticket counter
7. staircase
8. fire escape staircase

Escalator

Commercial

Exterior view

Passageway

Completion Date: 2008

Architect: Morphogenesis

195

India Glycols Limited

The office design for the corporate office for India Glycols embodies the issues concerning the workplace today, and explores the paradigm of the office space as a social activity. Sited in a non–contextual suburban area of Delhi, the setting led to the development of an introverted scheme that would address environmental and socio–economic issues from first principles.

As is the nature of most bespoke corporate developments, the building had to exemplify the brand identity and corporate ideology of equity and transparency in the workplace as an integral part of the architectural vocabulary. Conceived as a solid perimeter scheme with a more fluid interior, the morphology blurs the interface between the inside and outside. The built form optimises the natural day lighting and helps to define the programmatic requirements of the office. A stacking system is used to generate a variety of open spaces, such as courtyards, verandahs and terraces, which help to structure the office spaces. A central spine traversing the built volume serves as the common activity zone, with other departments branching out. The design's conceptual strength comes from the spatial organisation which creates overlaps between the exterior and the interior and between the various programmatic requirements, hence creating a vibrant and creative work environment.

Night view of the inner courtyard

External spaces

Shaded outer façade with small slit windows

Photo: Edmund Sumner

Exterior shot

Reception area

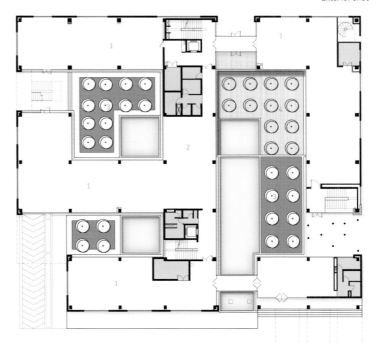

1. workstation
2. common spine
3. landscape greens
4. deck below

Corporate

Completion Date: 2009

Architect: Sanjay Bharwaj (morphogenesis)

General View

Avana Apartment

This sixteen–storey apartment project is located in Kemang area in South Jakarta, an established neighbourhood famous for its collection of mature trees and vast greeneries. The initial concept of an eight-storey apartment with balconies was abandoned for half a year in 2006 before the client decided to appoint Aboday Architects (Indonesia) to revive the project. As its first project in Indonesia, Aboday decided to retain only the project's internal modular unit plan, while changing the rest of external design, including rising it to sixteen storeys as a result of intense negotiation with local building regulator.

Living in an apartment unit way above ground is some kind of new experience for local people who used to the idea of staying in landed property, hence the introduction of extensive balcony surrounding each unit, mimicking a "yard" in "normal" house. Comprising sixty-four units ranging between 180 square metres to 460 square metres (for the penthouse), with each spacious private space and service area, this apartment is an epitome of landed house that stacked on top of each other creating a home in the sky. The idea of a fluid internal–external space is also explored in every space creation on this building. A six-metre-high lobby, which opens directly to its public pool and garden, starts this experience on the ground floor when people enter the building, leading to a glass–enclosed private lobby. This concept of internal–external space is further explored in each unit above. There is almost no visible boundary between internal unit, balcony (and even the sky...), as a result of extensive use of tempered clear glass panel for door, window and balcony's railing.

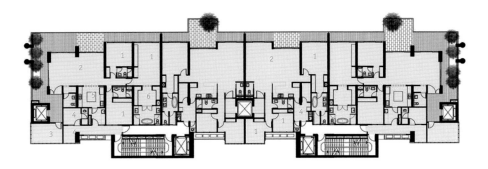

1. bedroom
2. living & dining room
3. study room
4. service area
5. kitchen
6. master bathroom

Details

Façade

Photo: Happy Lim Photography

Residential

Interior

Completion Date: 2009

Architect: ABODAY (www.aboday.com)

Villa Paya–Paya, Seminyak, Bali

This villa is located in Seminyak, a bustling residential area in the heart of Bali, Indonesia. The site bordered on the north by a six–metre public road, and by a pangkung (dried, old river in Balinese) on the south. The client requested to have a holiday home for the small family of four, with a simple programme: large living and dining, large servant quarter, a master bedroom with huge bathroom and two smaller bedrooms.

The sloping site gives an advantage to the design. Aboday, as an architect, doesn't want to have an imposing building. The villa needs to respect human scale and main road as main way to the temple. This road is sometimes crowded during the Hindu celebration as a shortcut to the nearby temple, and anything taller than coconut trees will be an intrusion to their ritual. The two–level villa appears as a friendly single–storey building from the road, sunk in the rest of the room programme on its ground level. Instead of evoking the surrounding typical Balinese building of slooping coconut leaf roof, Aboday choose a simple concrete white box as the façade of the building. The traditional sloping roof is still used in the master bedroom pavilion with its wood structure, hidden behind the white box façade, as an element of surprise among the domination of white forms.

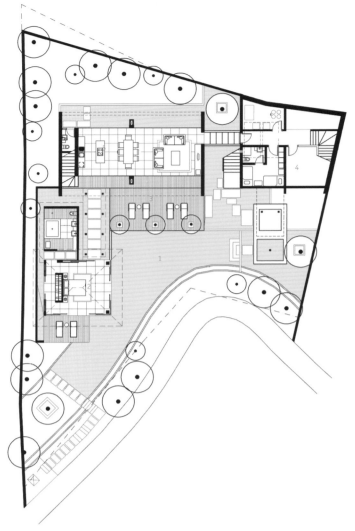

1. swimming pool
2. master bedroom
3. pool deck
4. store room
5. dining room
6. master bedroom

Photo: Happy Lim Photography

Residential

Completion Date: 2008

Architect: ABODAY (www.aboday.com)

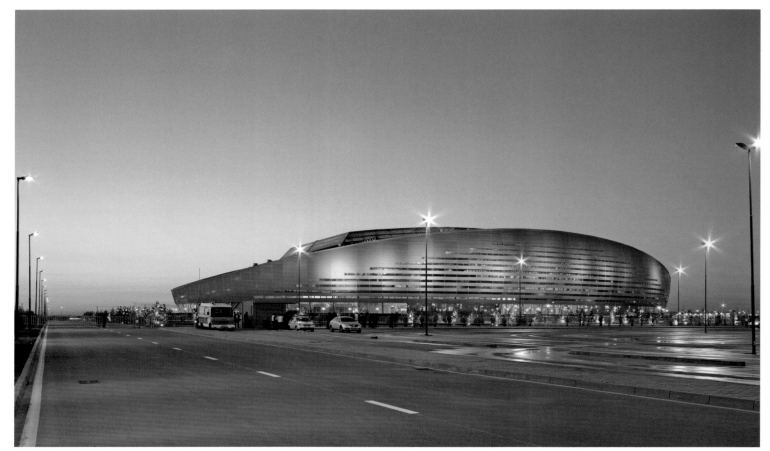

A new scene in Astana tallying with the synergy of sports, games, hospitality, nature and contemporary architecture

Astana Arena

Apart from its functional features, the Astana Arena is designed specifically for Astana City to be a symbolic building that reflects the modern and contemporary aspects of the new capital of Kazakhstan. The design introduces innovative solutions adopting high technology principles for operational management, interaction with the environment and especially with harsh climatic conditions of the geography. An operable roof system that functions independently from the fixed roof is programmed in order to protect the green area and provide eligible conditions for the spectators and players.

The Arena can be used for different sports and gathering purposes but it is mainly programmed as a soccer field, which will be covered with high–quality artificial grass that fits the FIFA and UEFA criteria.

Aligning with the elliptical outer form, the circulation line creates dynamic and peaceful areas. Entering and leaving the Arena, people will be able to walk in or out via a safe and secure path and spectators will be welcomed and discharged via twenty-four separate portals around the Arena. 30,000 people can enter and exit at the same time. Six separate zones, behind the different levels of the stand areas, are spared as concourse that open to food kiosks, restaurants and sufficient number of restrooms. Car parks and service roads for 1,411 cars are planned on 71,650 square metres, outside of these secure spaces where the ticket offices are located. A 9,000-square-metre VIP and media car park is secured behind the west wing.

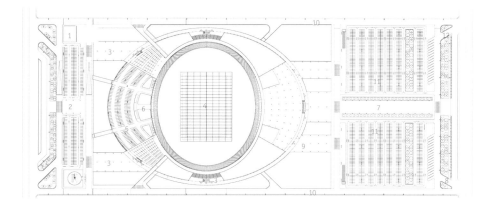

1. heating Centre
2. public car park , 340 cars
3. home team entrance
4. media car park , 65 cars
5. VIP car park, 136 cars
6. mixed zone
7. pedestrian walkway & landscape
8. public exit
9. emergency entrance & exit
10. emergency ring road
11. public car park, 532 cars
12. public entrance

A symbolic building that reflects the contemporary aspects of the new capital of Kazakhstan

Operable roof system over the elliptical outer form

One of the spacious entrances for 30, 000 spectators to enter and exit

Photo: Cemal Emden

Completion Date: 2009

Architect: Tabanlıoalu Architects, Melkan Gürsel & Murat Tabanlıoalu

Business Centre Tbilisi

A successful businessman in Georgia planned to build a "business centre" as the base of his business in a hill overlooking Tobilisi city, and held an international architectural design competition. As the result, Shin Takamatsu was designated. The business centre is not a mere office building. It consists of guest house, multipurpose hall, large and small conference room, fitness gym, pool, dance hall, indoor tennis court, relaxation space, and the owner's enormous residence. Besides, the client required the best security system and the best existence of architecture. It is a kind of a fortress. The architect is strong at creation of architecture as fortress. Though sizes are different, the architect replied to the requirements with all cultivated methods. The method was said "to be the Strengthening method of Forms". The effect is proved by the metallic dignified appearance which suddenly appeared on the hill.

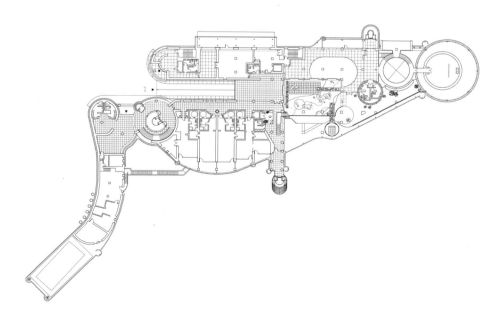

1. entrance
2. WC
3. lobby

Photo: Shin Takamatsu + Shin Takamatsu Architect and Associates Co., Ltd.

Complex

Architect: Shin Takamatsu + Shin Takamatsu Architect and Associates Co., Ltd.

Completion Date: 2008

Façade

Night view

0–14

Located along the extension of Dubai Creek, occupying a prominent location on the waterfront esplanade, 0–14, a 22–storey-tall commercial tower perched on a two–storey podium, broke ground in February 2007, and comprises over 300,000 square feet of office space for the Dubai Business Bay. The concrete shell of 0–14 provides an efficient structural exoskeleton that frees the core from the burden of lateral forces and creates highly efficient, column–free open spaces in the building's interior. By moving the lateral bracing for the building to the perimeter, the core, which is traditionally enlarged to receive lateral loading in most curtain wall office towers, can be minimised for only vertical loading, utilities and transportation. Additionally, the typical curtain–wall tower configuration results in floor plates that must be thickened to carry lateral loads to the core, yet in 0–14 these can be minimised to only respond to span and vibration. Consequently, the future tenants can arrange the flexible floor space according to their individual needs.

The main shell is organised as a diagrid, the efficiency of which is wed to a system of continuous variation of openings, always maintaining a minimum structural member, adding material locally where necessary and taking away where possible. This efficiency and modulation enable the shell to create a wide range of atmospheric and visual effects in the structure without changing the basic structural form, allowing for systematic analysis and construction.

1. rooftop garden
2. mechanical
3. prayer room
4. offices
5. landscape
6. offices
7. interior bridges
8. drop–off
9. parking entrance

Bird's eye view by night

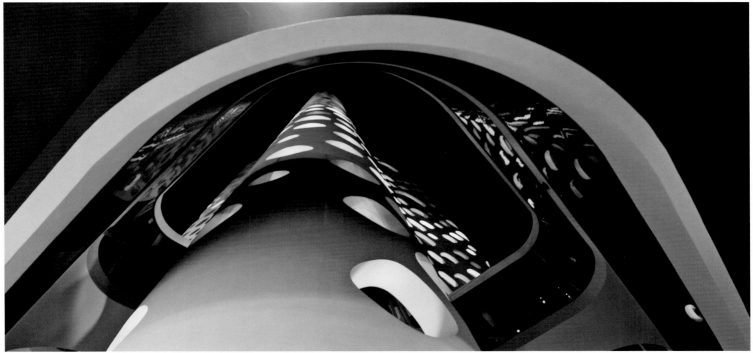

Façade details

Façade details

Photo: Reiser + Umemoto (1st photo), and Sebastian Opitz (photos 2–5, night photos)

Architect: Principals, Jesse Reiser + Nanako Umemoto; Design Team, Mitsuhisa Matsunaga, Kutan Ayata, Jason Scroggin, Cooper Mack, Michael Overby, Roland Snooks, Michael Young; Assistants and Interns, Tina Tung, Raha Talebi, Yan Wai Chu

Corporate

Completion Date: 2010

Abu Dhabi Investment Authority Headquarters (ADIA)

ADIA's future requirements demand a large single floor plate with a large central common zone on each floor for meeting and social interaction. This central zone has become the vertical atrium garden, the heart of the scheme unifies the whole building and represents the organisation and its openness. The design concept further refines the idea of creating an indigenous form, a form inspired by the special character of this waterfront site and the buildings importance as an international headquarters. The key to the design is the acknowledgement of the profound importance of the sea in the development of the site and of the urban plan as a garden city. The growth of the city begun at the old fort besides the headquarters.

The gardens of the fort and those adjacent to them create a wide green zone with further reinforces the seaward connection. The site is incorporated into this garden zone. The scheme has two great arms or fingers reaching into the sea; the extensive ground floor planting reinforces the original urban landscape strategy, tying the site to the urban plan. The success of this urban design strategy for landscaping has earned Abu Dhabi the title "Garden of the Gulf".

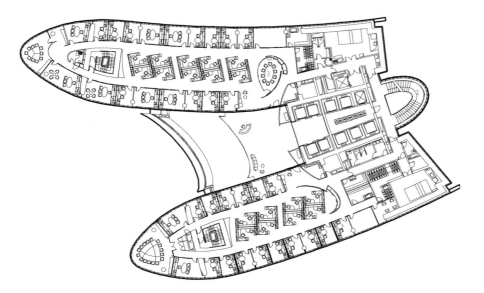

1. stairs
2. office
3. meeting room

General view

Front view

Corridor and countyard

Stairs and courtyard

Stairs

Photo: H.G. Esch

Completion Date: 2007

Architect: Kohn Pedersen Fox Associates (International) PA

General view

Night view

Bahrain World Trade Centre

The Bahrain World Trade Centre forms the focal point of a master plan to rejuvenate an existing hotel and shopping mall on a prestigious site overlooking the Arabian Gulf in the downtown central business district of Manama, Bahrain. The concept design of the Bahrain World Trade Centre towers was inspired by the traditional Arabian "Wind Towers" in that the very shape of the buildings harness the unobstructed prevailing onshore breeze from the Gulf, providing a renewable source of energy for the project.

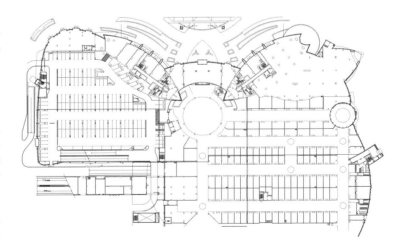

The two fifty-storey sail-shaped office towers taper to a height of 240 metres and support three twenty-nine-metre diameter horizontal–axis wind turbines. The towers are harmoniously integrated on top of a three–storey sculpted podium and basement which accommodate a new shopping centre, restaurants, business centres and car parking.

The elliptical plan forms and sail–like profiles act as aerofoils, funnelling the onshore breeze between them as well as creating a negative pressure behind, thus accelerating the wind velocity between the two towers. Vertically, the sculpting of the towers is also a function of airflow dynamics. As they taper upwards, their aerofoil sections reduce. This effect, when combined with the increasing velocity of the onshore breeze at increasing heights, creates a near equal regime of wind velocity on each of the three turbines. Understanding and utilising this phenomenon has been one of the key factors that has allowed the practical integration of wind turbine generators in a commercial building design.

Connection

Entrance

Hall

Suliman S. Olayan School of Business, American University of Beirut

The building includes, first, a large green oval carefully located on the axis of existing steps that will become a major access to the sea, connecting students from the Faculty of Engineering and Architecture, and beyond to the Corniche's elevated edge. Second, the design creates an L-shaped four-storey building with a traversable ground plane consisting of four enclosed pieces. These are grouped around the school's central space, a triangular open courtyard. Porous and transparent, the ground floor promotes collegiality, containing the school's lobby, auditorium, café and terrace, as well as student facilities, mailboxes and related social programmes.

To clarify wayfinding and the building's legibility, the undergraduate education facilities are located on the first floor, graduate education, the MBA programme on the second, and the Executive Education programme on the third floor, which also contains the Dean's Office in its corner. The triangular courtyard joins these three levels, and each overlooks the space, enriching it with their different lives.

The image of the building is one of vernacular precedent and contemporary vision. The "hanging" façade, made of pre-cast blocks replicates the warmth of the local Forni limestone present in the campus, while the openings of the screen-like skin recall the wooden mashrabiya that are characteristic of the region.

Corniche view from northwest

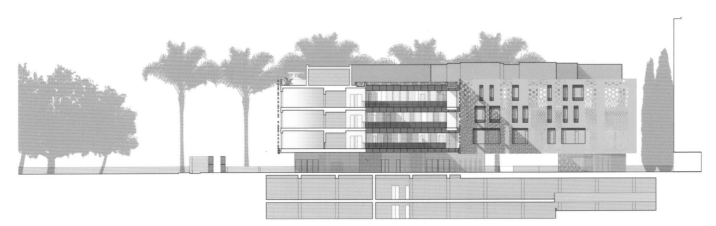

Section through atrium

Building entrance from west with corniche below

View of auditorium with courtyard beyond

View of ground–floor glass volumes with interior courtyard beyond

Photo: Fares Jammal, Clement Tannouri, Machado and Silvetti Associates

Completion Date: 2009

Design Architect: Machado and Silvetti Associates, Boston, Massachusetts
Executive Architect: Builders Design Consultants, Beirut, Lebanon

Night view of west exterior

Deichmann Centre for Social Interaction & Spitzer–Salant School of Social Work at Ben–Gurion University of the Negev, Beer–Sheva, Israel

The Spitzer–Salant School of Social Work and the Deichmann Centre for Social interaction were designed and built as an integrated project located on the campus of Ben–Gurion University in Beer–Sheva, the main city and gateway to the Negev desert in south Israel. The goal of the Centre for Social Interaction is to open the university to the city, to tie academic life with the history of Beer–Sheva, and to encourage all forms of art and education, while providing a sustainable environment.

Responding to its urban context, the sculpted façade establishes a distinctive identity to the campus's new entrance through a piazza that links the town of Beer–Sheva with the campus. By sinking the piazza and the complex below street level, the adjacent highway noise is buffered. Rainwater catchments were situated throughout the site, where the collected runoff is used to supplement landscape irrigation.

The complex has a bold and sculptural spirit, with a tilted concrete wall sitting in water supporting a floating zinc clad structure. A freestanding concrete ramp originating at the piazza level leads through the buildings to the main campus. Since concrete and zinc are environmentally friendly building materials, they were a natural choice for the sustainable construction of this project. The materials perform well in desert climate, as they are UV–resistant, maintenance–free and guarantee longevity and timeless beauty. The first layer of concrete walls on the west elevation defines a coherent formal edge to the piazza. Visitors to the building experience an alternating rhythm between solid concrete walls and several visual voids recessed in cast shadows. The physical presence of these concrete walls creates a structure that feels grounded yet shielded from the desert sun, while meeting budget constraints through the use of common and inexpensive local building techniques.

Beyond the first layer, walls become organic free forms and transparent, with a curved metal wall penetrating through large sheets of glass into the buildings, establishing an undisturbed visual connection between indoor and outdoor. Natural light is introduced into the interiors, through the shifted layers of walls accentuated by the change of materials between concrete glass and zinc.

Ground floor plan
1. courtyard
2. entrance
3. exhibition area
4. theatre/auditorium
5. computer lab
6. seminar
7. reading room
8. computer room
9. art class
10. staff office
11. storage
12. mechanical
13. dressing
14. sitting area
15. working open space
16. water

Night shot of the cute

Exterior context

East exterior view

Photo: Amit Geron
Post Production: Paul Chamberlain

Educational

Completion Date: 2008

Architect: Vert Architects / Raquel Vert, Principal Architect
In Collaboration With Axelrod–Grobman Architects / Irit Axelrod, Yasha Grobman (Israel)
Consultants: Piazza–Chyutin Architects, Yaron Ari Landscape Architect

Buildings melt with nature

University of Cyprus – School of Economics and Public Administration and School of Classical Studies

The Schools for Public Administration and Economics are designed as two long and narrow buildings, parallel to each other and perpendicular to the central pedestrian spine defined by the master plan, while the School for Classical Studies and the teaching halls are placed in a third building forming an angle with the other two, in order to create open space between them and allow for views towards the pedestrian way at the north–west site boundary. They form part of the new University campus master plan of the city of Nicosia.

The basic design concept is the creation of a diagonal axis (bridge) which interconnects the schools, while at the same time intersecting them in such a manner that independent units can be positioned on either side of the axis. The buildings follow the natural slope of the ground and form two–storey volumes as seen from the pedestrian spine to the north–west and four–storey volumes as seen from the south–east limit of the site. The composition includes parking facilities with planting as a prolongation of the Schools of Public Administration and Economics, and a lake for the creation of a pleasant microclimate and the reduction of temperatures during the hot summer season. Agreeable comfort conditions within the buildings are provided by the careful design of natural lighting, ventilation and shading.

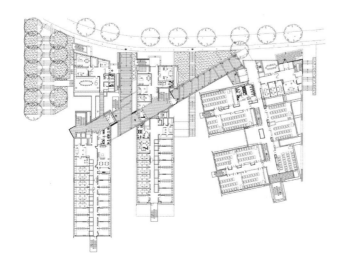

1. entrance
2. offices
3. training rooms
4. toilets/kitchen
5. laboratories
6. meeting room
7. library

Connecting bridges

Stairs

Lecture theatre and auditorium

Photo: Alexandros N. Tombazis and Associates Architects Ltd, Athens, Greece

Architect: Alexandros N. Tombazis and Associates Architects Ltd, Athens, Greece + Alekos Gabrielides and Associates Architects, Nicosia, Cyprus

Completion Date: 2010

Educational

217

Façade

Dalaman International Airport Terminal

The project which strived to deal with the boredom and feeling of emptiness created by the standardness of terminal buildings, aimed to problematise the international airport conventions in the project by making use of the region's rich landscape, climatic characteristics and the specificity of its tourism activities.

The plan was developed by differing from the customary massive orders of terminal buildings, which are conditioned by the disproportionate sizes of the narrow and long piers and the relatively shorter and wider halls; the design formed man-made valleys of the gaps between the interior spaces and the fragmented exterior masses. These gaps enabled the continuity of the region's landscape using its natural form outside and its abstraction inside. Other significant inputs were the fact that the terminal, which has a capacity of five million passengers, would almost only be used during the summer, and that the circulation of arriving and departing passengers were envisaged to be on different floors, the visual fluidity between the interior spaces and different levels, ensuring that the commercial units be attractive.

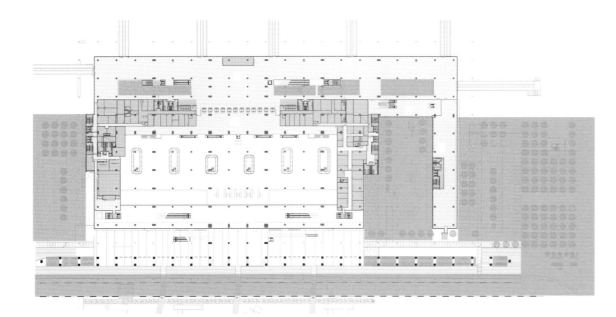

Bridge

Hall

Back view

Photo: Ali Bekman, Thomas Mayer

Completion Date: 2006

Architect: EAA–Emre Arolat Architects

External view

Ipekyol Textile Factory

The service entrance leads into the building from the road to Kırklareli and pedestrian access from the busy E–5 Highway on the other side. The sales unit, situated close to the road, again in the direction of the E–5, was connected to the main building by an overhang which covered and thus defined the walkway.

As are usually used in similar buildings, here too the main components were the vertical reinforced concrete load–bearing systems, a lightweight steel structure cover placed on top of them and the coffered system on the façades; the exterior surface took shape through a grammar established by the clear distinction between areas open or closed to the exterior.

The administrative section, which commonly is visually detached from the production building through the use of different surface languages, due to the conventional approach to such facilities, was more directly associated with production in this project and thus, instead of different buildings a large mass took shape. This mass, which reaches the outer borders of the lot, because of the constraints of the land, was implicitly loosened thanks to linear gardens located between sections. The main purpose of these gardens was that they be used by the staff during breaks and that natural light and air enter work places; it was intended that the gardens separate areas and that thanks to their transparent frames visual fluidity would be achieved. And due to the limitations of local production possibilities, innovative experimentations in building materials and production methods were especially avoided.

Building detail

Exterior detail

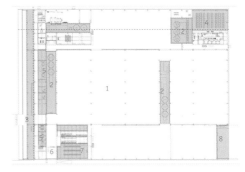

1. production area
2. inner garden
3. entrance hall
4. cafeteria
5. offices
6. staff entrance
7. changing room
8. service entrance

Interior

Santral Istanbul Museum of Contemporary Arts

Istanbul Bilgi University seeked for the renovation of Silahtaraga Power Plant, a typical modern industrial setting to be transformed into a museum, recreational and educational centre. Among the various buildings that were dealt with in this context, the two large boiler houses were handled with an interpretation that implied to their new function, in a way of abstraction in the design. The two buildings, that were detached but stood very close to each other to complete the surrounding building mass, were planned in a way proper to the volumetric existence of their older functions, but with a kind of "timeless" approach on surface qualities.

Just like the old buildings, new structures are composed of a dense and heavy inner core and a light, semi-transparent exterior sheathing that covers the core without touching to the possible extend. Instead of the punced state created by the walls and windows on the surfaces of the old buildings, a metal mesh that this time homogenises the sense of the whole building is simply placed on the concrete base. In this sense, it was considered that the buildings should evoke a kind of insignaficance by intervening into the aura of the environment at daytime, but should turn out to be a simple lighthouse with the interior lighting of the museum that makes the metal mesh invisible at night time.

Photo: EAA–Emre Arolat Architects, nevzat sayın (nsmh)

Cultural

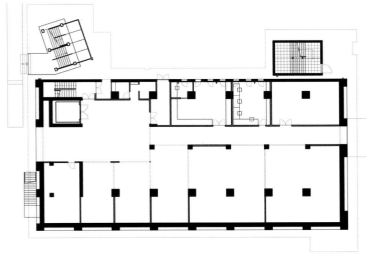
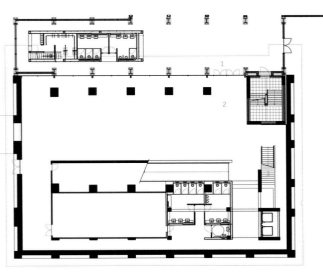

1. entrance 2. hall 3. stairs

Completion Date: 2007

Architect: EAA–Emre Arolat Architects, nevzat sayın (nsmh)

General view

Bursa Wholesale Greengrocers and Fishmongers Market

The municipality of Bursa required a new, modern facility for the wholesale trade of fruits and vegetables, as well as separate facility for fish and other seafoods. The building would consolidate these commercial activities, providing the city with a centralised control point from which to monitor the Bursa's food supply. The design of Bursa's wholesale greengrocer's and fishmonger's market maintains the idiom of the high, vaulted bazaar, connecting the new buildings symbolically and functionally with long-standing Central Asian architectural and cultural traditions. The complex patterns of vehicle, material, and pedestrian traffic are carefully coordinated within fluid, elliptical shapes, which in turn are bordered by brokers' offices. The ra-tional form of the 350-metre-long greengrocer's market is designed to facilitate easy orientation, efficient exchange and optimal routing of foodstuffs from suppliers to retailers and restaurateurs – all of then keep down transaction costs. But it is also a good place to work: an animated space and architecture that is representative of the energy and productivity of the labourers, as well as of the city of Bursa.

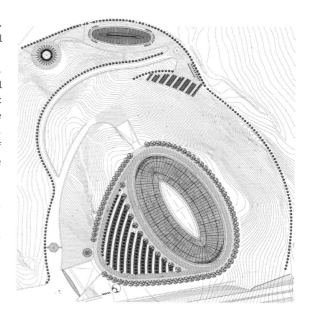

At the same time, the configuration of the naturally-ventilated spaces allows the municipality to ensure the efficient, safe distribution of food products to its citizens. By consolidating the wholesale trade of produce and fish for the city of Bursa in a single location, the municipality is able to monitor the goods for quality and also to ensure that health regulations are followed.

Bird's eye view

External view

Interior view

Photo: Tuncer Çakmaklı, Aziz Safi, Gürkan Akay, Fehmi Ferit, Seyfettin Bal

Complex

Completion Date: 2007

Architect: Tuncer Çakmaklı

General view

7800 Cesme Residences & Hotel

Main mass of 7800 Cesme Residences & Hotel has been made close to the border of the road, so that the frontal large beach and the natural environment has left as it exists as possible. The linear block of five storeys, has been transformed double sided by an internal street on which both vertical and horizontal circulation are organised.

Instead of being self–centralised and prominent by visual structural form, attractive and awaiting to gain its power by this kind of attention, what is aimed in the project is a kind of structure that tends to hide behind the landscape layer which covers it and in this way chooses to get rid of all the burden of concepts that might be defined as style, taste and genre of architecture.

Two different blind systems were designed in order to prevent the north and south façades that constitute the units' point of view, from sunlight and wind. Both of these systems, which are made as simplified as possible, became the most important elements of the exterior perception.

1. dock
2. landscape
3. hotel

Bridge

View of sunset

Hotel

Completion Date: 2008

Architect: EAA–Emre Arolat Architects

Façade

General view

Forum Çamlik

Forum Çamlik, in the city of Denizli (Çamlık), has a 3,420-square-metre supermarket and 32,000-square-metre lease able areas. It has a total construction area of 73,000 square metres. In the mall exist 7,700-square-metre Anchor, 600-square-metre MSU, 9,700-square-metre shop, 2,355-square-metre restaurants and food court, 800-square-metre leisure area and 2,140-square-metre cinemas.

Mall has four main entrances, one on the ground floor from "Democracy Square", two on the first floor and the last one on the second floor. The entrances and exits for the closed car park will be made on the side of "Democracy Square"; open car park entrances and exits will be positioned on the south of the building, where the food court is located. The Face Veneer is a colour combination of the materials of glass, metal, bricks and stones. The building has exciting movements within vertical and horizontal changes in placement. Especially the cinema side view has an artistic sculpture with its turquoise colour.

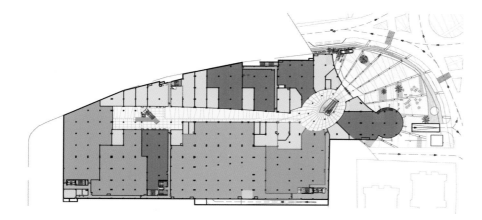

Night view

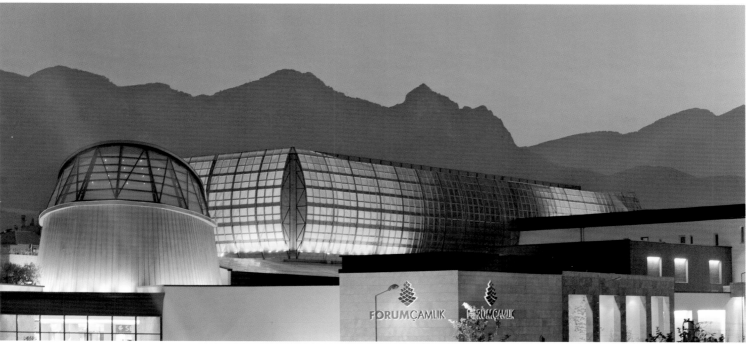

External detail

Interior view

Exterior view

Enter

Enter is an IT college in the town of Sipoo, close to Helsinki. The L–shaped pavilion–like building forms the last corner of an existing school campus.

The urban setting is dominated by two curved yards: a larger one towards the campus garden and a smaller courtyard connected to the main road. The two curved glass façades open up the school towards the community. The students and teachers see the community and are seen. The campus garden serves as learning area, featuring a wireless network and green islands. Fruit trees with white flowers celebrate the graduation in the end of May.

The street–side façade is broken up in smaller volumes to relate to the scale of the surrounding villas. The warm tone of the wooden surfaces is reminiscent of early–20th–century school buildings.

A-cast-on site concrete stair forms the centre of action in the building. It is topped by a large conical top light. A small mediatheaque and a café in the southern wing open up towars the central lobby. The class rooms are reduced in their material palette into industrial IT workshops.

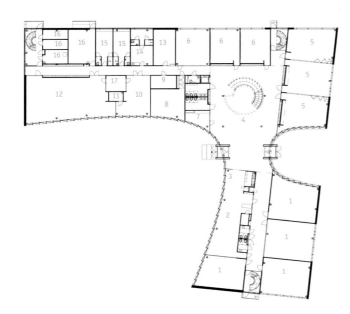

1. IT classroom
2. library
3. café
4. lobby
5. hall / languages
6. theory classroom
7. janitor
8. IT laboratory
9. servers
10. mechanics
11. welding
12. electrical laboratory
13. storage
14. facilities
15. dressing rooms
16. technical facilities
17. teachers' room

Exterior view

View from window

Exterior view

Staircase

Viikki Church

The church is located at the termination point of a narrowing landscape space, along the edge of a new square. The architecture evokes impressions of the Finnish forest. The eaves following the roof shapes reflect the forms of the treetops surrounding them. The approach to the church from the square takes a route past the bell tower and arrangements of vines. In the halls of the building the rising lines of the timber structures, resembling foliage, meet the systems of beams that define the space with light filtering through the structural members. The spaces, made of a single material, are hollowed out within the building like clearings in a forest.

The church design is based on the winning entrance to an architectural competition for the Latokartano Centre in Viikki, organised in 2000. The competition aimed to find suitable townscape and functional concepts for the civic and public service buildings of the area. The design brief also included proposals for the organisation of a public square, a park and commercial buildings on the competition site. In the chosen entrance the public buildings form rectangular shapes that delineate the square and the park, their light–coloured brick surfaces differentiating them from the wooden church rising in their midst.

Exterior

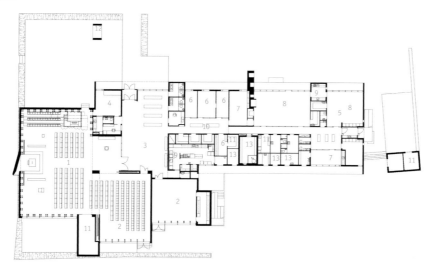

1. church hall
2. parish hall
3. entrance hall
4. sacristy
5. hall porter
6. office
7. meeting room
8. club room
9. kitchen
10. waiting room
11. storage
12. bell tower
13. technical facilities

Wall

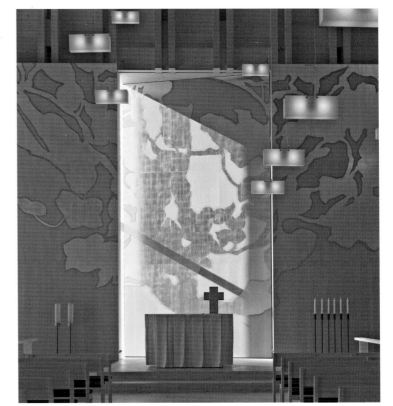

Altar and art work

View to landscape

Axial view of church hall

Photo: Arno de la Chapelle photos, Kimmo Räisänen photos

Architect: JKMM Architects

Completion Date: 2005

Cultural

Outside view

Knut Hamsun Centre

Dedicated to Norway's most inventive 20th-century writer and recipient of the Nobel Prize in Literature, the 2,700-square-metre Knut Hamsun Centre is located above the Arctic Circle by the village of Presteid of Hamaroy, near the farm where Hamsun grew up. The building includes exhibition areas, a library and reading room, a café, and a 230-seat auditorium for museum and community use.

The concept for the museum, "Building as a Body: Battleground of Invisible Forces," is realised from both inside and out. The wood exterior is punctuated by hidden impulses piercing through the surface. The concrete structure with stained white interiors is illuminated by diagonal rays of sunlight calculated to ricochet through the section on certain days of the year. Strange, surprising and phenomenal experiences in space perspective and light will provide an inspiring frame for the exhibitions.

The tarred black wood exterior skin alludes to Norwegian Medieval wooden stave churches, and in the roof garden, long chutes of bamboo refer to traditional Norwegian sod roofs. The spine of the building body, constructed from perforated brass, is the central lift, providing handicapped and service access to all parts of the building. The building includes a community auditorium which is connected to the main building via a passageway accessed through the lower lobby, which takes advantage of the topography, allowing for natural light along the circulation route.

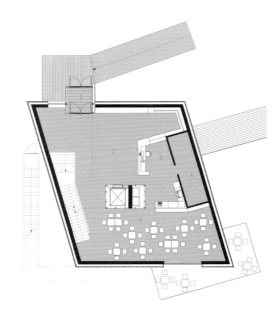

1. entrance
2. lobby
3. reception
4. café
5. kitchen

Outside view

Outside view

Outside view

Interior

Photo: Iwan Baan

Cultural

Completion Date: 2009

Architect: Steven Holl Architects

General view

The Energy Hotel

The power plant and adjacent dining hall, designed by the renowned architect Geir Grung in the 1960s is listed among the twelve most significant modern buildings in Norway. New owners took over the dining hall to transform it into an exclusive hotel in 2006. Its generally good condition led to a philosophy of minimal intervention. Only non-original or elements added later have been replaced or modified. New elements have been designed by re-using materials from the power plant, e.g. cables, wires and ceramic insulators. Helen & Hard invited three artists to develope parts of the interior with the intention to add more layers of exquisite value; the light weight, moveable reception by Marli Mul, a flexible textile roomdivider of Yngve Holen and furniture in the conference room of Randy Naylor. In this process Helen & Hard had the role of a curator and negotiated between the artists and the clients interests.

Part view

Moveable reception

Photo: Helen & Hard

Lobby

Completion Date: 2007

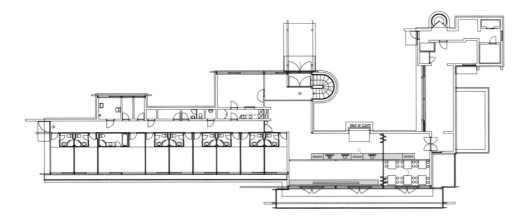

1. entrance
2. washing room
3. dining
4. stairs
5. reception

Architect: Helen & Hard

View from the south

Advice-House

Advice-House is the first completed building in the Lysholt Park, a new business-park north of Vejle, and is, with its proximity to the motorway, designated to act as landmark and eye-catcher for the entire development. The Advice-House interior is 5,000 square metres of open and flexible office layout, where various tenants share the same large space, which offers dramatic perspectives and angles. The building is shaped around two angled office wings, separated by an equally angled atrium, resulting in a plan resembling a hexagon with one angle pushed inwards. The two wings are connected by walkways across the atrium, and the floors' continuous window-bands give a high degree of freedom in the space-planning. A large, north-facing glazed gable gives passers by a glimpse into the dynamic void, day or night, and the open and transparent interior is also naturally ventilated.

The building's unusual geometry makes for a dramatic and changing appearance when cars are passing by on the motorway, and this mutability in form and shadows is further heightened by the colouring and texturing of the façades, designed to catch the light. The cladding-strips are composed of a "random" sequence of a total of thirteen differently-proportioned cladding panels, some of which are folded diagonally to create a triangulated pattern. The panels are mounted horizontally at staggered intervals, creating a glittering array of colours, light and shadows.

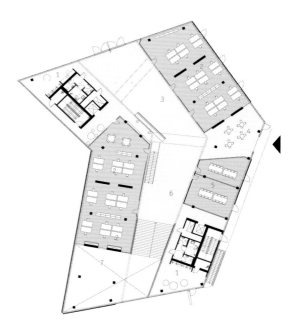

1. lounge
2. office
3. reception
4. entrance
5. meeting room
6. atrium
7. canteen

Seen from the passing motorway

The two wings connected by walkways

The interior is an open and flexible office layout

Photo: Julian Weyer

Corporate

Completion Date: 2009

Architect: C. F. Møller Architects

Green Lighthouse

Green Lighthouse is Denmark's first CO_2-neutral public building is home to the Faculty of Science at the University of Copenhagen. The building's circular shape and the adjustable louvres of the façade mirror the course of the sun. The sun being the predominant source of energy is the overriding design concept behind the new building. Green Lighthouse is based on a whole new experiment with an energy concept, consisting of a supply combination of district heating, photovoltaics, solarheating and cooling and seasonal storage.

To achieve carbon neutrality, many green design features were incorporated to reduce energy use and provide a holistic and healthy indoor environment for students and faculty. The building itself was oriented to maximise its solar resources, while windows and doors are recessed and covered with automatic solar shades to minimise direct solar heat gain inside the building. Plentiful daylight and natural ventilation are provided by means of the carefully-placed VELUX skylights, Velfac windows and the generous atrium. Finally, sensibly-integrated state-of-the-art technology has been applied: heat recovery systems, photovoltaic panels, solar heating, LED lighting, phase change materials, geothermal heat are just some of the technologies that are seamlessly integrated into the building. Seventy percent of the reduction of the energy consumption is the direct consequence of architectural design.

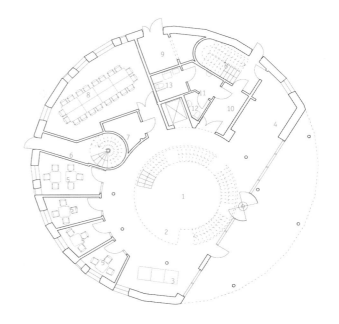

1. main stairs
2. students' lounge/working area
3. students' lounge/quiet area
4. reception
5. meeting rooms
6. fire escapes
7. printing room
8. auditorium
9. plant room
10. garderobe
11. lavatory
12. WC
13. disabled WC

Photo: Adam Moerk

Completion Date: 2009

Architect: Christensen & Co.

Night view

Birkerod Sports and Leisure Centre

The Birkerod Sports Centre in Rudersdal Municipality close to Copenhagen is a modern sports and culture complex that sets new standards in terms of both practicality and architecture. Fitness, yoga, team handball, concerts and other cultural events are all in a setting of one modern sculptural entity designed by SHL architects.

The façade's long sweeping lines and striking sculptural roof contours evoke a sense of movement and activity, creating a direct link between the building's design and its core function. Upon entering, the space appears bright, airy and open. The interiors are filled with natural light, and transparency creates a sense of permeability and activity.

The sports and activity centre is a multifunctional structure. The new building includes a large multipurpose hall with enough space to accommodate two handball courts with accompanying mobile spectator stands, as well as a VIP lounge. The centre also houses two smaller halls. This means the complex can not only accommodate major sporting events, concerts and other cultural events, but also be adapted for school sporting events and local sports initiatives requiring smaller, more intimate settings.

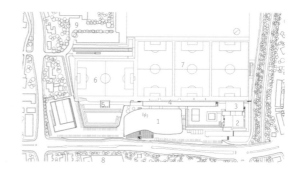

1. Sports Centre
2. existing public swimming pool
3. tranining and hot water pool
4. existing stand
5. grand stand
6. show pitch
7. training pitch
8. public school
9. high school

General view

Entrance

Swimming pool

Reception

Photo: schmidt hammer lassen architects

Completion Date: 2008

Architect: schmidt hammer lassen architects

Stepped ramp and canopy on south side

Vogaskóli School

The new extension is founded on the principles of open schooling. The building is centred on a double-height hall surrounded on the lower floor by library, music, kitchen and administration areas and teaching zones for the youngest and middle age groups on the upper. Divisions between areas are minimised and if necessary are of glass or movable partitions. A grand stair connects the hall to the upper level and this can be used either as an audience platform or a stage.

As a consequence of the deep plan, the periphery is predominately glazed with full height windows interspersed with attenuated grilles. The exception is the more massive, north fair-faced-concrete façade due to the proximity of the noisy Skeidavogs road. The heart of the building receives additional daylight through the clearstorey windows in the hall.

The main entrance is located at the junction of the existing building and the new extension. Students may be dropped-off securely in the entrance court and the same route serves the basement staff car park. The entrance is also connected to the school grounds on the south side of the buildings where the land has been lowered to create an external space for teaching and play, sheltered from the inclement weather. On fine days teaching on the upper levels can be extended outside on the east-facing balcony that also doubles as a secure fire escape route.

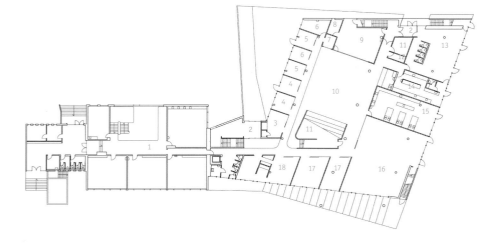

1. existing building
2. entrance lobby
3. reception
4. headmaster
5. office
6. meeting room
7. DJ booth
8. music practice room
9. music
10. hall
11. store
12. cleaners
13. staff room
14. kitchen
15. teaching kitchen
16. library
17. seminar
18. special teaching

Stepped ramp and canopy on south side

Entrance

Photo: Sigurgeir Sigurjónsson

Completion Date: 2007

Architect: Studio Granda Architects

Hall

In the daylight

The Long Barn Studio

The building is a simple glazed rectangular unit with frameless 3.2-metre-high glazed panels along its main elevations, which hold a very slight green tint to reflect the seasons of the surrounding glorious landscape. Internally, they provide all those who are lucky enough to enter with a panoramic view that is breathtaking.

Like bookends, the building is capped at both ends with full height larch cladding, the course of the building intersects a series of larch timber "pods" which house meeting rooms, a library, a printing area and a WC. Harping back to the adjacent barn building's history, the new studio utilises cor-ten detailing, further enhancing the sense of place, and reflecting the old and discarded agricultural machinery and steelwork.

Floating Wenge storage pods sit dividing reception, to kitchenette to work spaces, Knoll floating wide and deep desking with bespoke cabinets integrating designers files, tools and wate bin, married with wireless screen built-in computers and wireless keyboard ensure all is at hand in this exclusive user friendly environment.

The studio utilises rainwater harvesting, its own wind turbine, whole building air heat recovery circulation system, central vacuum and centralised lighting control. Utilising low energy lighting, organic paints and non-toxic chemical sealers further reinstates the philosophy of Nicolas Tye Architects. Their passion for this is clearly evident in their own building, an achievement that many companies long for.

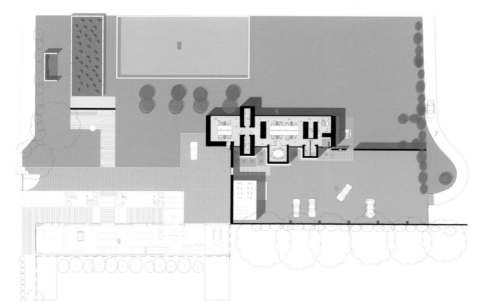

1. pond
2. vegetable garden
3. reed bed
4. wind turbine
5. Long Barn Studio
6. external dining area
7. vehicular access from road
8. studio parking
9. the long barn

In the sunset

Office

Book shelves

Photo: Philip Bier / Bier Photography London

Completion Date: 2007

Architect: Nicolas Tye Architects

Exterior view

University of Oxford New Biochemistry Building

The distinctive 12,000-square-metre facility with its glass façades and coloured glass fins brings together 300 lecturers, researchers and students previously based in a number of separate buildings. Inside, a 400 -square-metre atrium with breakout spaces and specially commissioned artworks encourages collaboration between the researchers.

The Biochemistry Department at Oxford University is the largest in the UK and is internationally renowned for its research in the understanding of DNA, cell growth and immunity. Previously the department's scientists have had to conduct research in outmoded buildings spread across the Science Area in the centre of Oxford.

The brief for the new building was to achieve a new ethos of "interdisciplinary working" where the exchange of ideas is promoted in a large collaborative environment. At the same time space was required to enable the research groups to focus on their cutting–edge work in state–of–the–art laboratories.

1. main laboratory
2. write up spaces
3. support/specialist laboratory
4. atrium
5. plant
6. ancilliary space
7. seminar/meeting room
8. café
9. offices

Coloured glass fins fixed vertically within the mullions wrap the full perimeter of the building

The exterior glass façade around the entrance courtyard, with Nicky Hirst's artwork The Glass Menagerie

Nicky Hirst's artwork Portal features on the glazed wall of the atrium

The atrium with the installation, 10,000,000 by Annie Cattrell

Photo: Tim Crocker (opposite, top-left), Keith Collie (top right, bottom left, bottom right)

Educational

Completion Date: 2009

Architect: Hawkins\Brown

Façade

BDP Manchester Studio

The building provides large open–plan studio space and ancillary accommodation including a hub space at ground floor level. This interactive area including café, staff restaurant and extended reception space, overlooks the canal at raised ground level.

A striking feature of the building is the punctuated stainless–steel south façade that rises above the Ducie Street colonnade to contain the open–plan studio areas before sweeping over to form the roof of the building. The reflective external finish, heavily insulated build–up and narrow vertical apertures all serve to minimise solar heat gain, and to maximise privacy with the residential buildings opposite.

By contrast, the northern façade of the building is transparent. The floor–to–soffit glazing takes maximum advantage of north light to illuminate the full extent of studio spaces and reveals wonderful views of the city centre. A fully–glazed circulation staircase cantilevered over the canal provides the circulation for all floors.

Sustainability has been a key driver in all aspects of the design and delivery of the new studio which is an expressive response to context and microclimate. Rainwater is harvested from the roof and used to flush toilets throughout the building. It is the first naturally ventilated and night time cooled office building in Manchester to achieve an Excellent BREEAM rating.

Working area

Reception

Photo: Martine Hamilton Knight

Corporate

Completion Date: 2008

Architect: BDP

Royal Alexandra Children's Hospital

The site was a very tight handkerchief of land wedged between two roads and a number of existing buildings. Planning constraints dictated a maximum height. The very steep hill overlooking the Channel was the location's great saving grace, affording a sunny panoramic sweep over the sea and historic Brighton. The introduction of an atrium at the heart of the hospital initially seemed unfeasible as it sacrificed a significant amount of area. Addressing this shortfall the designers generated the idea of bowing the building out as it grew upwards, which chimed nicely with the desirability of shallower plan spaces on the lower levels.

As the design began to take shape, it soon became known amongst the team as the "Children's Ark", an image that crystallised a number of important themes: from the idea of a "sustainable" community centred around the family to the nautical spirit of Brighton and the boat-like form of the building. With its soft, rounded corners and sheltering roof, it projected a reassuring and optimistic image, around which the designers could integrate all the elements of the brief in a coherent and appealing way that would resonate with children, families and staff. At the centre of the hospital, the atrium binds all levels together, ensures good day-lighting throughout the building and creates a strong sense of the whole, which is immediately perceived by anyone entering the Alex or moving up through it in the public lifts.

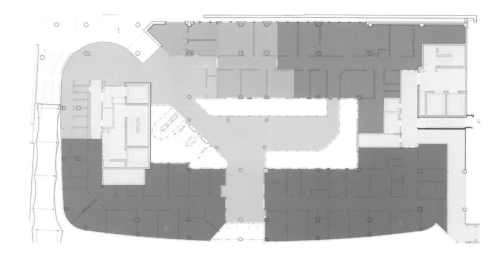

1. main entrance
2. café
3. stairs
4. adjoining main Hospital Theatre block
5. outpatients department

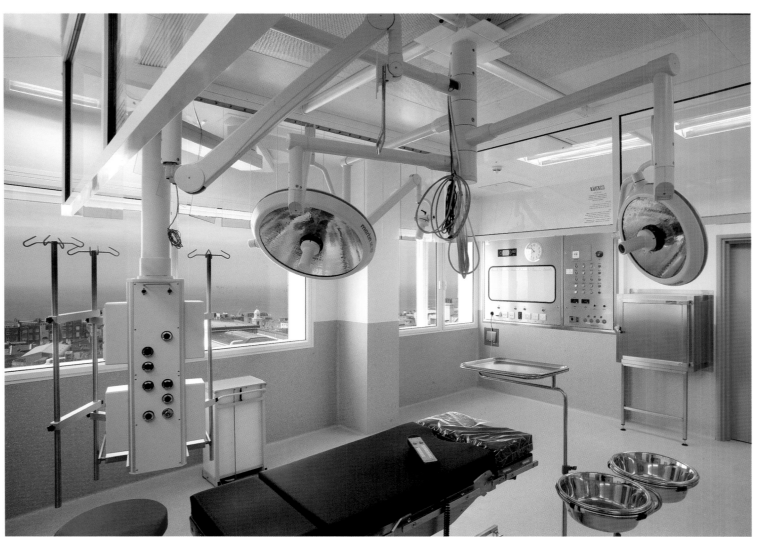

Photo: David Barbour

Hospital

Architect: BDP

Completion Date: 2007

General view

Institute of Cancer Studies, UCL

Conceptually, the building design was influenced by its role as a cancer institute and the relationship between science and the study of cancer. In particular there was an interest in the images that have been generated by the processes used in modern medical research and which have now become part of the culture. Images of cells, wave patterns and the chromosome permeate the forms of the building. For example, the terracotta louvre–bank suspended across the main façade has a rhythm that can not only be read as a vertical "bar code" configuration or genetic sequence image, but also reflect the waveform that is so significant to modern science. Likewise, concrete soffits are left exposed, retaining the details of their own construction and revealing points of reinforcement reflective of the mechanisms and cellular structures of biology: they are literally scooped out where the material serves no structural purpose.

The main entrance is located at the juncture between the reinstated wall flank of the Grade II listed building and the new Institute. This gap is glazed with a single glass sheet spanning from the new structure to the old. It reveals a highly engineered staircase that provides the main circulation core and an architectural focal point. The transparency of this circulation area articulates it as an open, shared space that is visually accessible from the street. This emphasises the Institute as a live and active building. The staircase itself consists of cast stainless steel treads cantilevered from a structural spine of pre–cast concrete to create a dramatic feature.

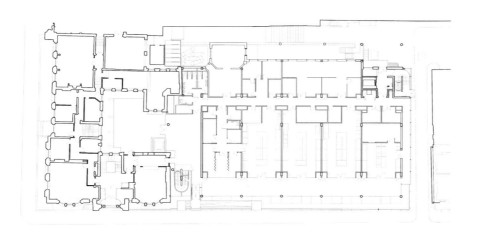

Ground floor plan

Front view

Corridor

Photo: Mark Humphries

Completion Date: 2007

Architect: Grimshaw Architects

Stairway

View form Sandford

Multi–Purpose Hall, Sandford Park School

The Multi–Purpose Hall creates a new identity for the school from Sandford Road, advantageously reinforcing the school within its suburban context of Ranelagh. Located at the middle ground between the gate lodge and school house, it allowed for the insertion of a contemporary architectural volume to mediate between the different generations of school appendages.

The brief was to provide a multi–purpose hall for use by various school departments including sport; music; recitals, theatrical performance, examinations, assembly, and ancillary presentations. The space was for an equivalent Department of Education and Science 406-square-metre sports hall allowing for three badminton / single basketball court, with ancillary storage and changing facilities. Due to the context and functions, the quality of both internal and external acoustics was critical. Noise penetration onto neighbouring properties required an increase in the mass of internal walls and roof, and reverberation times internally were reduced through the softening of internal finishes.

Externally the expression of materiality has been reduced to enhance the juxtaposition between the hall and the immediate context. The use of a fibre cement cladding meant the entire form could be homogenously wrapped with only the entrance screen and Profilit glazing of the hall being inserted into the skin. A visual connection is created between the footpath and the hall through the suppression of the internal floor level. It is through this separation of ground that an enhanced spatial arrangement is made between the external school environment and the new hall.

Front elevation's night view

Entrance foyer exterior

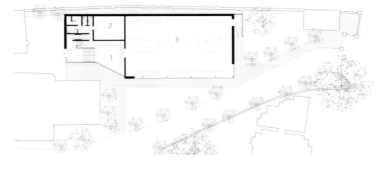

Exterior + interior connection

Foyer, assembly space

Ground floor plan
1. plant
2. store
3. multi-purpose hall
4. foyer

Upper floor plan
1. changing 1
2. changing 2
3. sports office

Photo: Rós Kavanagh

Educational

Completion Date: 2009

Architect: DTA Architects
Team: Colin Mackay, Derek Tynan, Dermot Reynolds, David Graham

View across the street

Salvation Army Chelmsford

The project pioneers modern methods of construction in its use of cross–laminated timber panel system KLH. The system is akin to jumbo plywood and offers all the advantages of reinforced concrete construction without the environmental cost. All walls and floor plates arrived on site as prefabricated panels with cut–outs for doors and windows, ready for quick assembly, allowing the building's frame to be erected in just twenty-four days.

The two most conspicuous elements of the scheme which maximise the cross–laminated technology are the entrance canopy on the north elevation, which provides lateral stability to the front elevation, and the building's signature undulating butterfly roof, which rises to accommodate six generously sized dormer windows, measuring 4.2 metres wide. The butterfly roof is further dramatised by a zinc cladding, which cloaks the building and sweeps down and anchors it on its north elevation on Baddow Road and south elevation on Parkway. The zinc cloak forms a striking enclosure, which gives the building a very robust toughened and urbanistic character and distinguishes it from the surrounding brick buildings.

The building's toughened zinc shell breaks at the Baddow Road entrance lintel where floor–to–ceiling glazing creates a dialogue between the foyer café and the street, projecting an image of openness crucial to the work of the organisation.

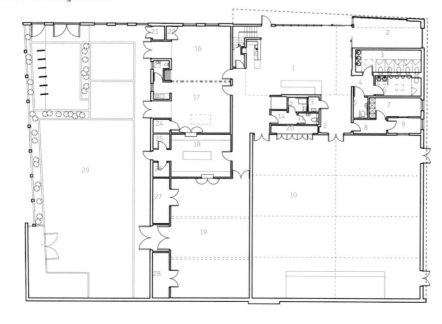

1. foyer
2. multi–purpose room
3. female WC
4. toilet lobby
5. male WC
6. disable WC
7. centre manager
8. lobby
9. drop in space/cry room
10. worship hall
11. WC
12. baby change
13. cleaner
14. lobby
15. 20.22. 24.27.28.store
16. lounge
17. 19.hall
18. kitchen
21. bin store
23. baby WC
25. cool store
26. dry store
29. courtyard

Aerial view

Entrance

Photo: Keith Collie

Completion Date: 2009

Architect: Hudson Architects

Folkestone Academy

The new Folkestone Academy will offer a range of curriculum, teaching and learning facilities that combine the best features of the independent education sector with the Pastoral System of intra–school support and encouragement. A core curriculum – based on the National Curriculum – will be supplemented by specialisations in the Creative Arts and European Culture and Language. As with other schools in the academy programme, Folkestone Academy will also contribute to the regeneration of the local area by offering a range of services to the wider community.

A total of 1,480 pupils – aged between eleven and nineteen – will be accommodated in eight Houses. The sophisticated pastoral system lies at the heart of the Academy's philosophy, with each student benefiting from a level of individual support that comes from a small readily–identifiable group which offers them guidance. Pupils will be encouraged to identify with their House, returning there for breaks and meals – when healthy diets for all pupils is a priority. The architectural design supports this system by providing each House with separate dedicated facilities, including outside space for social activities, within the overall building form.

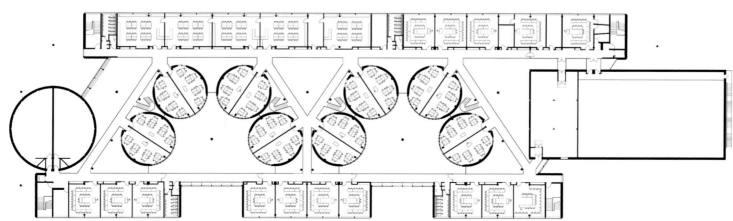

Photo: Nigel Young/Foster + Partners

Completion Date: 2007

Architect: Foster + Partners

Aerial view of school

Hazelwood School

Hazelwood School is an education facility for up to sixty students with multiple disabilities. The students are aged between three and nineteen and the school provides education from nursery through to secondary stages. The school itself and the Life Skills House (an independent facility used for life learning and respite) have a combined area of 2,665 square metres and are set within a landscaped green adjacent to Bellahouston Park.

The design of the building has focused on creating a safe, stimulating environment for its pupils and staff. The focus and ambition from both client and architect at the outset was to develop a building that would eliminate as much as possible the institutional feel that a project of this nature inherently possesses. The designers worked to avoid conventional/standard details, creating a solution bespoke to the project requirements and developing a building that entirely embodied the users' needs.

The existing site was surrounded by mature lime trees and had a large lime tree and three beach trees in the centre. The building snakes through the site, curving around the existing trees. Its form creates a series of small garden spaces suitable to the small class sizes and maximises the potential for more intimate external teaching environments. Internally the curved form of the building reduces the visual scale of the main circulation spaces and helps remove the institutional feel that one long corridor would create – in addition, this also significantly reduces visual confusion by limiting the extents of the space.

1. hydrotherapy pool
2. shower
3. gym
4. physiotherapist room
5. disabled WC
6. doctors room
7. kitchen
8. depute head teacher
9. head teacher
10. staff entrance
11. dining/multi–purpose space/assembly
12. staff room

North elevation

Aerial view of school

Sensory wall designed to aid mobility training

Photo: Andrew Lee

Completion Date: 2007

Architect: gm+ad architects

Langley Academy

The Langley Academy is an exemple of sustainable design, a theme which is showcased by the building itself. The Academy's curriculum highlights rowing, cricket and science and is the first academy to specialise in museum learning. As well as running its own museum, ancient artefacts and objects are brought into the classroom to spark questions, debate, analysis and provide connections across the curriculum. The scheme also provides unparallelled access to significant cultural institutions across the country, involving hundreds of students.

With an enclosed full–height atrium at the heart of the three–storey building, the social life of the school revolves around this assembly space for 1,100 students. A recurrent element in several other Foster + Partners' academy buildings, the atrium is defined by a sense of transparency and openness – like a gallery of learning – which in this case also resonates with the museum theme. Inside the atrium there are three yellow drums raised above the floor on circular columns. These two–storey pods house the Academy's ten science laboratories, reinforcing the importance of science teaching. A dedicated sports and culture block contains specialist facilities for music and drama including a fully–equipped theatre, a TV and sound recording studio, soundproof practice rooms and a rehearsal space, sports hall and lecture theatre. The academy's two light and airy covered streets extend from the atrium and are lined with thirty-eight classrooms.

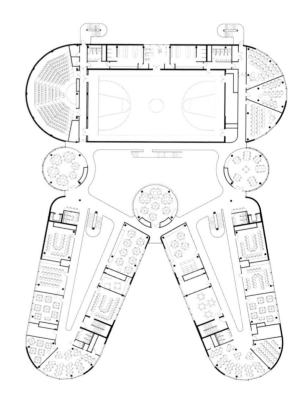

Ground floor plan
1. stairs
2. WC
3. multi–purpose hall

Photo: Nigel Young/Foster + Partners

Completion Date: 2008

Architect: Foster + Partners

Façade

David Mellor Design Museum

The new David Mellor Design Museum is at Hathersage in the Peak District National Park. The new building has been designed to show the whole historic collection, privately owned by the Mellor family, of David Mellor's designs form the 1950s onwards and includes more recent work of his son, Corin Mellor. More broadly the building will help to reinvigorate local Sheffield traditions of cutlery making, forming a visible link between modern design history and present-day production. The building will have the effect of safeguarding existing and creating new jobs.

The main structure of the building is composed of a steel frame supporting a linear lead-pitched roof. Onto the steel frame reclaimed pitch pine, which the client already owned, was bolted to form a composite flitched structure for both columns and roof. Beneath an overhanging steel gutter, which also serves to shade the building, full-height glazed doors allow the linear building to be opened up. At the bottom of these doors, both inside and out, a pitch pine bench is supported from the steel frame to provide a sheltered space along the south front of the building. Toilets, shops and the exhibition displays are accommodated in the rear, north-facing section of the building and the interior design and fabrication of the building was undertaken by the client.

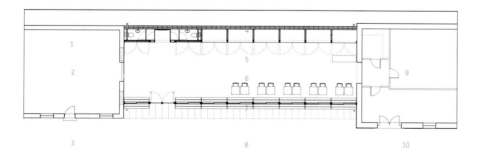

1. existing window
2. wall
3. existing shop building
4. exhibition
5. flexible exhibition space
6. seating
7. outside seating
8. new visitor centre
9. wall
10. existing retort building

Exterior with trees

Interior

Night view of exterior

Photo: Phil Sayer

Completion Date: 2006

Architect: Hopkins Architects

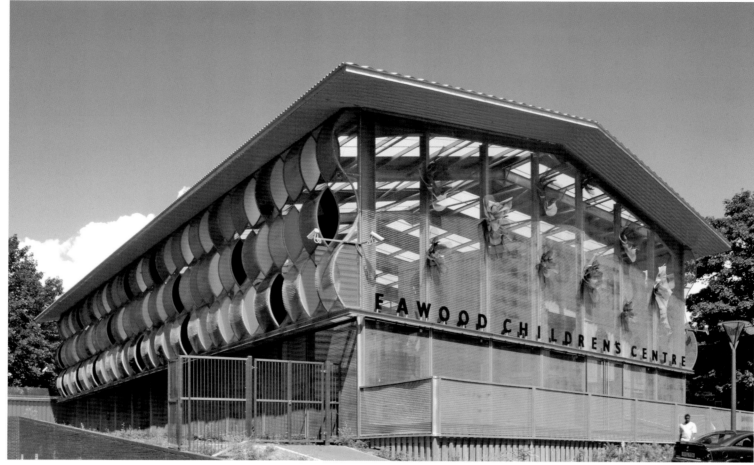

Southwest daytime view

Fawood Children's Centre

The Fawood Children's Centre is an integral part of the overall masterplan for the Stonebridge estate, in Harlesden North London. Planned demolition of the neighbouring housing blocks took place in 2007 and a new park was developed. The Fawood Children's Centre is sited within the new parkland where acts as a focal point in the landscape. It was proposed that the new park will include nature trails and adventure play areas, and that the play areas within the park be located adjacent to the Children's Centre for shared use.

The Children's Centre is located adjacent to the site for a proposed new Health and Community building, also designed by Alsop, which is intended to be an important community focus within the overall regeneration of Stonebridge.

The brief from Stonebridge Housing Action Trust (HAT) was for a nursery school that would replace and expand existing nursery and community facilities on the Estate. The new Fawood Children's Centre, was to provide, under one roof a nursery for three–five year olds: nursery facilities for autistic and special needs children, and a Children's Centre with adult learning services – a base for community education workers and consultation services. This brief was in line with the Government's Sure Start proposals, which advocate combining, within one facility, play and educational experiences for nursery age children, with supporting amenities for the local community, parents and childcare workers.

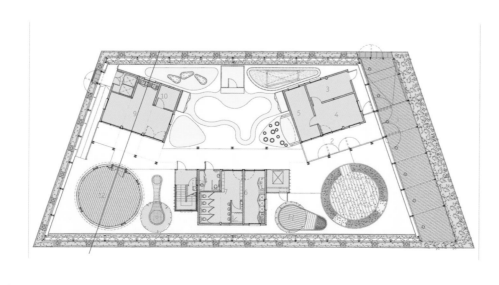

1. entrance deck
2. reception lobby
3. administration/deputy head teacher office
4. head teacher office
5. meeting / office
6. kitchen
7. cloarkroom /children WC
8. unisex disabled WC
9. nurserry accommodetion
10. existing retort building
11. bin store
12. nursery accommodation: yurt

South elevation

Stage

Photo: Alan Lai of Alsop Design Ltd, Roderick Coyne of Alsop Design Ltd.

Educational

Completion Date: 2005

Architect: Alsop.

Main façade

Bryanston School

The New Science School is located within the picturesque grounds of Bryanston School. It houses the three main science disciplines, part of the maths department, and a shared lecture theatre.

The semi–circular plan for the building grew out of the aspiration to conclude the formal axis of the Norman Shaw main building and its later additions, whilst addressing the informal series of individual buildings along the route of the main drive. The three–storey building makes use of the naturally sloping landscape by having the main entrance on the middle floor so that only two levels are visible from the main school courtyard. The building focuses on a central south–facing science garden that features a pond and geodesic greenhouse.

The building has a simple construction of load–bearing brick and block walls, concrete floor slabs and a zinc–clad pitched roof. The main façade to the inner courtyard is solid load–bearing brickwork in English Bond using a high lime–content mortar. The concrete floors bear via pads onto brickwork piers, and flat arches span above window openings.

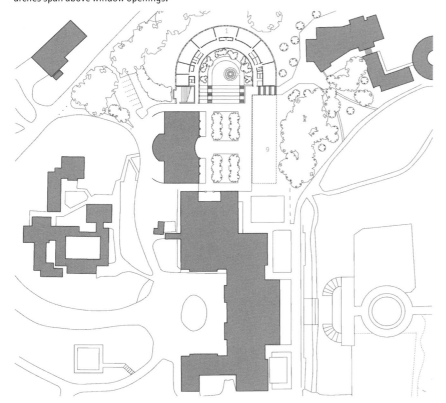

1. new science school
2. main building
3. CDT
4. Coade hall
5. arts and drama
6. art school
7. music school
8. estates
9. future music school

External view

External walkway

External view

Photo: Anthony Weller

Completion Date: 2007

Architect: Hopkins Architects

Falmouth School Design & Technology Building

Designed by Urban Salon, the project came out of the Sorrell Foundation's 'joined up design for school programme where pupils are given control and responsibility as clients. The 95-square-metre extension is a solid prefabricated cross-laminated timber construction with the timber exposed to the interior and standing seam pre-weathered zinc to the exterior. The timber structure was chosen for its environmental performance and was designed with half lap joints and has no visible fixings in the building. The ceiling within the extension rises from 3.2 metres to 5.2 metres, allowing even north light to flood the space, and creates the distinctive saw-tooth form of the building. The only steel structural elements are T-sections that support the ridge of the roof panels from the timber beams below. Specialist contractor KLH manufactured the timber structure off site. This modular construction method meant that the structure was assembled on site within two weeks.

The existing Design & Technology studio was upgraded as part of the scheme. The refurbishment rather than wholescale removal of the existing workshops had the added benefit of less waste and lower embodied energy in building materials required. Coupled with the use of the prefabricated elements, this led to less construction time and less disruption to students and their education. The existing block now has a new roof, wood-fibre insulation, double glazing to prevent heat loss in winter and solar shading to the south of the building to prevent summer overheating.

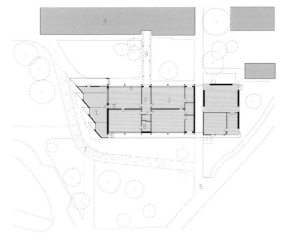

1. design studio extension
2. original design technology block a
3. original design technology block b
4. main school buildings
5. pedestrian entrance
6. polycarbonate canopy above
7. new pathway with markings
8. new disabled toilet
9. existing covered walkway

Photo: Gareth Gardner

Architect: Urbansalon Architects

Completion Date: 2008

Educational

Exterior

John Lewis Department Store and Cineplex and Pedestrian Bridges

Department stores are conventionally designed as blank enclosures to allow retailers the flexibility to rearrange their interior layouts. However, the physical experience of shops is an increasingly important consideration to compliment the convenience of online shopping. The concept for the John Lewis Department store is a net curtain, providing privacy to the interior without blocking natural light.

The design of the store provides the retail flexibility required without removing the urban experience from shopping. The store cladding is designed as a double-glazed façade with a pattern introduced, making it like a net curtain. This allows for a controlled transparency between the store interiors and the city, allowing views of the exterior and natural light to penetrate the retail floors whilst future-proofing the store towards changes in layout. Thus, the store is able to reconfigure its interiors without compromising on its exterior appearance.

In order to establish a consistent identity between the cinema and department store, the curtain concept is extended to the cinema. This curtain both associates the cinema and department store and resonates with the theatre curtains which were a traditional interior feature of cinemas.

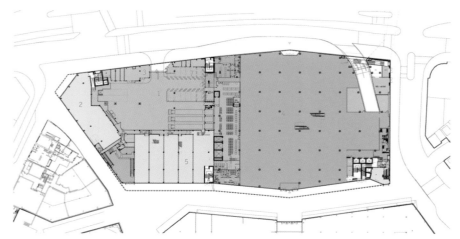

1. service yard
2. retail
3. services
4. department store
5. retail units
6. cinema
7. Vaughan Way

View from the street

Façade with bridge

Photo: Satoru Mishima, Peter Jeffree, Helene Binet and Lube Saveski

Completion Date: 2008

Architect: Foreign Office Architects

Edinburgh Academy – New Nursery and After School Facility

The nursery is arranged entirely on the ground floor and the main teaching accommodation is in three linked rooms, one of which, for the two to three–year–old group, is capable of sub–division. Each of these rooms gives onto landscaped play terraces and also has external covered space and internal bay window spaces. In the centre of the plan are all the necessary services and storage and on the entrance elevation is a large cloakroom arrival point for distributing the children to the different classrooms. The entrance lobby is supervised by the staff room for security. A small dining room and kitchen is also shown for the use of the two to three year olds; the remainder of the children use the junior school's refectory facilities.

The After School and Holiday Care facilities for older children are also to be relocated on the first floor above the new nursery school and these consist of a series of linked rooms for group and individual activities. A floating roof covers the whole building with a line of roof light illuminating the circulation in the middle of the plan.

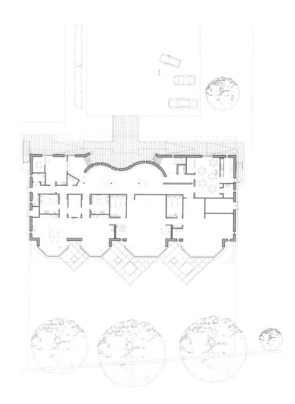

1. park
2. landscape
3. dining
4. entrance
5. WC

Photo: Richard Murphy Architects Ltd.

Completion Date: 2009

Architect: Richard Murphy, James Mason, Dominik George

Stratheden Eighteen-Bed Dementia and Mental Health Unit

The proposal is to provide a low security residential dementia unit in the grounds of Stratheden Hospital. The accommodation consists of eighteen single bedrooms with en–suite shower rooms and associated accommodation for both patients and staff. The building is single storey with a U–shaped plan. Bedrooms are split into the two wings and the communal facilities located centrally. The whole building focuses on a south–facing secure garden for patients with the southern edge of the garden walled and framing the view south towards Walton Hill and White Hill. The design allows for patients to wander freely around the building and into the secure sensory garden. The circulation around the garden has small alcoves with built–in seating for patients to stop and sit and look out into the garden.

Each bedroom has a bay window with views out into the grounds of Stratheden. Secondary light comes into each individual room via a roof light located below the pitched roof ridge line. Each bedroom is identifiable by individual pitched roofs giving the patients a sense of their own identity within the building. All the other accommodation and circulation areas have flat roofs at different heights.

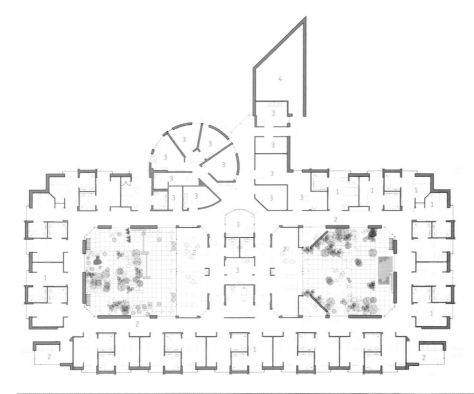

1. bedroom
2. patient areas
3. staff/consulting
4. services

Exterior

Courtyard

Garden

Reception

Photo: Richard Murphy Architects Ltd.

Architect: Richard Murphy Architects Ltd.

Hospital

Completion Date: 2009

General view

Kirkintilloch Adult Learning Centre

The aim of the project was to provide an open learning environment which draws in potential students from all sectors of society and to provide a new home for the classes already located within Kirkintilloch by Strathkelvin Further Education Centre.

The building is laid out as a linear plan with a two-storey block to the south side housing classrooms and offices. Against this sits a lean-to structure which houses the open learning facilities and projects out onto the canal bank.

The entrance to Phase 1 (previously to one end of the linear plan) is now positioned in the centre of the completed building. The reception orientates the visitor and first-time student within the main double-height space, allowing a clear reading of the building to be made with the majority of the classrooms and computer resource space to the left and the café and other administration offices to the right. A void behind the reception, through which the stair descends past a seated area, which protrudes out over the canal, makes connection to the lowest level which houses the open resource areas.

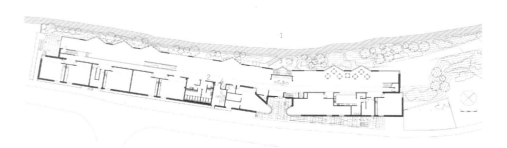

1. entrance
2. WC
3. services
4. stair

Exterior detail

Entrance

Photo: Richard Murphy Architects Ltd.

Educational

Adult learning space

Architect: Richard Murphy Architects Ltd.

Completion Date: 2009

General view

Wakering Road Foyer

Wakering Road Foyer provides 116 bedsits for disadvantaged young people. The foyer tackles social exclusion among vulnerable sixteen to twenty-five-year-old through housing and training programmes that transform their lives. It accommodates young people with a range of support needs, including young parents, ex-drug users, wheelchair users and those with minor mental-health difficulties. Residents spend up to two years there to gain independence before moving on to a home of their own.

The massing allows sunlight into all of the dwellings, distances the dwellings and offices from the noise of Northern Relief Road, and reinforces the street edges. The L-shaped building, made up of a two- and a nine-storey block, creates a sheltered garden at ground level and a sunny roof garden. The interaction of the two- and nine-storey blocks is expressed by two distinct materials. Fibre-reinforced-concrete rainscreen cladding dresses the taller wing, while curtain walling defines the low-lying wing.

The landscaped garden is for residents and staff, with a secure play area reserved for the adjacent crèche. Trees and an existing embankment screen the garden from Northern Relief Road. The second-floor roof garden, for the young parents and their babies, includes a lawn and "living roof" to encourage biodiversity, as well as a pavilion for all-weather use. The landscaping promotes sustainable urban drainage, reducing surface-water run-off with planting and permeable paving.

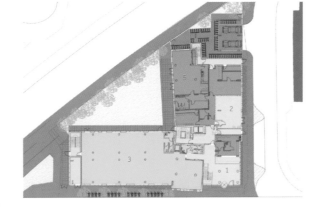

1. reception
2. refuse room
3. office for partner organisations
4. public WC
5. crèche

View from street

Main entrance

Completion Date: 2009

Architect: Jestico + Whiles

Main entrance from outside

North view

Kielder Observatory

The design brief called for an inexpensive building, not only suitable to house two telescopes and a warm room, primarily intended for amateurs and outreach work, but also suitable for scientific research. The design had to achieve a positive relation to the exposed setting on top of Black Fell overlooking Kielder Water and had to include both the facilities needed in this remote site and a "social space" for interaction and presentations, while being accessible both literally and culturally.

Timber was chosen as the material for the observatory early in the design process. Besides being a low carbon material and the obvious relation to its forest setting, the architects wanted a low-tech engineering aesthetic for the observatory, the opposite of the NASA-inspired world of high tech, high-expense and exclusive science. Instead, the architects wanted to evoke the curious, ad hoc structures that have served as observatories down the ages, and to the timber structures of the rural/industrial landscape at Kielder, the pit props of small coal mines and the timber trestle bridges of the railway that served them. The architects felt that a beautifully handcrafted timber building with "Victorian" engineering would be more inspiring in this setting than seamless, glossy domes.

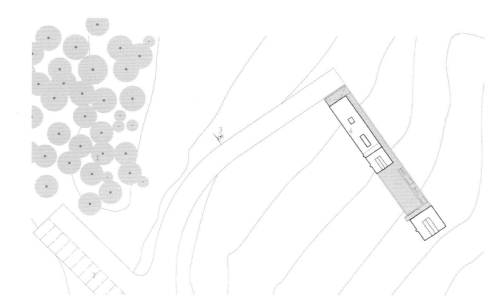

1. forestry plantation
2. parking
3. wind turbine
4. observatory

Telescope

Rotated

Southwest view

Photo: David Grandorge

Completion Date: 2008

Architect: Charles Barclay Architects

New Flower Market – Mercabarna–Flor

While the roof is the big integrating element of this market, in the interior three conceptually different markets are located, each of them with its own specific characteristics and logistic and technical conditions, according to the product on sale. One part is meant for the Cut Flower Market, with modern industrial cooling systems, where the temperatures can be maintained between 2 °C and 15 °C, since the product has a fast turnover with a selling time of only three days.

On the other end of the complex the Plant Market is located, designed with heating systems with a radiant industrial floor, one of the biggest in Europe with 4,000 square metres. It has passive cooling systems that introduce humidity, which guarantee that the temperatures will never be below 15 °C, or above 26 °C, especially designed for the needs of this product that requires more selling time, about fifteen days. This means that besides being a vending zone, this sector is also a storage zone or greenhouse during this period of time.Finally in the middle of these two opposite sectors the Accessory Market is located, an especially delicate sector, because of its elevated fire risk. Due to the fact that they work with dried flowers and that the sale requests a considerable storage area, this subsector has especially been designed to detect and extinguish fire.

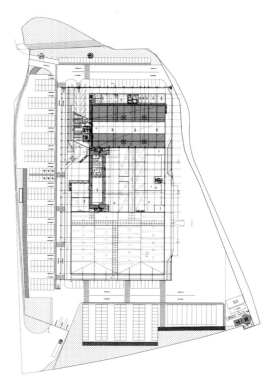

1. entrance
2. store

Photo: Willy Müller Architects

Completion Date: 2008

Architect: Willy Müller Architects

Overall view

Side look

Torres de Hércules

Located in the Bay of Algeciras (Cadiz), the new construction, which is surrounded by a man–made lake, is composed of two identical twenty–storey cylindrical towers, joined by a crystalline prism which houses the hallways connecting the two buildings. Its outer appearance is configured by the structure of the building, a gigantic lattice which completely surrounds the perimeter. There are the giant letters of the legend "Non Plus Ultra". Their job is to protect the inside of the building from excess solar radiation while providing panoramic views of the Bay of Algeciras, the Rock of Gibraltar, and the Serrania. This grid extends past the building's limits, as a "unique element" protecting the terrace roof–top deck, while at the same time acting as a base for possible energy collecting and telecommunications systems.

On the top floor, eighty metres up, will be a lookout restaurant. Above this, a panoramic roof–top deck will boast unique views over the Straight of Gibraltar, Mount Musa and the Alcornocales Natural Park. The building has a main entrance for pedestrians and cars which provides a clear view of the towers. The 200–spot ground–level parking lot is located on the other side of the towers and is organised around a landscaped area.

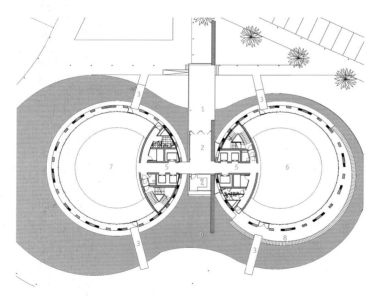

1. main entrance/canopy
2. entrance lobby
3. side entrance/bridges
4. reception
5. lift lobby
6. cafeteria/bar
7. commercials
8. terrace
9. water

Details

Stairs

Inside view

Photo: Rafael de La-Hoz Castanys

Corporate

Completion Date: 2009

Architect: Rafael de La-Hoz Castanys

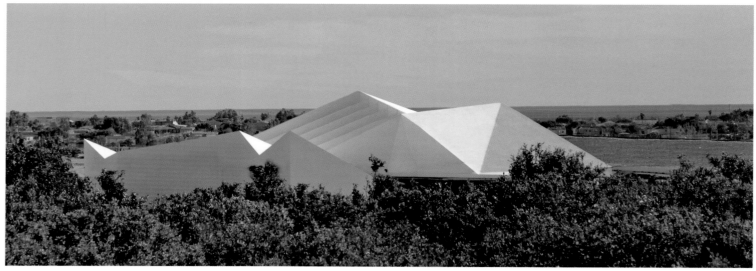

Exterior

The Azahar Group Headquarters

The parent company originated from Castellón and, given its growth and expansion, was eager to have a corporate headquarters that would reflect its environmental and artistic commitment. With this as a framework and with the availability of a 5.6–hectare piece of land next to the N–340 highway, Half way between Castellón and Benicàssim, the project contemplates three interventions: the covered greenhouses and exterior nursery plantations; a building for services complementary to the activities developed by the company; and the group's corporate headquarters.

The headquarters is erected as an icon building maintaining a close relationship with the landscape. To both the north and west, the topography of the mountains serves as a backdrop for the building, against which the geometrical roofs repeatedly stand out. From a distance their facetted shape and outline help situate the building in the landscape. Orientated on the east–west axis, the building is structured as two wings united by a central body around two open patios of a very different sort. The first as a "parade ground" or external reception area for users and visitors, and the rear one landscaped and for more private use. The four wings that accommodate the company's different departments converge in a main hall which, as well as acting as a distributor, is a large exhibition space.

An important environmental feature of the building is the channelling of water from all the roofs and the outside areas to a cistern–reservoir, the latter being used in the watering of exteriors and nursery plantings on the plot of land.

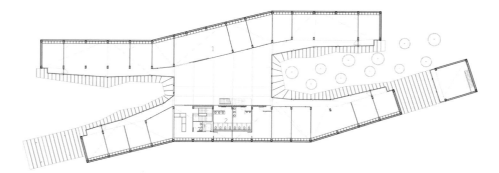

Ground floor plan
1. office
2. toilet

Exterior

Night view of the exterior

Outside view of the offices

Interior lobby

Photo: Alejo Bagué

Completion Date: 2009

Architect: Carlos Ferrater – Núria Ayala

General night view

Abertis Headquarters

The brand–new building for Abertis, the second phase of Barcelona's "Logistic Parc", a 11,000-square-metre office building accommodates in its five floors the different business areas of the company.

The Abertis building is a part of a whole new–edge landscape, and three buildings with a continuous façade to the Ronda Litoral, form an interior plaza that conforms a patio protected from the highway. In this new phase three buildings conform an angled façade towards the highway, a dynamic, solid and transparent façade, in an attempt to capture the paradoxes of a new urban landscape.

It is an optimised ground plan with a feature, central greek cross–shaped open space. This space allows access from the lobby to the flexible working zones. It has some elements in common. The efficiency ratios exist from the beginning, reflecting the relationship between the gross and the usable space as ratio, the result of studies on economical and architectural functionality for a building.

There is a strong tendency to reduce price and quality. Of course, ask some of them, for example, Dior, Cartier, Rochas, Shiseido, Parisbas, Swift, JP Morgan, AXA and Chateau Lafitte Rothschild: all these companies have multiplied the final value of their buildings. The double skin façade was proposed some years ago, and has been used in many projects. Even though it was inspired, only ideally, in the great Egyptian or Medieval historical walls, the double glass façade has in common with these walls the element of thickness, acting as container, as barrier. We don't find these components in the single glass walls.

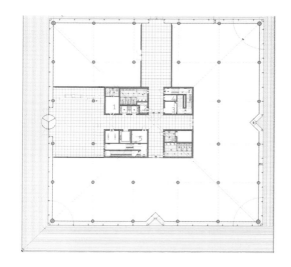

1. local control system
2. installation mechanism
3. installation electricity
4. local maintenance
5. installation telecommunications

General daytime view

Photo: Carlos Casariego

Completion Date: 2007

Architect: Ricardo Bofill Taller De Arquitectura

Façade details

Interior view

293

Exterior

Orense Swimming Pools for Vigo University

The plot chosen is at the highest point of the university campus, a location that gives it a special value in the relationship between the city of Orense and the campus, currently encumbered by the presence of a busy road between them. Opting for a programme orientated towards leisure, and that may thereby serve both the university community and the people of Orense, it will help to heighten the value of the building as an element of urban interaction.

This special location has inspired the main conceptual and formal decisions of the project. The proposal is drawn up as a vast platform that looks onto the campus, and the whole organisation of functions is indebted to this idea. The users will be able to see the campus and its buildings from this raised platform containing the swimming pools. The platform is designed with bold projections supported by a strong base that, aside from spanning the existing drops, shapes the pools and contains all the water treatment services and necessary systems for the correct performance of the programme. The contrast between this massive, topographic base and the cantilevering light glass surfaces surrounding the public level of swimming pools is one the basic formal arguments of the project.

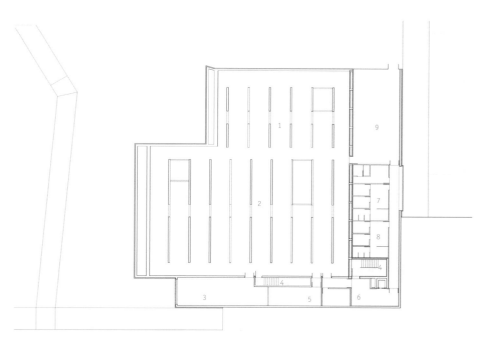

1. swimming pool a
2. swimming pool b
3. rest room
4. stairs
5. personnel room
6. administration office
7. men's room and showers
8. women's room and showers
9. rest hall

General view

Exterior

Swimming pool

Swimming pool

Photo: Pedro Pegenaute, Roland Halbe

Completion Date: 2008

Architect: Francisco José Mangado Beloqui

Archeological Museum of Álava

The building adjoins the Palace of Bendaña, today the Naipes Fournier museum. Access to the building is through the same courtyard that leads to the Palace and conveys the full scope of the project. The proposal includes extending the courtyard surface area in order to upgrade the access area. This does not encroach on the whole court, however, taking only a narrow strip for an appendix perpendicular to the main building. As well as housing auxiliary programmes, this addition provides a more attractive access façade than the current party walls of the neighbouring constructions. Thanks to the sloping terrain, the courtyard is reached through a bridge over a garden that allows light to penetrate to the lower areas that otherwise would be permanently in shadow.

The areas housing the various activities, including the library and workshops, are located on the ground level orientated towards the street, and have an independent access. The assembly hall and galleries for temporary exhibitions are on the same level as the public entrance shared with the Naipes Fournier museum. The permanent exhibition halls are on the upper levels. The stairs linking the different levels define part of the façade onto the access courtyard. The outer walls comprise a series of different layers. The façade facing the access courtyard is bronze grilles, a material with clear archaeological references. In the middle, a double-layered wall of silkscreen printed glass contains the stairs that offer visitors views of the courtyards. In contrast, the façade fronting the street is more hermetic, comprising an outer layer of opaque prefabricated bronze louvres, with openings where needed, and an inner layer formed by a thick wall containing the display cabinets and systems. In this way the internal exhibition spaces are unencumbered and only traversed by translucent light prisms.

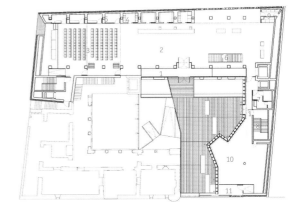

1. entrance foyer
2. entrance –reception
3. mul–tipurpose hall–auditorium
4. coat check
5. simultaneous translation room
6. circulation
7. toilets
8. stair shaft
9. hvac
10. temporary exhibition hall
11. foyer

General view

Cast bronze pieces configure the outer façades that define the access court

Photo: Pedro Pegenaute, Cesar San Millán

Cultural

Access

Interior view

Architect: Francisco Mangado / Mangado y Asociados

Completion Date: 2009

Insular Athletics Stadium

The sports building's location produces a large entrance square under which the indoor facilities are housed. The Elite Performance Centre is placed beneath a large horizontal platform set midway up the slope, using the existing incline. A repetitive construction system of concrete screens reduces the budget for a project in which the structural component is extremely important. High-resistance materials will permit intense public usage of the facilities with minimal upkeep. The Elite Performance Centre will have natural ventilation and lighting through patios and skylights. The athletics track meets the dimensions and guidelines required by the National Sports Council, with perimeter training belts. The inner track will have flexible usage, including partial usage for gymnastics. A linear network of services and dressing rooms separates the athletics field from the EPC, permitting alternate usage by both. An amenities block and a small canteen with independent access are placed in line in the top section of the tiers. The living quarters set in the southeast part of the allotment make the most of the slopes, aspects and views. There are four distinct entrances: the main public entrance, the athletes entrance, the direct entrance for marathons and external events and the service entrances.

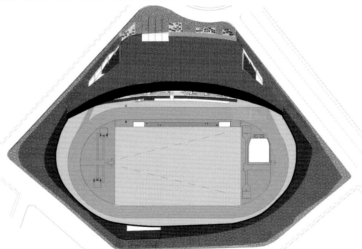

Photo: AMP Arquitectos

Completion Date: 2007

Architect: AMP Arquitectos

Private House in Menorca

Being a summer house, the main idea is not only to create the interior spaces of the house, but to distribute all outer space. The interior spaces seek good relations with the outside world, colonising their surroundings and their views.

Inspired by the typical Menorca "tanca", stone walls divisions of the realm, the plot is organised from a space frame, fully passable, based on a trace orthogonal, combining floors, platforms, water, trees, plants, tanca, pergolas, walls and the house itself. By combining these elements the architects are encountering this approach in which each piece is delimited and acquires its own identity within a harmonious whole. The diversity of outdoor stays provides the site with a space balanced richness.

The house is situated in the centre of the outer solar stays divided in two, front and rear. The hall of the house with two large openings on each side operates as a mixed external–internal transition. Falls outside the pavement creat a passage that connects the backyard with the front porch.

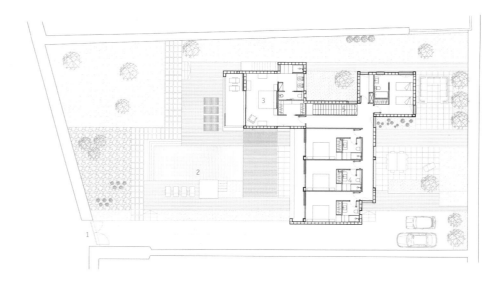

1. entrance
2. living room
3. bedroom
4. WC
5. stair

Photo: Pablo Serrano Elorduy

Completion Date: 2009

Architect: Pablo Serrano Elorduy

Bird view

Terminal 1 of Barcelona Airport

Designed by Ricardo Bofill, Barcelona Airport's new Terminal 1 is one of the best projects in his long career history.

The impressive infrastructure created stands out for its spaciousness and functional nature, the spaces inside it interrelating in a clear and orderly manner, offering the visitor great ease of movement. The general design, simple and minimalist, is the ideal framework for Nu benches, located in several of the terminal's spaces. The Bicilínea bicycle racks (designed by Beth Galí), situated outside the terminal, are also based on a design with well-defined lines.

Forged anchors galvanised steel ten-millimetre-thick dimensional control equipped and provided with expansive blocks M-16 and stainless hardware. Primary structure uprights and beams extruded aluminum, alloy 6063, adequately sized to withstand a wind load of 110 kg/m^2, bearing joints in both directions. Double glazed skin externally with twelve-millimetre tempered glass, restrained by structural silicone independent portavidrios frameworks for each hole. Inner skin consists of two glass sheets colourless practicable, which shall be operated and kept open with shock gas. The intermediate ventilation chamber shall have seventy-millimetre holes for inlet and outlet ventilation.

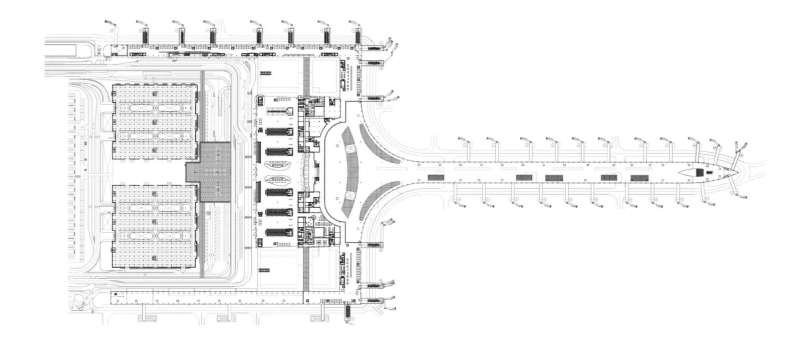

Front view

Service areas

Lounge of an airport

Inside view of service areas

Photo: Carlos Casariego

Completion Date: 2007

Architect: Ricardo Bofill Taller De Arquitectura

Façade

Pontevedra Campus

In the planning of the Campus of Pontevedra, the geometries shaping "local traces" and a nature still with potential, super put on the intention of creating an atmosphere that results from the permeability and presence of the environmental peculiarities, added to the decision to make the diverse activities of the university life take part among them, through two mechanisms: visual continuities in horizontal and vertical section, and conversion of circulation spaces in relation areas.

It leads to taking the most of reliving the river as organiser of the city, to deal and to propose the campus as community space of culture and leisure, and to recover the area of the campus and the river as park and as defined ecozone.

The central area of the campus is pedestrianised and creates a central–covered main square covered as a place that holds different events, which "sews" the buildings isolated. The landscape treatment joins the values of the natural space with the cultural place, coming together an ecozone of bank with a constructed garden, and the campus joins across entail with the river in the net bank path network that connect, with the city.

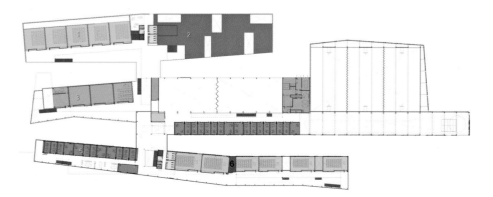

1. lecture room
2. university library
3. work room/lab
4. office
5. stairs/lifts

Corridor

Details of openings

Photo: Manuel González Vicente

Completion Date: 2010

Architect: Irisarri+Piñera Arquitectos

Gym

General view

Headquarters of the Environment Service and Public Spaces

The building houses the Forestry and Natural Areas Departments of Zaragoza City Council. Situated in the centre of the city, next to the Almozara bridge, the site has considerable differences in level, about five metres between the avenue and the square at the upper level and the Ebro riverbank park. The relationship with the adjacent urban spaces and the topographic features of the site become active conditions for the implementation of the building; it can clearly be seen in the project section that the extension of the public space of the entrance is also expresed, via the roof and the configuration of the building as a platform—viewpoint onto the Ebro River.

Given the differences in level of the site, the main entrance to the building is on the upper floor, which houses the administrative spaces and the environmental hall. The main hall joins and separates spaces, enabling them to be used independently. The restricted access offices of the Forestry and Natural Areas Departments are located below the entrance level, in the basement. This lower floor has pedestrian and vehicle access from the Riverbank Park.

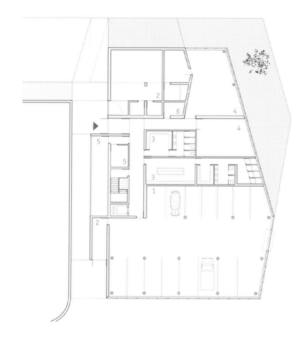

1. garage
2. warehouse
3. locker room
4. staff rooms
5. installations
6. utility room

Elevation from Europe Square

Open-air amphitheatre

View from Europe Square

Photo: Pedro Pegenaute

Completion Date: 2009

Architect: Magén Arquitectos (Jaime Magén, Fco. Javier Magén)

General vew

Kindergarten in Rosales Del Canal

The Kindergarten in Rosales del Canal is located in an area of residential growth in the southwest of Zaragoza. The two main ideas that existed at the start of the project are based on children's special perception of the constructed environment. The first idea tries to combine the general volumetrics of the public facility with the domestic scale that must accompany the child. The second has to do with the sensorial relationship between children and architecture.

The basic unit of the school is the classroom. Its form responds both to the primary identification of the sloping roofing and to the advantages of height and additional lighting in the classrooms. The shape of the roofing of the classrooms is repeated to cover significant spaces that occupy a larger surface area such as the multipurpose hall and the dining-room.

The general configuration of the building clearly responds to organisational criteria, placing the classrooms around the patio, with service spaces situated between them and communicated on the inside with the corridor and on the outside with the patio, via the continuous exterior porch. The lobby, the multipurpose hall and an administrative area composed of the reception, the teachers' room and the administration complete the functional programme.

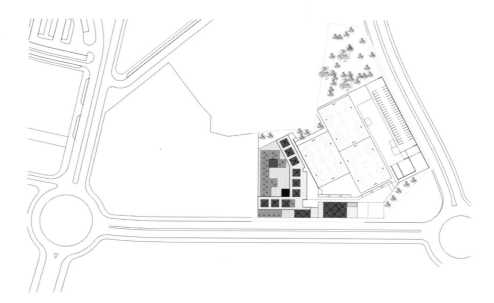

Courtyard

Wall

Interior

Classroom

Photo: Jesús Granada

Architect: Magén Arquitectos (Jaime Magén, Fco. Javier Magén)

Educational

Completion Date: 2009

309

44 Social Housing Tauste (Zaragoza)

The building is located at the south urban edge of Tauste, which is situated fifty kilometres away from Zaragoza. The project avoids the direct dialogue in a formal way with the closest out of context surrounding – the site borders at the north with a green space, at the south with housing buildings, at the east with an industry zone and at the west with the access road from Zaragoza and the municipal sports centre. The interior public space establishes connections with the adjacent spaces to get an appropriate integration in the place.

With the purpose of dealing with the urban character of the interior of the city block, two restrictions are proposed: the first one is to fit the garage of the semi–basement floor in the same width as the other floors, renouncing the allowed highest occupation, in order not to reduce the dimensions of the public space; the second one is to free a big porch at the north side, under the building, which relates the interior space with the pre–existence green space. This opening, together with the openings situated at the west and the south of the site, the trees and the urban furniture, helps understand the interior of the block as a public space.

Daytime view from the street

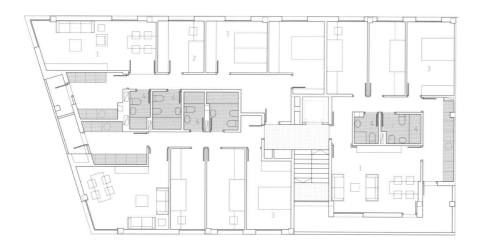

1. living room
2. study
3. bedroom
4. toilet

Building exterior

Entrance

Interior

Photo: Jesús Granada

Architect: Magén Arquitectos

Residential

Completion Date: 2010

Buildings with entrance

BTEK — Interpretation Centre for Technology

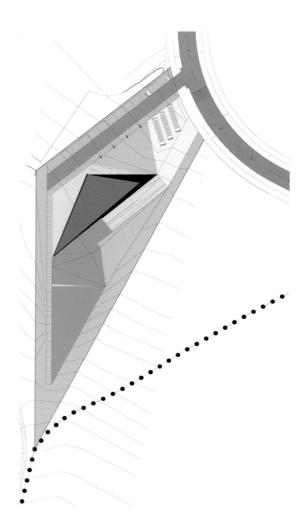

BTEK is an interpretation centre for new technologies, aimed at student visitors. The Centre's promoter, Parque Tecnológico, S.A., (Technology Park) set out the following as the most important guidelines:

The site's location, on one of the highest points of the Vizcaya Technology Park and close to the Bilbao airport's flight path for takeoffs and landings, helps with the aim of making the building a landmark in its landscape.

The building consists of two apparently uninterrupted pyramid–shaped volumes that connect below ground level.

+ The first is a heavy, black volume that emerges from the earth; it is enclosed by three metallic façades and completely covered with solar panels that form a patterned network.
+ The second volume, contrasting with the first, is formed by two façades of curtain walling with an artificial grass–covered roof that starts off as an extension of the terrain and continues on to cover the entire site.
+ Artificial grass also covers the below–ground–level connection, allowing it to merge with the site and its surroundings.

The five galleries are designed to be visited sequentially. In order to serve for a wide variety of possible exhibitions and contents, the galleries have been designed with very different characteristics: from those with ceilings at a conventional height to galleries with variable–height ceilings, reaching up to sixteen metres of clear height, and with or without natural lighting.

Roof

Building with landscape

Detail

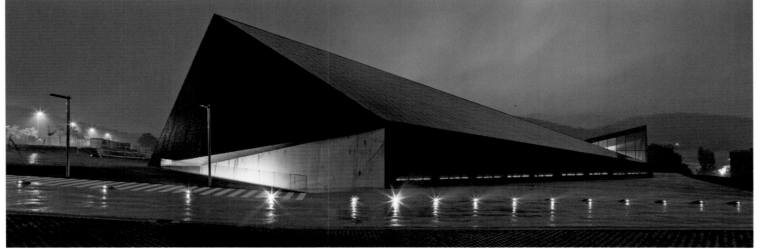

Night view

Mora River Aquarium

Given the blazing Alentejo sun and the need to create shade, the building was devised as a compact and monolithic volume with a pitched shelter of thin white pre-cast concrete porticos with single spans of thirty-three metres, evoking the profile of the canonical Alentejo whitewash barns known as "montes". The shading and cross ventilation systems along with the water circuits foster the reduction of cooling energy, the sustainable increase of humidity and the wellbeing of animal and plant life.

Standing on a massive concrete plinth with a built-in stairway-cum-ramp entrance, the pitched shed veils a set of mute boxes that contain the programme, namely reception, ticketing and shop, cafeteria, changing exhibits hall, documentation centre, research and education, live exhibits, multimedia and a small auditorium. Inside, the exhibition spaces tend to be dark, in order to minimise UV impact on the live exhibits and allow visitors an in-depth viewing of the aquariums. The outdoor void between these programme boxes and the pitched shed generates not only accelerated viewpoints onto the outside but also a promenade that culminates in the passage through a bridge over the lake which, in itself, is also a live exhibit of animals and plants collected and nurtured in the region. The live exhibits, the main feature of an aquarium, reproduce, through complex life support systems, the habitat conditions of different regions allowing to exhibit side-by-side the various animals and plants. On the basement, these support systems guaranty stability of water temperature, pH, quality control and filtering for each habitat parameter, including a duct gallery below each exhibit to supply and monitor the water.

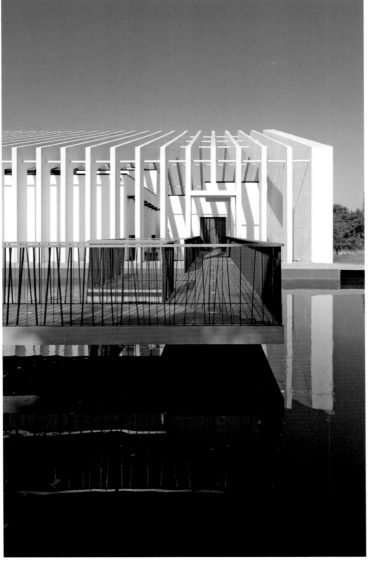

Photo: Sérgio Guerra and Fernando Guerra

Recreational

Completion Date: 2006

Architect: Promontorio Architects

Antas Educative Centre

The spatial and architectural design of the building of the new Antas Education Centre were formalised in several bodies, each containing part of the programme in accordance with principles of internal organisation, functionality, form and image, given the type of building and its specificity. This conception took into account the morphology of the terrain, solar orientation, access and links to surrounding bodies. It's a building consisting of several bodies expressed by a "simple architecture" that will build a close relationship with the exterior spaces. It was intended to create in the spaces between the various bodies the visual relationship between interior and exterior reducing relations with the urban surroundings.

There was an intention to turn into how the building relates to the exterior. However, there are some links to the outside also. The settlement found answers to a matrix that structuralise a functional organiasation of the school as a function of the planned programme and constraint imposed by various land levels.

Southeast view

General plan
1. entrance
2. gym
3. atrium
4. playing field
5. kindergarten
6. classrooms / kitchen and dining
7. outdoor recreation
8. classrooms / covered playground

Children's outdoor play area

Night view of children's outdoor play area

Circulation space to classrooms

Photo: Barbosa & Benigno

Educational

Completion Date: 2010

Architect: AVA – Architects

Night view

Le Prisme

The building is a new venue for theatre, concerts, fairs and sports events. It contains retractable seating and demountable stage for versatility. The main space can accommodate up to 4,500 people during performances. As it is never permanently inhabited, the building is essentially a chamber for ephemeral events.

It is an instantly recognisable object. Three ribbons of concrete that vary in height and texture define the building. The ribbons delineate the different zones of the building: entrance, hall, storage and back of house facilities, and also create a series of residual spaces that contain services machinery and technical access. Inside, a twelve–metre–high ribbon defines a rectangle that is the hall. The hall is column free, measuring forty metres wide by sixty metres long. Externally the upper ribbon is made of prefabricated concrete panels with a regular grid of glass bricks.

During the day, the sunlight plays with the 25,000 bespoke pyramid–shaped glass bricks, producing glimmering effects and dramatic shadows. In the evening, the building awakens as the Fresnel lens–like surfaces of the glass bricks that amplify the intensity of the coloured lighting scheme, producing a glittering façade.

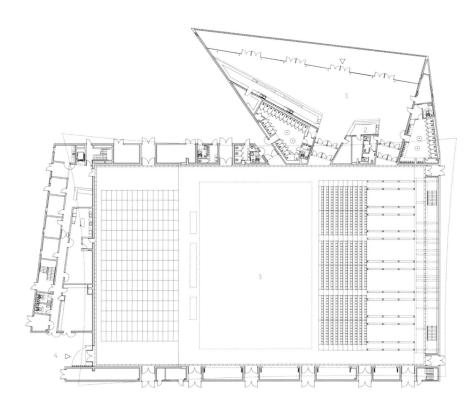

1. entrance foyer
2. reception desk
3. multi-purpose hall
4. delivery

Front view

Interior

Enrance

Photo: Helene Binet, Brisac Gonzalez Architects

Completion Date: 2007

Architect: Brisac Gonzalez

CCVH–Gignac

At the entrance to the city of Gignac, the stake consists in positioning on this place a urban complex, a village around a square. Every building has an independent access to the garden, is autonomous and has its own identity. The traffic of vehicles is channelled around the entity allowing the heart to become only pedestrian.

A particular care is brought to the set–up of buildings. The main constructions are facing north/south to facilitate the natural ventilation. This choice of set–up has two other objectives: shelter the central garden by protecting it from the North wind, and then maintain views on the tower of Gignac, the Pic Saint Baudille and the low valley of Hérault.

Only the building used for the Communauté de Communes is perpendicular, it marks the city entrance and the access to the site, it closes the internal garden. The medical pole and the pole of services face each other around the central garden. Their composition is symmetric, unitarian, modular and evolutionary. This allows to answer both the climatic comfort and the respect for the surrounding built heritage. Zinc, stone and concrete are the essential materials of this composition and make echo for the traditional materials of the place, both for the houses and for the agricultural structures.

Central garden and community building

Community building

Community building

1-8. community building

Photo: Paul KOZLOWSKI

Completion Date: 2009

Architect: N+B Architectes

Night view

General view

Limoges Concert Hall

The Concert Hall in Limoges' outer envelope is made of wood arcs and translucent rigid polycarbonate sheets and the inner envelope of wood.

The use of wood was suggested by the location of the hall, in a clearing within a large forest surrounded by trees over 200 years old. The region also has an active timber industry. In addition, the soft translucency of the polycarbonate complemented the wooden frame by allowing light to filter in and out of the building. The strategy establishes reciprocity between concept and context.

The configuration of the double envelope with circulation in–between is a scheme that is advantageous for both acoustical and thermal reasons. The detached and fragmented envelope opens in two directions, towards both the forest and the road. Between the two envelopes are the movement vectors: two ramps, one extending downward toward the lower tiers of the auditorium, and the other upward toward the upper tiers. Additionally, two straight "flying" staircases extend directly toward the top row of seats.

Interior

Night view

Exterior view

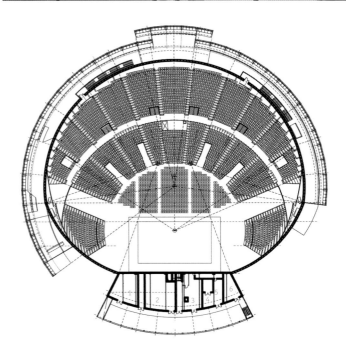

1. local engine
2. boiler room
3. local CTA
4. local TGBTS
5. local TGBTS
6. local transformer

Whole scene of the exterior

Boulogne Billancourt

The first building within the Trapeze masterplan at Boulogne Billancourt, in the southeast of Paris, this seven-storey office development occupies a prime position within the mixed-use development. The building has an expressed white concrete structure, with a steel and glass façade. It is divided between two volumes, connected by a glazed, full-height atrium containing a café and two restaurants for staff. This dynamic space incorporates panoramic lifts and suspended walkways, which appear to float at double-height intervals to allow uninterrupted views out to the river or the park. Above the entrance, giant translucent brise-soleils filter daylight down into the atrium, while a wave-formed geometric façade on the east and west elevations comprise curved vertical panels of alternate translucent and fritted glass.

A rooftop pavilion to the east and the expansive south-facing balconies are accessible from the office floors and take advantage of the riverside location. The 22,000 square metres of interior floor space provides a mixture of cellular and open-plan configurations. The internal arrangement is flexible – the floor plates can be split either vertically or horizontally to accommodate multiple tenants. A fringe of shops enlivens the ground level and the boulevard between the river and the building has been landscaped to provide a waterside promenade.

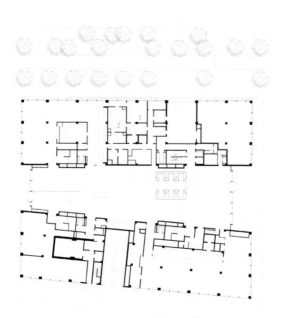

1. office
2. lounge
3. staircase

France

Europe

Whole scene

Photo: Foster + Partners

Interior

Completion Date: 2008

Architec: Foster + Partners

Hall

General view

Centre Dramatique National de Montreuil

The building complex, closed like a fist, has its correspondence in a series of spaces which expand and contract on the interior, reminiscent of the implausible spaces Alice in Wonderland traversed.

In the entrance area, the ceiling above the reception desk has multiple folds, similar to a geological zone of convergence, where tectonic plates are on a collision course but manage to slide past each other. In the stairway, gyrating concrete volumes are bathed in Caravaggioesque light. Dark and light, empty and full, this red space expands horizontally, ultimately leading to the auditorium, and then contracts until it becomes lost in the darkness of the foyer. Breaches in the building envelope occasionally offer up views to the city and allow daylight to penetrate deep into the space.

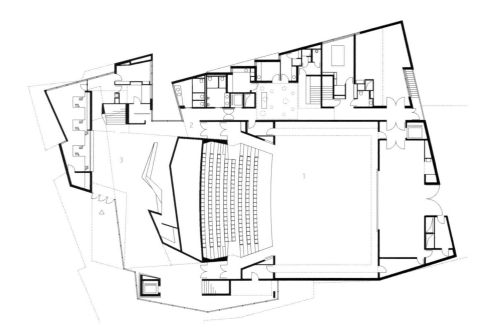

1. salle
2. toilet
3. stairs

Interior

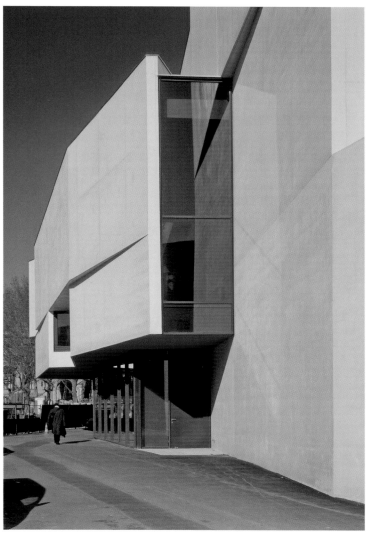

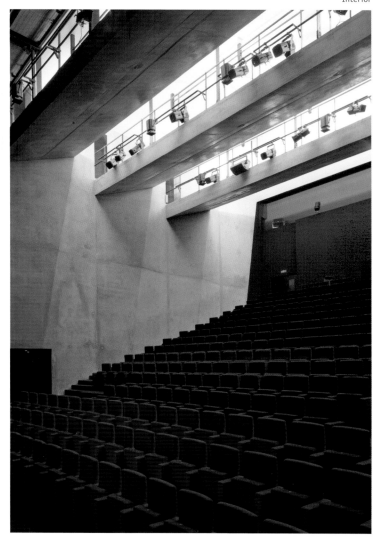

Entrance

Salle

General view

Chapel Mussonville

Mussonville Chapel was built in 1880. The small theatre located in the chapel had to be improved and create new functions (reception, dressing rooms, equipment rooms, etc.). To ensure that these additions are not read as "warts" hung in the chapel, the extension has been made in the form of a "cloister" in which the various functions services take place.

A square grid, which consists of concrete columns of the equivalent sections in the foothills of the chapel, was developed from the chapel and deployed on three sides. In this constructive frame dictated by the chapel, the "brutality" of the constructed elements – joinery galvanised steel poles with coffered concrete planks of raw wood, compacted gravel floor, and chestnut logs provides consistency and a basis stronger in the park that surrounds Mussonville. The empty space created by this provision allows to extend the festivities outside. In the suburbs, a square enclosure formed by screen walls made of logs raw untreated fixed on a tubular frame, was galvanised to close or open space of the chapel, providing a "grid" vision on the spacious park.

Wall

Night view

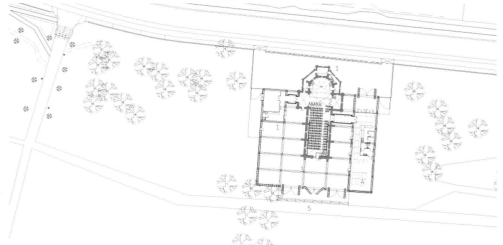

1. loge
2. scene
3. loge
4. parvis
5. reception

Photo: Arthur Pequin

Completion Date: 2008

Architect: atelier d'architecture King Kong

Garden

European Investment Bank

The new headquarters building for the European Investment Bank (EIB), with its compelling 13,000-square-metre glass roof, extends Sir Denys Lasdun's existing buildings on Luxembourg's Kirchberg plateau. It provides 72,500 square metres of office space and other facilities for up to 750 employees.

The striking tubular glass roof spans the entire, 170-metre-long and 50-metre-wide structure. In combination with an extremely lightweight glass and steel superstructure, it offers a maximum of daylight and transparency. In addition, the building's zigzag plan encourages a non-hierarchical office layout that promotes interaction and communication. This unrivalled office environment is carried by an environmental programme that reflects a progressive approach towards sustainability in architecture.

Key to the new headquarters' ecological concept is the glass roof which curves around the floor plates to create the atriums in the V-shaped "gaps" of the building wings. The landscaped winter gardens on the valley side are unheated and act as climate buffers. In contrast, the atriums on the boulevard side serve as circulation spaces; hence temperatures have to be kept at a comfortable level. Both winter gardens and "warm" atriums are naturally ventilated through openable flaps in the shell to draw fresh air into the building and to reduce heat gain especially in the summer months.

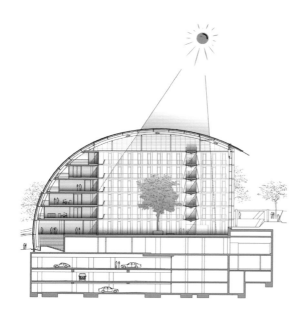

Photo: Ingenhoven Architects

Completion Date: 2008

Architect: Ingenhoven Architects

General view of hotel

SOF Park Inn Hotel Complex

October 8th 2009 marks the opening of SOF, the new Hotel Park Inn, Krakow, Poland designed by the architects team of J. MAYER H. Architects, GD&K Consulting Sp. z o.o. and OVOTZ Design LAB. The hotel is being constructed in the city centre, at the intersection of important transport routes. The hotel is located in the vicinity of the planned Congress Centre as well as near to the Wawel Castel and the historical Jewish district. It offers splendid views onto the old city centre. The new porperty is characterised by clear horizontal lines, picking out the panorama view as a central theme. The façade is emphasised by black and white aluminium stripes, seperated by dark glass windows.

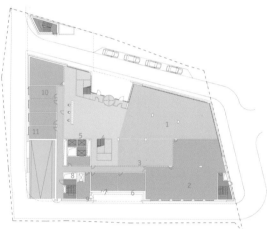

1. restaurant
2. kitchen
3. bar
4. lobby
5. reception
6. canteen
7. waste
8. service
9. delivery
10. toilet
11. office

Side view

Photo: Jakub Kaczmarczyk, Ovotz design Lab (www.ovotz.pl)

Park Inn

Park Inn and entrance

Architect: J. MAYER H. Architects, GD&K Consulting Sp. z o.o., Ovotz Design Lab

Completion Date: 2009

View of the house from the driveway

Aatrial House

One-hectare site near the forest, where the building is designed has only one weak point: south-west access. An obvious conflict developed between the driveway and the garden. The idea arose to lower the driveway in order to separate it from the garden. This prompted another idea of a driveway leading inside to the ground floor level, from underneath the building, which became possible thanks to the creation of an inner atrium with the driveway in it.

New type of the house
As a result, the building opens up onto all sides with its terraces in an unrestricted manner, and the only way to get into the garden is through the atrium and the house.

Structure and materials
The gateway is situated in the highest point of the site sloping to the east side. The ten-metre-wide driveway follows slope's declivity. The building was situated on the garden level. For the sake of neighbouring buildings, typical Polish "cube houses" arisen in 1970s, the structure of the house results from various transformations of a cube.

As a result of stretching and bending particular surfaces of the cube, all the walls, floors and ceilings were defined, together with inner atrium and terraces. This principle of formation has not only created the structure of the house, but also defined interior and exterior architecture, including use of materials. The building is a reinforced concrete monolith, and concrete is at the same time the finishing material of the transformed cube, while all additional elements are finished with dark ebony.

Kitchen and dining room

View of the driveway leading inside to the ground floor level

View of the atrium

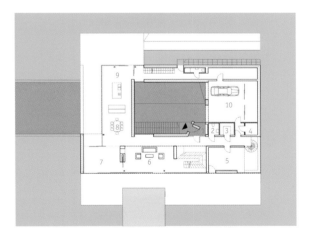

1. entrance
2. toilet
3. wardrobe
4. storage
5. study
6. television room
7. living area
8. dining area
9. kitchen
10. garage

Backyard façade

Photo: Kwk Promes

Completion Date: 2007

Architect: Kwk Promes

Outrial House

The context and investor's expectations made designers to treat grass as a material. One part of the grassy plot is cut out and treated as the roof for basic functions. At the end of design work the investor wished to find a place for an orangery and a small recording studio. Due to "cutting a notch and bending" to inside, the roof became an atrium reached from the inside of the house. The smooth roof created space similar to bandstand that can be used to outdoor jam sessions. The very similar process was used to design the recording studio.

OUTrium – the new type of space
The green space smoothly penetrates into the interior which joins the merits of a traditional atrium with the outdoor garden. OUTrium – as it was called – lets inhabitants be pleased with the outside and stays the inside of the house strictly joined with the living room at the same time.

Technology
The selection of technologies was based on the investor's principles who wanted a simple house. The house is built in white plaster inside and outside walls. The green roof is a good isolation that reduces the loss of heat in winter and cools the house in summer. It assures a very positive microclimate inside the house.

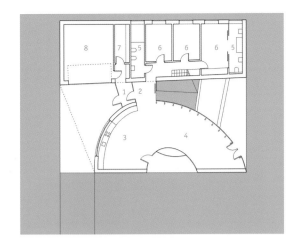

1. entrance
2. hall
3. kitchen with dining area
4. living area
5. bathroom
6. bedroom
7. storage
8. garage

The southwest façade

View of the house from the road

The stairs leading to the roof with one mesh across which grows the grass

Living room with stairs leading to the green roof

Main entrance to the house

Photo: KWK PROMES

Completion Date: 2007

Architect: Kwk Promes

Façade

Safe House

Location
The house is situated in a small village at the outskirts of Warsaw. The surroundings are dominated with usual "Polish cubes" from the 1960s and old wooden barns.

Idea
The clients' top priority was to gain the feeling of maximum security in their future house, which determined the building's outlook and performance. The house took the form of a cuboid in which parts of the exterior walls are movable. When the house opens up to the garden, eastern and western side walls move towards the exterior fence creating a courtyard.

After crossing the gate, one has to wait in this safety zone before being let inside the house. In the same time, there is no risk of children escaping to the street area in an uncontrolled way while playing in the garden.

Movable elements interfering with the site layout
The innovation of this idea consists in the interference of the movable walls with the urban structure of the plot. Consequently, when the house is closed (at night for example), the safe zone is limited to the house's outline. In the daytime, as a result of the walls opening, it extends to the garden surrounding the house.

New type of building
The sliding walls are not dependent on the form of the building. That is why this patent can be applied to both modern and traditional, single- and multi-storeyed houses covered with roofs of different geometry. This universal solution gives a new type of building where not the form but the way of functioning is the most important. The name "safe house" gains a new meaning now.

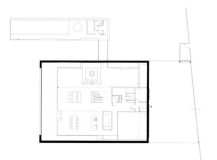

1. entrance
2. living area
3. dining area
4. kitchen
5. toilet
6. wardrobe
7. television space
8. fireplace
9. garage
10. storage
11. swimming pool

Open house

South terrace

Open shutters show widely open inner space

Completion Date: 2009

Photo: Kwk Promes

Architect: Kwk Promes

Sustainable House at Lake Laka

This simple sustainable house – like a chameleon – blends with its surrounding area on Laka Lake. Colourful planks within the timber façade reflect the tones of the landscape. The window reveals, clad in fibre cement, framed images of the countryside. Analogical to most creatures, the building is symmetrical outside, although the internal zones – according to function – are arranged asymmetrically.

The built form is designed to optimise the absorbance of solar energy. Approximately 80% of the building envelope is facing to the sun. The single-storey living space on the ground floor is externally clad with untreated larch boarding. Solar energy is gained there by the set-in glazed patio. Solar collection panels are located on the roof and a photovoltaic system is planed for the future. The dark façade of the "black box" – a three-storey structure clad with charcoal coloured fibre cement panels – is warmed by the sun, reducing heat loss to the environment. The passive and active solar energy concepts and a high standard of thermal insulation are enhanced by a ventilation plant with thermal recovery system.

The design of the project was determinated by the twin goals of low life cycle costs and a reduction in construction costs. All details are simple, but well thought out. The house did not cost more than a conventional one in Poland. Cost-saving was made by the application of traditional building techniques and the use of local materials and recycled building elements.

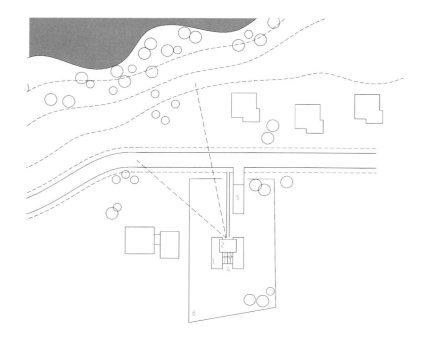

1. green roofs
2. solar "black box"
3. winter garden
4. terrace
5. parking space
6. garden

Completion Date: 2008

Architect: Peter Piotr Kuczia

Front view

Andel's Hotel Lodz

The impressive weaving mill building was originally established in 1878 as part of a cotton factory complex. Due to subsequent turn of historical events, the building was forgotten and covered by the dust of history for many years. In 2009, the former cotton mill has been transformed into a sophisticated hotel by OP ARCHITEKTEN. It includes 278 designer style rooms and suites, 3,100 square metres of conference space, ballroom for 800 people and fine-dining restaurants and bars with seats for more than 450 people, swimming pool and wellness centre.

OP ARCHITEKTEN completely redesigned the roof area, proposing a wellness centre, event space and sun terrace. A lot of glass elements and skylights ensure that public space, including four-level atrium is properly lit by the great amount of natural light. Located on the roof of the building the big ballroom of 1,300 square metres is one of the largest hotel halls in Poland. To meet the needs of various occupants the place is fully customisable and acoustically separated from the rest of the building.

The most characteristic element of the roof area is a unique glass-enclosed pool, placed in a former fire water tank. The tank's unusual location allows for exceptional experience of the flow of spaces, where the pool-area ties together with the skyline of the city, impressive red-brick scenography of the façades and the elegant new landscape of the roof.

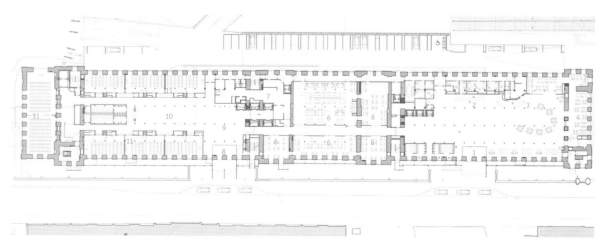

1. main entrance
2. reception
3. lobby bar
4. café, bar
5. offices
6. restaurants
7. kitchen
8. conference entrance
9. conference lobby
10. prefunction
11. conference rooms

Roof top

Plant

Ballroom

Restaurant

Photo: Op Architekten

Completion Date: 2009

Architect: Op Architekten

General view

Basalt Wine – Laposa Cellar

The wines of the Laposa Cellar following the millennium became well known amongst Hungarian wine drinkers under the brand name "Bazaltbor" or Basalt wine. The building is composed of connected panel elements, which were cast as monolithic visible concrete. The neutrality and rigidity of this are primarily detectable in the internal spaces and their relationship. There were two places where the ornamentation was necessary: when meeting the outside and at the cellar section for barrel maturation. For the former, following the principle of being like a model, the differentiation of the façades and the roof is missing; their homogenous covering is made up of prefabricated fine concrete facing panels, with a slightly transformed pattern of grapevines climbing and twining around them. If natural lighting needs to be provided in the inside spaces, the bands in the reinforced concrete model, following its geometry, were replaced by a light structure and glass cladding and the facing panel by a perforated metal sheet. Naturally the same grapevine pattern continues on this latter one, pulling it together into a unified surface.

The other ornament is to be found in the inside, in the deepest branch of the cellar. Although this space is of a longitudinal nature with a barrel shape, like a traditional cellar, its axis is broken several times and its structure is from reinforced concrete as part of the model. This bent–broken surface is covered by a brick layer characteristic of traditional cellars, but not according to the principles of tectonic order and brick binding, but diagonally, appearing as a woven fabric.

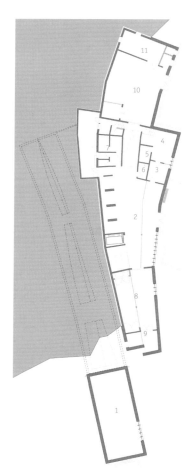

1. airspace
2. manipulation area
3. lab
4. storage
5. storage
6. WC
7. changing room
8. bottling area
9. technical room
10. warehouse
11. technical room

View with landscape

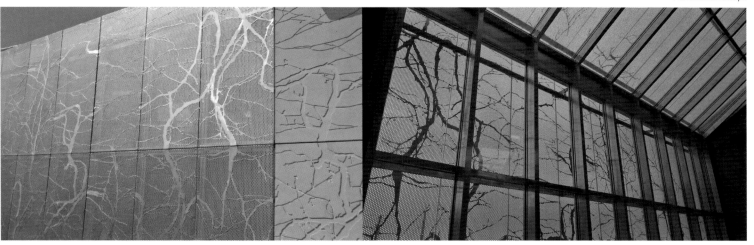

Details

Wall

Passageway

Photo: Zsolt Batár

Completion Date: 2010

Architect: Plant–Atelier Peter Kis

Exterior glass façade

UNIQA Vital Business Centre

The new head office is located close to the previous one at the junction of two important traffic arteries in District XIII, Lehel út and Róbert Károly körút. The office building constructed by property developer Raiffeisen Evolution in twenty-two months, named the Vital Business Centre, has net usable floor space of 18,000 square metres. The nine–storey building houses all of UNIQA's divisions, while 40% of the usable floor space will be let to other companies. Companies renting the space so far include a pharmacy and a diagnostics centre. Árpád Ferdinánd explained that while designing the building he was guided by the principle of transparency. Transparency is one of the cornerstones of UNIQA's business philosophy, and is conveyed in the Vital Business Centre by many glass surfaces and expansive rooms, the architect said. Lighting up the night, a distinctive feature of the building is its LED façade, allowing colourful images and messages to be displayed on the street–facing side of the office building every evening. Although the idea is not new, it is unique in its scale: with some 80,000 pixels, the Vital Business Centre currently boasts Europe's largest LED façade.

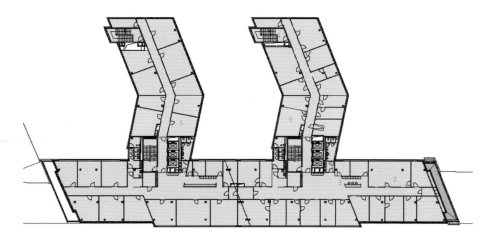

1. entrance
2. lounge
3. reception
4. management
5. office area

Front

Detail

Interior

Photo: Istvan Oravecz

Corporate

Completion Date: 2009

Architect: Ferdinand and Ferdinand Architects

Benozzo Gozzoli Museum

The new design of this building, which has a total area of about 400 square metres, closely follows the ground traces of the old building and it is luckily detached from the buildings around because it is located in an empty space which is a sort of square.

The building is rooted to the ground through a functional island–shaped base which solves the problem of urban furnishing meant in the classical sense (benches, flower pots, etc.). The curvilinear base takes over the space around the building and, at the same time, people take over a little of the museum's space: the base becomes a bench, a play area for children and adults, a theatre for small outdoor events. The building had to be entirely coated with cotto; in this way, it refers to materials and finishes of some of the local churches.

Inside, the museum is spread over four floors, three above ground and one underground. The ground floor is partly characterised by a low ceiling: a shaded area which quickly runs to the full–height space where the "Tabernacolo della Visitazione" is placed. This is illuminated by a cascade of natural light coming from the skylight in the ceiling. On the first floor, recessed into the corner–wall, we find the "Tabernacolo della Madonna della Tosse" which looks like a television screen. The staircase linking the floors, becomes a kind of visual path which frames the Tabernacles (now lacking their original context), according to new and constantly changing perspectives. It stops on the first floor, and then starts again on the opposite side thus reaching a room on the second floor, a naturally suitable space for small exhibitions and educational workshops.

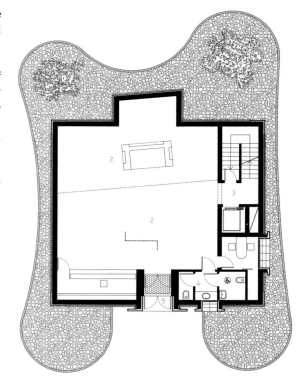

1. landscape
2. exibition room
3. staircase
4. toilet
5. entrance

Exterior

Its island–shaped base closely follows the floor plan of the preceding building

Façade

Night view

Photo: Massimo Mariani

Completion Date: 2009

Architect: Massimo Mariani

General view

New Branch of the Cooperative Credit Bank
11 Kilometres of Chain....

The architecture seems like an ode to clarity, transparency, to conceptual essence itself, while at the same time never losing sight of that direct functional relationship with the public, not just words from a bank worker's manual, but the real public; an old man, a parent a child, all with differing needs. There is a wide, luminous open informal space given over to a children's play area, quite a novelty in a bank, besides the obligatory comfortable sofas at the entrance. Wherever one goes from the counters to the meeting rooms one is breathing in that atmosphere of ordinary domesticity that never descends into the banal or predictable.

The inclusion of the chains on the façade, 11 linear kilometres, are no mere stylistic or aesthetic pretence, no external second skin. The idea is much more considered. The whole building, changes, shimmers and modifies its physical consistency. The curtain of chains hanging from on high fluctuates lightly letting off a gentle ringing, like Tibetan prayer bells. It captures the light bringing it inside, moulding it, and changing it, thus transforming the massive potentially heavy interior so that the whole building becomes a gigantic semitransparent lamp. In direct sunlight they act as protective sunshades.

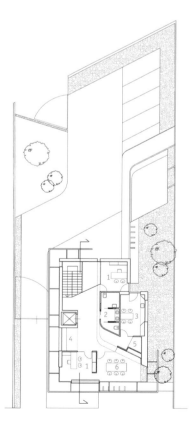

1. office
2. toilet
3. kitchen
4. waiting area
5. storage
6. meeting room

Details

Profile

Interior

Landscape deck

Photo: Alberto Piovano

Corporate

Completion Date: 2007

Architect: Studio KUADRA (www.kuadra.it)

Schreckbichl

The existing façade of the winery "Kellerei Schreckbichl" remains unaltered in its shape and its windowcases. A new structure will be suspended in front of this at a horizontal distance of fifty centimetres – a timber and metal structure.

The façade is a playful mix of spacings, colours, openings and shadows. This results in a rhythmic assemblage of forty-five metres total length and nine metres height. The black and red steel plates accentuate the window openings through their tilts and depths, focusing the views on production facilities, entrance, offices, reception and the sky. In contrast with the previous flat appearance of the façade, the differently sized openings produce a surprising and vivacious plasticity. The timber surfaces are inspired by the oak barrels, recreating a theme which adds a warm, inviting character to the building. At night the dynamic façade is immersed in light, again in a playful combination of colour and shadow.

The central element is a tilted plane, which represents the backbone of the staircase, the stairs themselves being integrated in this plane. A glass railing and the lighting from below create the impression that the staircase leads upward, beyond the printed image, in a seemingly weightless manner. A visitors' sofa has also been accommodated in the tilted plane, which bends and continues as a horizontal feature, thus rendering the reception and presentation area a unique visual entity.

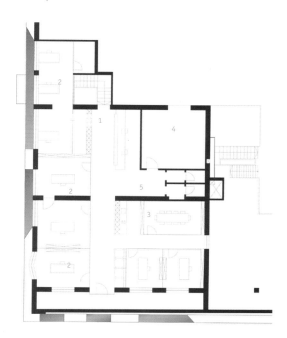

1. stairs
2. office
3. meeting room
4. storge
5. entrance

External detail

External view

Front view

Industrial

Interior wine shelf

Completion Date: 2007

Architect: bergmeisterwolf Architekten

Matzneller

Three buildings are integrated among themselves. The areas of contact are forming the terraces. Different materials meet in a harmony of colours. The dihedral of the bodies is creating a tunnel–like atmosphere towards the green interior courtyard.

The plaster emphasises the individual volumes: brownish and strongly structured beneath, the admixed copper vitriol (bluestone) creating a bluish colouring, an association to the vine that used to grow here. A wooden slatted frame is connecting the individual buildings as well as the inside and outside. The glassy cube, separated from the living area, is planned to be the library, the office and the guestroom all in one. Windows in the shape of a belt allow the daylight to penetrate the underlying sports room.

The main bodies are connected by a staircase, the central element of this residence. A slot arises, a gorge made of glass panels, in which the wooden stairs are slotted and which are connecting everything from the upstairs until the cellar. The staircase is leading upstairs in a decorative way, right between the frameless glass panels and the OBS–panels painted with white varnish.

Exterior corridor

Building in the natural environment

Interior corridor

Stair

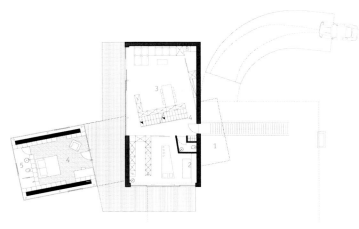

1. entrance 2. toilet 3. dining 4. bedroom 5. bathroom

Completion Date: 2008

Interior

Architect: bergmeisterwolf Architekten

External

Hi-tech Systems Headquarters

The new directional building has been designed to abstract itself from the common building scheme, rejecting analogies and mimesis, while intended to assume technology and innovation as its essence.

The traditional building techniques make room to the use of innovative materials or the different exploitation of the old ones, and, at the same time, to the overcoming of conventional building schemes. Through the opposition between the sculptural concrete shapes and the lightness of the glass and steel structures, the designers have chosen to characterise the internal and external space, pointing out a clear and essential architectural language.

The façade is mainly conceived to go between the aesthetic and conceptual definition of the architecture. Built totally in steel and structural glass and closed among big concrete walls the front is both like an optical and material screen of the building, both its external projection; the aim is to symbolise the Company's talent to be always in search of innovative and new solutions.

Interior

External

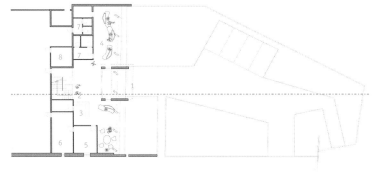

Interior

Interior

Photo: Enrico Muraro fotografo

1. entrance
2. access to upper floor
3. reception
4. waiting room
5. purchase office
6. office
7. toilet
8. café
9. delivery access
10. production area
11. technical office

Completion Date: 2007

Architect: UAU Office

Elsa Morante Library

The pre-existing building for the new Lonate Ceppino Public Library already belonged to Lonate Ceppino's historical heritage. On a rectangular plan, the two-level buildings housed the Civic Library on the ground floor, while the first floor had been left unused. From the outside, the main entrance façade has a higher decorative part which is independent from the roof structure. The design of the fronts is organised in horizontal bands at different heights, while on the north, south and west fronts a system of vertical pilasters apportions the windows on both floors.

Besides the east front, a new well-balanced volume has been built. The new volume's architecture is marked by a narrower profile on its top, with a sloping side that restrains to give more space to the historical building pitches. The dialogue between the volumes is the key and main theme leading the whole intervention. The relationship between the two is nourished by juxtaposition between matterness and lightness, solidity and instability, opaque and reflecting materials. The highlighting of differences underlines the peculiarities of both volumes, in a mutual figure–background relationship. The two buildings are connected through a glazed roofed little volume. The entrance is on the left side and a further wooden connection goes to the first floor.

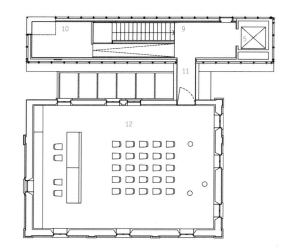

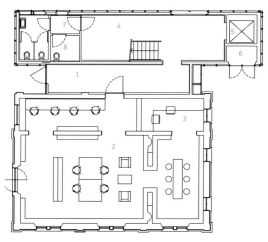

1. entrance hall 2. open-space library 3. reference office
4. staircase 5. lift 6. technical room
7. vestibule 8. bathroom 9. hall
10. study hall 11. raised walk 12. flexible room

Front view

Window

Side view

Photo: Luigi Filetici

Educational

Open-space library

Staircase

Completion Date: 2008

Architect: DAP Studio / Elena Sacco – Paolo Danelli

Building rooftop

Sloschek

The image of the concept is characterised by the landscape: three differently positioned cubes, connected by a levitating, protecting roof, are giving birth to an interplay of openings, insights and views and interspaces. Great stress is put on a good view of the steeples, the orchards in the valley and the mountain scenery. An excellent view towards the village, the vicinity and vice versa arises as a result of the spaces between the bodies and the roof. A "centre" emerges, a central location which opens itself towards the countryside and communicates with it. Different sizes of windows arise depending on the direction of view, which are defining the façade design.

Interior lounge

1. stairs
2. relaxing area
3. bathroom
4. dining table
5. entrance

Photo: Günter Richard Wett

Side view of the exterior

Completion Date: 2007

Architect: bergmeisterwolf Architekten

Rooftop connection

From the road on the south, the skeleton of the roof gives evidence of the history of the building

San Giorgio Library

Apart from functional requirements, the building is designed to give shape to the urban space around it: the issue was to inject and express a sense of modern–day culture in this kind of context while making only minor alterations: how to provide a "library" while introducing in the new architecture a sense of both the old factory and the idea of being the research instrument inherent in a library; bringing together past and future, well aware that there is no conceptual difference between designing something new and recovering the past, just in the number of constraints to be faced.

The structure involves three vaulted aisles covering 4,000 square metres. The competition called for its conversion into a library containing 350,000 books, 600 readers, 100 multimedia stations, a conference room for 100 seats, a children's space with outdoor spaces, offices and a coffee bar. It is re–designed keeping the old vertical structures while introducing wide floors, changing the vaulted roof into laminated wooden ribbing, setting a compact image on the longitudinal fronts, stripped down at the north and south terminals. The result is an overall image of a skeleton which draws out the old features and breaks them down.

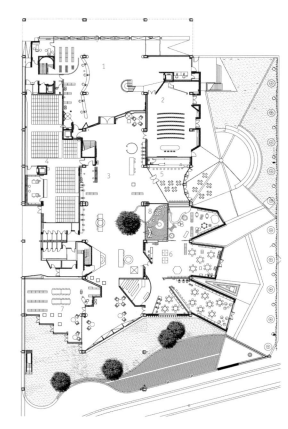

1. entrance
2. conference hall
3. central hall
4. book shop
5. coffee shop
6. children's library
7. mediateca
8. patio

Architectural relation between the library and the water and power plant

Photo: Pica Ciamarra Associati

The main hall on the ground floor, looking towards the large closed lecture hall on the second floor

Completion Date: 2007

Architect: Pica Ciamarra Associati, Franco Archidiacono, Federico Calabrese, Angelo Verderosa

The space for the children's library

Side façade

The Central Library of the University of Molise

The scheme of the Library and the main lecture Theatre of the University of Molise includes the design of external spaces with a sheltered pedestrian path and new parking areas. The main hall has two entrance spaces, one from the public open connection system of the University and the other directly from the Faculty of Social Sciences and has been designed for 480 seats and is used by the whole university.

The scheme is grafted onto the morphology of the site with two main blocks, the first being used for the offices and the second for the library, connected by two service and security stairs.

Architectural unity, in relation to the existing buildings, is granted by typological features and the use of materials like bricks and iron windows, yet used for the main buildings.

The block is connected to the University complex and to the parking area through a grid of pedestrian paths and a future pedestrian bridge that overcomes the main street in the University area.

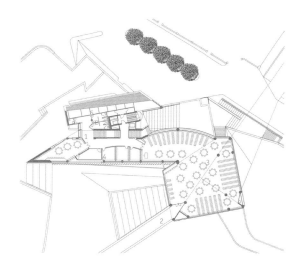

1. entrance stairs
2. entrance path
3. reading hall
4. study and research
5. administration

The main entrance

The main façade

The inner space

Photo: Pica Ciamarra Associati

Completion Date: 2009

Architect: Pica Ciamarra Associati

General view

Officine Maccaferri and Seci Energia

The new headquarters of Officine Maccaferri and Seci Energia is a building designed from the inside out. One of the unique features of this project was bringing two of the group's companies to share one building and finding the right balance between the independence of the individual companies and the group as a whole. The interior space was divided with fitted mobile walls that are partly glazed and partly opaque with a wood finish. This made it possible to make open spaces, closed offices, shared areas, meeting rooms and toilet areas, depending on the needs of the various work teams and different kinds of activities. Progetto CMR designed brightly lit, invigorating offices for about 160 people, focusing on the functional aspects and flexible solutions in anticipation of possible future changes. It optimised the division, arrangement and fitting out of each area and work station to ensure that every user has the highest level of comfort and wellbeing as well as providing optimal efficiency.

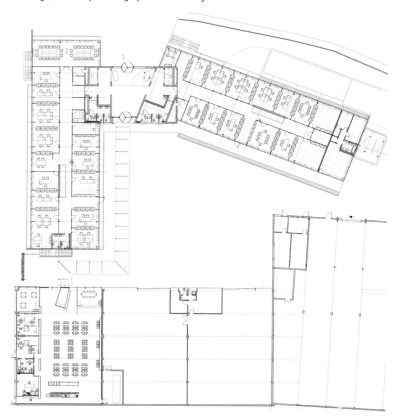

1. entrance
2. conference hall
3. office
4. WC

Entrance

Side view

Entrance and stairs

Stairs and corridor

Photo: Oscar Ferrari

Architect: Progetto CMR Massimo Roj Architects

Corporate

Completion Date: 2007

Birken-elementary School and School "am Grüngürtel": Nursery Building

In the borough of Spandau, Berlin, the existing schools, Birken-elementary school and school "am Grüngürtel" will be extended to open-all-day schools with a capacity of 155 pupils within a national funding scheme. The project is cofinanced by EFRE-funds. The spacious sports-and playgrounds in the heart of a heterogeneous urban block will be reorganised within the design concept.

Under a firm protecting roof made of exposed concrete the new building offers plenty of space for the extension of the Birken elementary school and the school "am Grüngürtel" to a open all day school with a capacity of 155 pupils. The new building with two floors in the Berlin borough of Spandau (total construction costs about 2.2 millions) was financed from funds of the programme"future, education and mentoring" (IZBB) and the "European fund for regional development"(EFRE).

Placed in the extension of a picturesque Berlin "Gründerzeit" street-scape, the building mediates between the classical block housing on the south side and the open urban structure with four-storey-high housing slabs from the 1950s in the north. Within the building scheme the extensive sport and recreation areas were rearranged inside the large heterogeneous urban block.

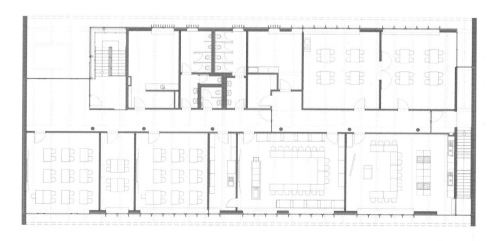

Photo: Werner Huthmacher

Completion Date: 2008

Architect: Huber Staudt Architekten

Hedwigshöhe Hospital

The intervention is based on the remodelling and extension of the existing hospital and on the design of the psychiatric units. In the open dialogue between the dense urban pattern and the spacious landscape, the new Hedwigshöhe Hospital is the turning point for Falkenberg. To contrast the existing structure, the two-storey pavilions of the psychiatric ward are playfully juxtaposed; the result is a small hospital city where the parataxis between old and new is evident.

The new psychiatric department is located north, on the slope of Flakenberg hill. Patients are welcomed in paired pavilions, each set as to create a slight crenelation toward the surrounding open landscape. The two levels follow the scale of close-by homes and their patios reach for a view over the landscape; the façades of the courts are wood and glass and wooden battens characterise the hospital. Along the external perimeter, the square windows are divided in three parts and slightly project from the wall. The scheme seems to support a positive contrast between the orderly layout of the existing structures and the vivacious layout of the psychiatric courts; the new sanitary structure establishes a conscious relationship with the landscape, the city and the final user.

Photo: Werner Huthmacher, Jordi Bernadó, huber staudt architekten bda

Architect: Huber Staudt Architekten Bda, Berlin, Germany
Manuel Brullet, Albert De Pineda, Barcelona, Spain

Hospital

Completion Date: 2008

Main entrance in the daytime

Media Centre Oberkirch

Three levels are connected with an open, organically formed stairwell. The centrally positioned open staircase is not only a movement and communication zone, but is an exposure element for the inside-recumbent zones of utilisation with the generously glazed upper light. The façades, with the large apertures, are understood like shop-windows, which permit varied and exciting views in the surrounding town space. The external, brighter window areas serve the reading zones and stay zones, partially furniture with an up-and-down movement is integrated which the visitor can use as a table or a bench. By the planning of the building it was respected beside the striking town planning architecture, particularly to create a high stay quality for the visitors in the building. In the whole building one finds the comfortable seating pieces of furniture, which also invite visitors in the free areas of the reading terraces for staying. As a sculptural architecture, which is modellised full of contrast, the building creates a sensuous experience space which should serve the citizens as a communicative centre where to all generations the varied media technologies and technologies of information are accessible.

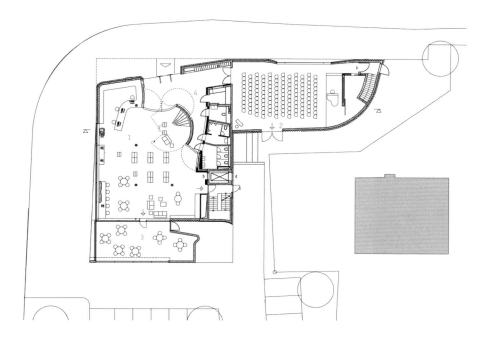

1. reception
2. festival room
3. terrace
4. passageway

Details of the façade

Details of the passage way on the ground floor

Details of the toplight

Main staircase and toplight third floor

Photo: Guido Gegg

Corporate

Completion Date: 2010

Architect: Wurm+Wurm Architekten Ingenieure Gmbh

Shopping Centre Stadtgalerie

Directly located at Heilbronn's pedestrian zone, the new shopping centre "Stadtgalerie" strengthens the inner-city location. The architectural sumptuously-designed building integrates itself well into the town-space as a two-split building presenting different body languages. The Stadtgalerie Heilbronn consists of three levels which invite to stroll, a sales area of 13,000 square metres, and an attractive offer of approximately seventy-five shops and stores, cafés, and restaurants. The underground car park offers 600 parking spaces.

The cubic building with its straight and hard edge and the rounded building with the curved and soft façade melt into each other and are well integrated in the existing town-space. The independence of the buildings is especially highlighted via the façade concept. Backlit light-slits are crossing the wall area in an erratic way and thereby open the building alignment in an optical way. In the darkness the alleyway suddenly becomes a light creation. The shape softens the bulk of the building, integrateing itself in a smooth way into the surrounding building structure. A penthouse with a filigree projecting roof marks the end of the arched building shell. Vertical coloured glass lamellae accentuate the outline. Due to the different day and night impressions, the building offers varying appearances.

The building at night

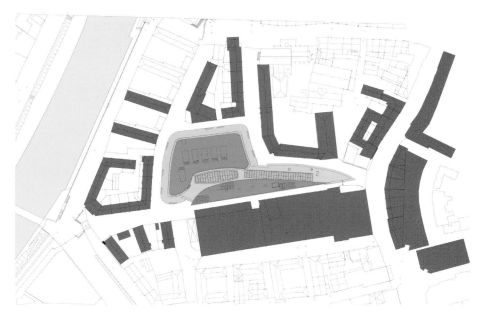

1. entrance
2. dining area
3. roof

Entrance

Front view

Interior

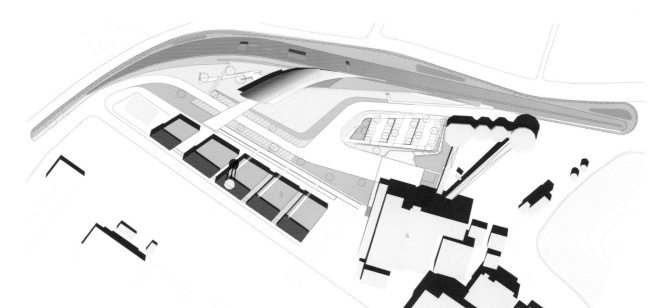

1. start in the lecture hall
2. historical trench
3. garages' views over the roof
4. waste bunker

ZMS Administration Building

The task to design a new administration building, reorganise the power station compound and create a new noise protection barrier offers the chance to dissolve the dichotomy of landscape and building to realise the deconstruction of those categories into one designed environment, to be experienced in a dynamic and curious fashion. Four hundred and fifty metres long and up to thirteen metres high, the central part of a noise protection wall with a forty-five-degree incline simultaneously constitutes a new administration building for over 140 metres. The superimposition of building and earth wall allows one to explore and experience the landscape of this entire ensemble on various levels.

An auditorium with a visitor centre unfolds from this landscape and opens up towards the power station compound. It separates from the earth wall on the upper level, resting on two radial supporting walls and cantilevers up to twenty metres over the landscape. A long panoramic glass façade leans towards the power station. The administration building underneath is sculpted into the earth wall. Meeting rooms and common areas penetrate through the wall to establish a relationship with the bordering village.

The main structural challenges arose from the fact that they had to create an earth wall of up to thirteen metres high that is capable of supporting not only itself at a forty-five-degree slope, but also to accommodate a building within it, situated at about six metres above grade. It was very important to cover the building in landscape and vegetation that appear to be continuous, without indication of the shape of the building underneath.

Main entrance

Courtyard

Lower foyer and stairs

Corridor

Photo: Archimedialab / Bernd Lederle

Completion Date: 2009

Architect: Archimedialab

New churchyard with new façade

Dornbusch Church

Dornbusch church is situated in a residential area in the north of Frankfurt. Due to the poor condition of this sixty–year–old church and the extreme decline in attendance at church services, a complete demolition and the new construction of a small "prayer room" as a replacement were under discussion. Planning studies were able to show, however, that the best choice is only a partial demolition. From a town planning point of view, a spatially and functionally intact ensemble remains – consisting of a community centre, "residual church" and tower: a new churchyard, with an attractive potential for public use, is created. The spacious area round the altar and the choir remains as the old / new church.

Reconstruction / New construction
The open side of the building, caused by the demolition work, is closed with a new wall or façade. The special nature of this location and the reduction process are made evident in that this new wall is marked with outlines and moulds of the "old" church, i.e. the structures which have been removed – such as the old entrance façade, altar and gallery – now form a sculpted structure out of the flat wall surface. Further factors contributing to the final form are room light exposure, completing construction features, the remaining building and the access to it.

The new wall is a mixed construction (reinforced concrete, masonry); the plasterwork surface corresponds with the plasticity of the concept. The new wall / entrance façade and the tranquil north wall as a counterpart are contrasted in light colours.

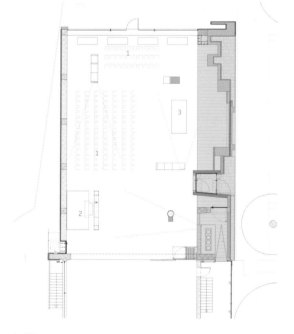

1. sitting area
2. reception
3. platform

Façade

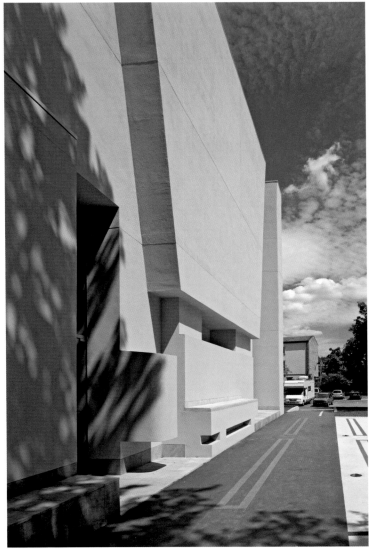

Exterior view

Side view

Photo: Christoph Kraneburg

Completion Date: 2006

Architect: MEIXNER SCHLÜTER WENDT Architecten

Façade

GFC Antriebssysteme GmbH Transfiguration and New Construction of a Production Hall with Service and Socialtract

GFC Antriebssysteme GmbH is looking back on more than 100 years history of developing and manufacturing of worm gear and hydraulic gear units at its enterprise location Coswig near Dresden. The existing production hall was established a faceless, simple box in standardised construction way from precast concrete parts. The existing building did no longer meet the requirements to modern jobs and the increased space requirement within the logistics area.

The designers decided to use the structure of armoured concrete, which was in a good condition, and to extend the original building with a two–storey administration building, logistics and stock area. The spatial connection between administration and production is made by wide glazings in both levels.

Different materials signify different functions. The administrative tract is coated by walls from exposed concrete, and production and logistics are characterised by the use of shingles from stainless steel and translucent boards from polycarbonate. The particular, large, calm surfaces stress the sculptural character of the whole body. The carrying structure of the office area is done as a grid from columns and beams from exposed concrete.

The support structure is slanting in two directions, forward and sidewise and thereby the façade along the railway line Dresden–Berlin creates a motion–impelling model. The movement arising from this skew is continued in the façade around the entire structure.

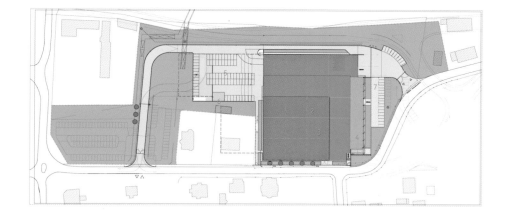

1. high–bay racking loading area
2. production hall
3. existing building
4. administration
5. 78 parkplatze
6. fahrrader
7. p3– 23 parkplatze

Night view

Back view

Entrance

Photo: Ester Havlova

Completion Date: 2009

Architect: Wurm + Wurm Architekten Ingenieure Gmbh

Exterior view of the canteen and sports hall

Evangelical Grammar School

The project comprises a two–storey grammar school with refectory and sports hall as a full–time school. The site for the new Evangelical Grammar School is located in the northeast outskirts of Bad Marienberg. To the west it borders on an area with other schools such as a primary school, a secondary modern and a junior high school. To the east and north begins open land, while to the south there is a youth hostel and a special school.

Both sections of the building – the angled school building in the north and the second building with the arts rooms, the sports hall and the refectory in the south – circumscribe a schoolyard that is open to the west. The school thus has a relationship with the other schools, while on the other hand pupils are welcomed symbolically "with open arms" due to the positioning of the building.

In general, natural materials are used which radiate warmth, brightness and lightness while still remaining sturdy. The choice of colours and materials, openness, generosity, freshness and colourfulness form the basis of a relaxed atmosphere for learning.

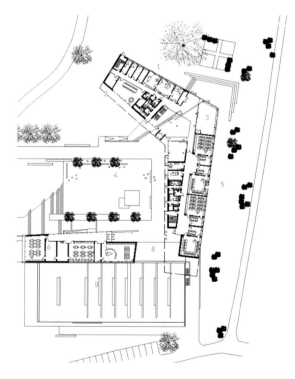

1. staff rooms
2. meeting room
3. entrance hall
4. playground
5. classroom
6. arts rooms
7. artisanry room
8. music room
9. sports hall

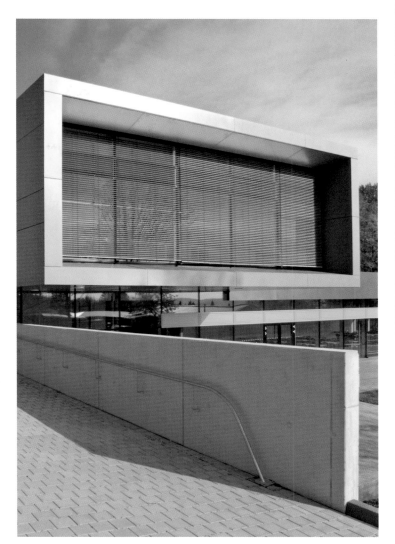

Exterior view on the angled school building

Striking wing

Photo: Guido Kasper, Constance, Germany

Educational

Architect: 4a Architekten GmbH, Stuttgart, Germany; Matthias Burkart, Alexander v. Salmuth, Ernst Ulrich Tillmanns; Project team: Andreas Behringer, Rike Hannes, Birgit Wäldin, Lars Goose

Completion Date: 2007

The great entrance hall can also be used as an assembly hall

Ener(gie)nger – Energy and Sustainability

The architect has named the project Ener(gie)nger – a coinage of the words Energie (Energy) and the name Gienger, the well established domestic engineering wholesale business. The geometry of a "band–spiral" creates a unique tunnel–like area, which by means of the side intersection surfaces exposed to light, throws a fascinating ray of light onto the slanting walls. The spiral begins at entrance of the Fa. Gienger showroom at the east of the building by means of a wide open projecting roof – opposite at the west side a similar opening is put to use for the cash–and–carry wholesale store.

The vibrant energy spiral stands for the energy within a fascinating area, with this area expressing the dynamics of new types of energy: The slanting external surfaces are fitted with both solar–thermal and photovoltaic panels – the latter of these could in the course of new developments, be fitted with products, which at the moment are still being devised. The outer shell is made up of solar panels, photovoltaic panels and metal and glass elements.

The core of the exhibition hall is not only the various bathrooms on display, but also the "educational energy trail" – an exhibition of current installations and equipment belonging to the energy–saving sector. Since its introduction, this "trail" has been accepted very quickly and intensively: it plays an important role in the understanding of technology, which in turn means that such technologies can actually be put to use.

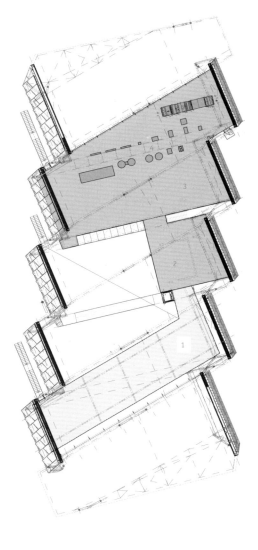

1. extension level
2. café
3. event
4. energy trail

Night view

Entrance

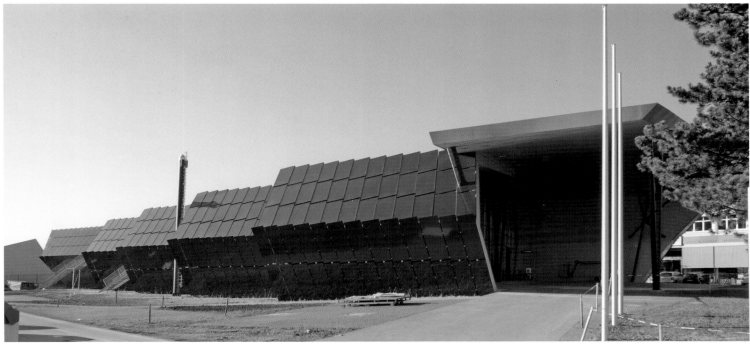

Façade

Interior

Photo: Roland Weegen

Architect: Peter Lorenz Ateliers

Completion Date: 2009

Cultural

Sipos Aktorik GmbH

The new building of the Sipos Aktorik GmbH is designed as a compact volume, embedded into the easily hilly landscape at Altdorf, which in its spatial effect, is more similar to a large mansion than a factory.

The building is divided into three parts: the assembly hall with attached automated store room, a two-storey administrative tract in front of that and a storage hall with goods receipt and goods issue afterwards to both ranges. The proximity of the individual operating ranges is to make possible a maximum of internal communication. The roof of the production hall is occupied with skylights shaped as a bar, so the lighting of the work stations reaches thereby daylight quality. This light impression on the inside is still strengthened by the bright colour of the construction.

On two sides ground-same, high window fronts with integrated glass doors enable contact wih the external space. The steel structure of the production hall is modular developed, whereby the manufacturing area is optionally expandable up to the double size. The functional separation between assembly area and the two-storey office area is abrogated by space-high glass walls. This conveys internal communication between these different working environments.

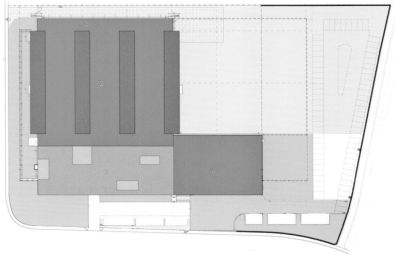

1. high–bay racking
2. production hall
3. administration
4. loading area

Photo: Ester Havlova

Completion Date: 2009

Architect: Wurm + Wurm Architekten Ingenieure GmbH

Residential Area at Pelargonienweg

The lot of the residential area is characterised by a newly created gently-waved topography which through the redeployment of excavations on the site can be styled like dunes. So emerges a landscape on the outskirts of the town with a special identity: the houses are embedded in a space sequence of soft hills and troughs, in a grove of apple, pear, cherry and nut trees. There are also common spaces in this gentle hilly landscape which could be used, for example, for green houses, must cellars and playgrounds. The architects obtain the opportunity to develop their buildings "on the slope" through the newly created three-dimensional landscape. The construction "plays" with the slopes in the landscape and a number of configurations through various combinations of the two basic types, each bringing its own particular qualities. They thereby achieve a differentiated and rhythmical building typology which in a sequence of linked and free standing combinations of the buildings creates ever-changing townscapes. In doing so, particular attention is paid to a relaxed ground-floor zone, the contact areas of the building are reduced, and a visual connection of the transportation spaces with the garden landscape through the construction is made possible.

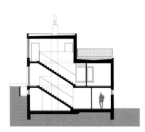

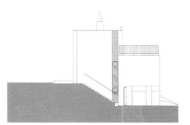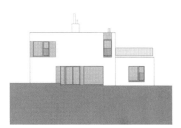

Architect: Josef Weichenberger architects

Completion Date: 2009

Photo: Lisa Rastl

Residential

University Mozarteum

The University was named after Wolfgang Amadeus Mozart and is a worldwide acknowledged training Centre for artists now for more than 160 years. Situated directly next to the Mirabell Gardens in Salzburg, the Mozarteum is part of the inner city ambience.

A stony solitaire is situated at the entrance and the Mirabellplatz Square is visually being led into the building. Entering the doorway of the hall is a special moment created by illumination effects through the floor. The hall is illuminated with down lighter from the shed–roof–construction. The lights are being arranged in bunches and can be activated as light isles in between which the students and concert guests might move animated by the light. A perron leads to the institute's areas. Open-access balconies with integrated light channels serve as attractive lounge zones. The walls appear to glow from cherry tree wood and therewith create a warm and festive character.

To make this outer illumination more visible, the façade of the solitaire is being shaded. The remaining three walls create an edged and bright solitaire. The light concept in context with the building makes a varied but calm and reserved impression. It wants to inspire and give room to the creativity of the occupants.

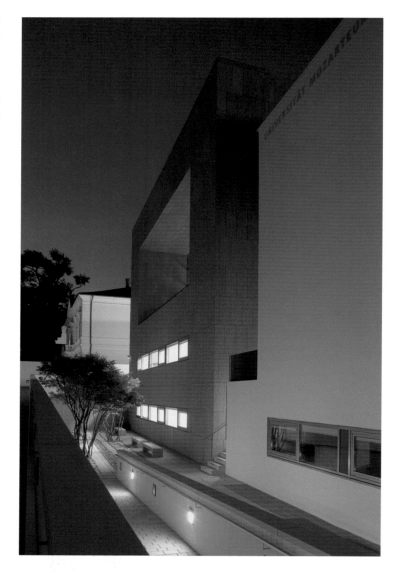

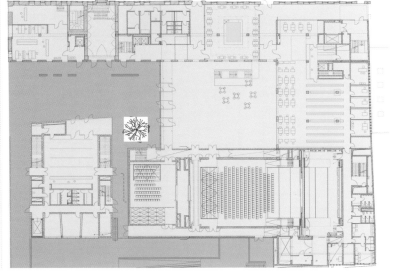

Architect: Rechenauer Architects, Munich
Lighting Design: Gabriele Allendorf – light identity, Munich

Photo: Andrew Phelps

Completion Date: 2006

Educational

Western elevation

Main Railway Station Innsbruck

Although for the most part the trains travel on viaducts above street level, the station represents a real barrier across the main orientation of the valley. The reaction to this sharply defined urban situation that is further complicated by the long, narrow railway station forecourt was a relatively low and very long building with an extremely open and regular lattice–like façade that is placed at the east side of the forecourt but shifted six metres further back. This means that it moves out of the existing street line and – employing a classic way of shaping space – can assert itself as a liberated, freestanding building against the rest of the dense high–rise development on Südtiroler Platz. The building measures are grouped in detail around the theme of permeability.

All the important functions, such as travel centre, waiting and retail areas are placed in the central, lowered part of the railway station concourse. On the one hand this allows a direct approach from the underground car park to the concourse and thus to the trains, while on the other it also permits an uninterrupted view of the platforms from the city and vice versa.

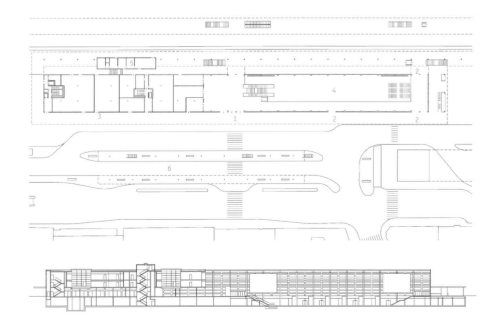

1. main entrance
2. access hall
3. access shops
4. hall
5. offices
6. bus stop

Southern elevation

Platform 1 at night

Station forecourt at night

Photo: Nikolaus Schletterer

Completion Date: 2004

Architect: Riegler Riewe Architects Pty. Ltd. / Florian Riegler, Roger Riewe

General view

Niederndorf Supermarket

Niederndorf is a small, rural village at the border between Austria and Germany. On the periphery of this village, there is a chance to realise a supermarket – urgently needed. The site lies between farmhouses, feedlots for cows and some residential areas. The client asked for a "cool marketplace" – protected from sun and heat.

Wood is the favourite building material in the Alps. Wood means homeland, cosiness and identity. The wooden stables do provide a clear local building identity. So the idea was to use decorticated pine trunks of the area: directly from the sawmill without any further treatment. This filter has several functions. It turned out to be the cheapest solution for sun protection, and is creating a public space and in some parts represents a curtain–wall façade.

The humanistic approach leads to the ideas of offering extra communicative areas for the clients. The "trunks" do separate an open space from the actual shopping area. Here the farmers can sell their X–mas trees, the local brass–band can play, and sometimes they offer some mulled wines, etc.

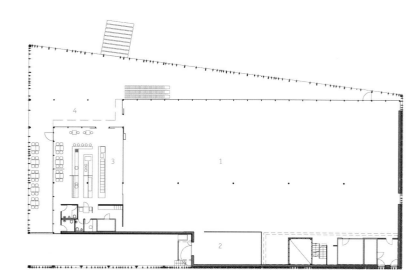

1. food market/sales area
2. bakery
3. store
4. canopied access

Canopied access

Sales area

Canopied access

Photo: Thomas Jantscher

Completion Date: 2008

Architect: Peter Lorenz Ateliers

Exterior plant

Villa A

The property is about 5,000 square metres in a protected green zone with an old tree population. The architects orientate the living areas towards southwest. This side is entirely open to the panoramic view over the city and the garden. On the north side, the building façade is closed with natural stonework to provide intimacy towards the street. Following the topography of the site, the house is partly caved in the ground. A central hall with an open staircase gives access to various areas on different levels.

Garage, building services, fitness area, guestroom and office are allocated in the lower, carved-in storey. Living, dining and kitchen area are distributed on three different levels on the middle part of the building. The sleeping rooms are situated in the roof structure on the upper level.

The architect's intention was to differentiate formally and structurally the upper floor from the other two levels below. The purpose was to contrast the different function in the building. The lower levels are mostly designated for living, lounging and dining. These activities are embedded with different levels into the topography of the land and have direct access to the surrounding garden. The earthy relationship led the architects to opt for massive concrete structure that is cladded with stone. Above these, bedrooms are embedded into a roof structure carried by steel columns, totally detached from the massive walls below, almost flying over the massive walls.

Dinner area

Side daylight

Photo: Manfred Seidl (seidl.m.foto@aon.at)

Exterior

Completion Date: 2008

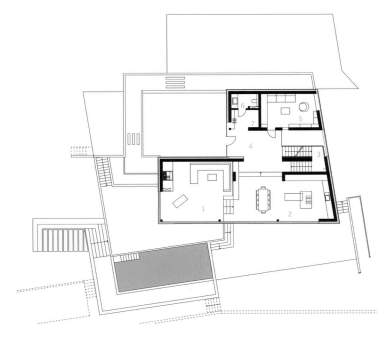

Architect: Najjar–Najjar Architekten

1. living area
2. dining area
3. staircase
4. entrance
5. saloon
6. WC
7. guard

Front view at night

Oase Liezen Sustainability in the Shopping Town

Over the past few years the major shopping town of Liezen has been developing with great energy. Now the new "Oase" on the main street offers a "haven of peace" to spend some time and linger: on a roofed "village square" in front of the centre, the square including a bistro as a café–restaurant. This complex is indeed a "small or refined" shopping centre with a real market hall. Due to its height and sense of space, it is one of the reminding historic examples in larger cities.

The centre is able to be accessed from two sides and has two parking facilities. At the pathway turning points, illuminated fountains provide a daylight effect similar to that of "forest clearings". Beyond the shelving the surrounding area's beautiful mountains are combined with the centre which make the customers feel free and at ease. H&M is spread out over two storeys – with a view around the market hall being provided. In between there is an attractive tobacconist's. Peter Lorenz finds that expressive architecture at this location is of importance: this is functionally important for a good identification of the customers with this "new marketplace" and also generates a relationship between customers and residents.

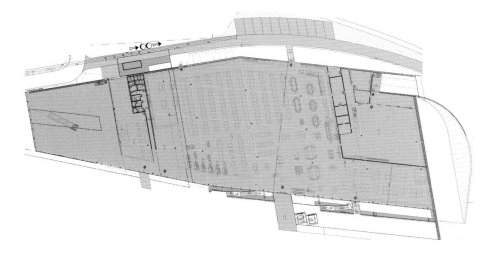

1. shop
2. café
3. traffic
4. food market/sales area
5. store
6. canopied access

Side view at night, with light projection on the pavement

Inside the mall

View inside the mall

Façade

Q19

Metaphors must always be used carefully in architecture. However, approaching Peter Lorenz's new local shopping centre in Döbling quarter, in Vienna, from the north side, the associations of ideas spontaneously come out: a stranded ship, a rusted tanker. Actually, it is just with these images that the architect has introduced this work to his client: ships corroded by time, standing still and quiet, as waiting that something would happen.

This image is proper only when one observes the building from the north side and far off. Thus one can see the long and powerful hull, flanked by two protruding spiral ramps to the south and the north side, leading to the covered parkings on the upper floors. The "rusty" façade is made of corten steel. One can also see the domes diffusing the light, which are porthole-shaped elements of different dimensions.

On the entrance side, the scene is completely different. Here the continuum is created between the old and the new building. The old building is the Samum cigarettes paper factory. It is joined by the new one all along its length and, on the north side, even beyond. To the northwest there is the main entrance, with a large forecourt (which has been extended to include an urban public space too) and the glass front structure with uprights and crossbars. The façade is covered by a second skin, made of blinds, working either as solar control device or as dynamic advertising LED panel, which is 22 metres wide and 7.5 metres high.

Inside q19 upper floor

Night view – entrance, connecting the old and the new part of the shopping centre

Façade – LED façade, entrance

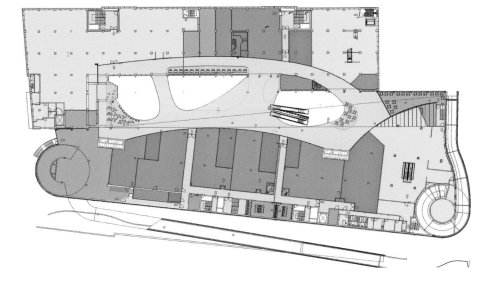

1. gross shop
2. dining area
3. shop
4. traffic zone
5. auxiliary area

Photo: Pia Odirizi

Completion Date: 2008

Architect: Peter Lorenz Ateliers

Commercial

Music Theatre

The mumuth theatre belongs to the university of music and performing arts graz which is a place where young musicians receive their instruction in the performing and musical arts.

The unit-based part of the organisation (the box) is situated on the right side, and the movement-based part (the blob) on the left side of the building as seen from the lichtenfelsgasse. There are two entrances: the everyday entrance on the park side which is used by students and staff, and the public entrance on the Lichtenfelsgasse which is used by the audience when there is a performance. On performance nights, the student entrance is transformed into a wardrobe using mobile closets. A removable ticketing desk and screen bulletin are placed underneath the staircase. The public ascends a wide staircase and enters a large foyer on the first floor. This foyer gives access to the multipurpose auditorium that can seat up to 450, and that is adaptable to a great variety of performances, ranging from solo instruments to opera to full orchestra.

First floor plan

General view

Public lobby, ground floor

Stairs

Photo: Christian Richters

Cultural

Completion Date: 2008

Architect: UNStudio

Night view

Buildings with entrance

Museum Liaunig

The museum entrance zone is orientated towards both the centre of Neuhaus and the nearby historical castle. The substantial viewing storage depot, where visitors are accompanied by a "wine cellar of art", is one of the main areas of the museum, stretching the whole length of the gently sloping approach to the main exhibition hall. This underground volume offers the possibility to organise a variety of exhibitions by virtue of flexible screens and lighting arrangements. The building's core is a 160-metre-long, fully daylit exhibition hall, with protected terraces at each end. The continuous thirteen-metre-wide, seven-metre-high room is covered by a translucent curved skin – an industrial element permitting daylight. The hall is organised with mobile exhibition panels. In the exhibition hall are separately sited the graphic collection and the gold collection.

Besides, the museum claims efficiency and sustainability by its utility of the excavated soil for its construction. Industrial materials like concrete, glass and sheet metal dominate the visible portion of the building. Moreover, set into the hill, the building benefits from the constant temperature of the ground. Rooflight is adopted to substitute artificial light as much as possible.

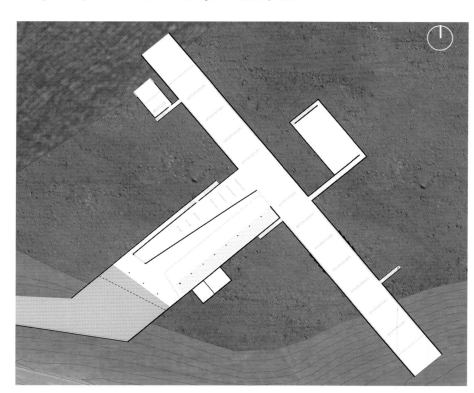

Roof

Building with landscape

Details

Entrance

Photo: Erwin Stättner

Completion Date: 2008

Architect: Erwin Stättner

House in Canobbio

Nestled on the Alpine slopes north of Lugano, this house is characterised by a volumetric architecture that emerges from the terrain and follows the natural contour of the land. Its constructed volumes embrace the land in an organic and fluent sequence of spaces, each relating to another and to the surrounding landscape. In order to communicate an identity and a language to the inhabitants, the project has a strong and precise form, and its clearly identifiable geometric structure delimits an organised development of spaces. Carved in a clear square geometry, the spaces meet the slope and extend in a spiral, fluent movement that continuously changes the perception of the space and its relationship to the exterior, offering striking panoramic views across the hinterland and to Lake Lugano.

The succession of spaces and play of perception in the house are ideas derived from those principles of the Japanese garden. By their design and their nature, Japanese gardens offer varying levels of awareness of and responsiveness to space by offering an experiential sequence of different sceneries. As in the gardens, the organisation of the spaces in the house is condensed yet continuous, and is intended to take the experience of being in the house beyond the rooted and enclosed domestic scale. In addition, the house also works on both an intimate and vast scale. The clients, desire for a shell–like home has been met; the house is very private, protected and not overlooked, and the generated form and volume of the house also create an open, generous outlook, embracing its setting and taking quiet ownership of its prospect .

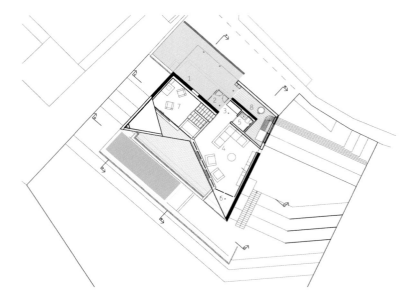

1. parking
2. covered entrance
3. entrance
4. living room
5. bathroom
6. terrace
7. void over reading room
8. heat pump

External view up to house from southwest slope

East façade with terraced gardens

View across terrace into kitchen and dining space

View into living space from main entrance

Photo: Enrico Cano

Completion Date: 2009

Architect: Davide Macullo Architects

General view

Lienihof Residential and Business Complex

The Lienihof complex, situated between Albis and Heinrich-Federer streets in Zurich-Wollishofen, Switzerland, is incorporated into a virtually similar building site. Its complex sequence of twenty corners in the structure reflects respect for the building regulations in force as well as for the polygonal form of the plot. The building shape, determined by necessity, is balanced by the courtyard which opens up towards the south, thus constituting an architectural force of its own. Surrounding balustrades express the character of this meandering visually horizontal construction. The pine-wood panelling of the balustrades painted in dark red is a reference to the traditional carpenter's workshop which once stood on the site.

Following the sophisticated form of the building, the different apartments are designed as complex figures, closely interwoven with each other so that together they build but a single form. This organic adjustment of the ground plans to the outer structure generates inner spaces which offer a variety of perspectives, views and insights – an architectural approach which leads to interesting inner promenades continuously changing their orientation while moving through the apartments.

Each of the upper floors comprises eleven different apartments which are accessed by three stairscases. The ground floor accomodates both business premises and an apartment for persons with nursing needs. A long hall linking streets, courtyard and the three staircases, creates a community space.

1. bedroom
2. washing room
3. bedroom
4. loggia
5. living
6. kitchen
7. bedroom

Corridor

View from far away

Photo: Adrian Streich Architekten AG, Zurich

Complex

Completion Date: 2007

Architect: Adrian Streich Architekten AG, Zurich, Roger Frei

Inner courtyard

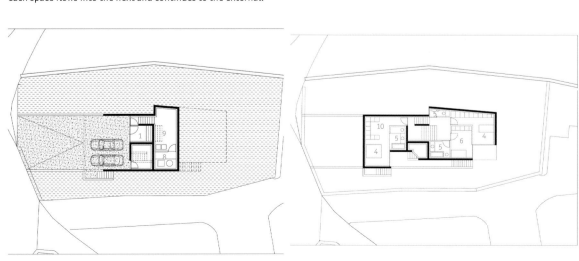

External view of the house in its Alpine context from the southeast

House in Lumino

Located in the Swiss Alpine village of Lumino, just north of Bellinzona, this house stands as a monolithic element, quietly complementing and echoing its context. The surrounding area is characterised by traditional stone built houses, many of which date back centuries and are marked by their use of this single construction material. The new house acts as a sort of bastion between the old core and the modern residential expansion.

In addition to the local scale references and material cues siphoned from the physical context, the concept and approach to the project was further influenced by the clients' expressed desire for a minimalist aesthetic. As such, the quality of the spaces in the house would be defined explicitly by the architecture and not by objects placed within it. The idea of the "minimalist monolith" was adopted as the conceptual generator of the project and became a principle applied to all elements of both the functional and construction programme, from the foundations up to the smallest finishing details.

The geometry of the plan is generated by two shifted parallelepipeds and follows the fall of the site. The double system of vertical connections, one internal and one external, relates all the spaces of the house in a spiral movement, and is in a constant play with its new inhabitants' perception of time and scale. What is interesting about the house is the ability of the spaces to expand and extend into the landscape, allowing the external become part of the composition. While the individual spaces may be defined geometrically, each space flows into the next and continues to the external.

1. entrance
2. living
3. kitchen
4. bedroom
5. bathroom
6. guest bedroom
7. terrace
8. laundry
9. mechanical room
10. storage
11. parking

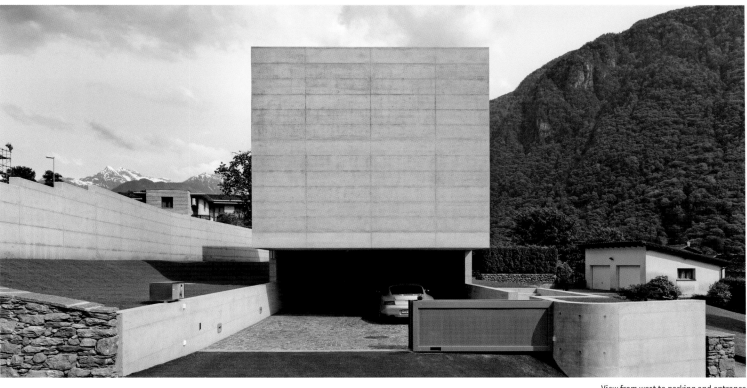

View from west to parking and entrance

View from kitchen through dining and out to terrace

View into living space

Photo: Enrico Cano

Architect: Davide Macullo Architects

Residential

Completion Date: 2009

New Industrial Development Centre

To the west of Neuchâtel, the landfill from the early 20th century spread over the lake is occupied by a centre of industrial production of Philip Morris. The project resulted in a cuboid of 106 metres long, thirty-three metres wide and twenty metres high. This particular configuration made of solid work on several levels is due to lack of space. The challenge of this realisation is simple: to provide the user with a tool capable of adapting to any new configuration of use and at a price of a conventional plant.

The proposal is based on a structural system capable of delivering significant ranges (sixteen metres) and integrating in its thickness and frame all the techniques necessary for the activity of this sophisticated development centre, namely the ventilation, electricity, gas, compressed air, dust removal related to the building, clean rooms and machinery.

Beyond its technical interest, this device offers a particular spatial quality and a quiet environment. The building envelope consists of a single material, namely the glass industry. This choice can optimally manage the confidentiality of the activity, quality natural light and indoor climate.

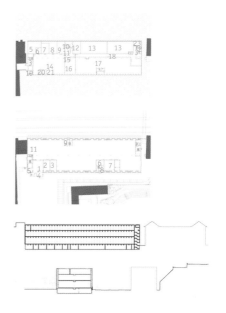

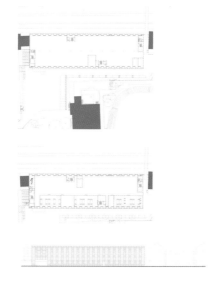

1. WC
2. lift
3. airlock
4. lift
5. heating distribution
6. informatics
7. power transformer
8. power distribution
9. airing +water treatment
10. technical
11. sprinkler
12. compressed air
13. stocking
14. south–west workshop
15. meeting room
16. CAD office
17. prototype zone
18. hallway + freezers
19. break room
20. meeting room
21. supervisor's office
22. cubbyhole
23. emergency power

South Façade, looking from the Neuchâtel Lake

Night view of the south façade

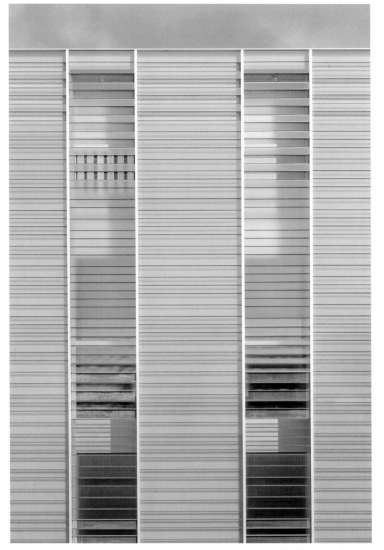

Details of the industrial glass

Inside view of the open zone

Photo: Thomas Jantscher

Corporate

Completion Date: 2009

Architect: Geninasca Delefortrie SA

Werdwies Residential Complex

The course of the river Limmat and the motorway represent two antipodes forming the boundaries of the insular microcosm of the Grünau Quarter in Zurich, Switzerland. The Werdwies Residential Complex provides the Quarter with an open centre characterised by the density of an inner space. The complex consists of seven rhythmically positioned prism–like constructions creating a sequence of built and open spaces. This leads to the emergence of several smaller and larger squares, each with its own character. A hard covering with integrated lawn areas forms the ground area of the exterior space and allows free movement within the residential complex. The planting of about 100 trees underlines the park–like character of the complex.

Each building comprises seven residential floors, having a total of 152 apartments in three different house types. The houses are distinguished by their staircases with loggias and stairwells. The spacious loggias create a dense relationship between interior and exterior spaces. At the same time, they mark the beginning of a principle of layers, generating a comprehensive modularity. Each apartment includes a sequence of rooms lighted from different directions, with areas for living, eating and sleeping. Simple layouts with long rooms and built–in cupboards extending over the whole length of the wall give the apartments a robust character.

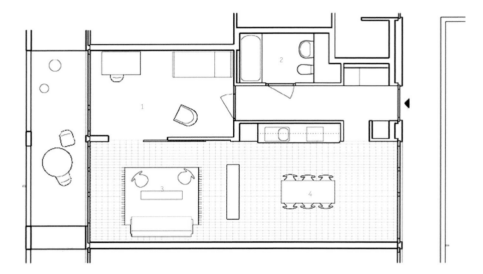

1. bedroom
2. washing room
3. living
4. kitchen and dining

Front view

Landscape

Courtyard

Dining

Photo: Adrian Streich Architekten AG, Zurich

Architect: Adrian Streich Architekten AG, Zurich

Residential

Completion Date: 2007

South view

Sempachersee Golf Club

This is the largest golf course in Switzerland. The architectural office Smolenicky & Partner was commissioned to design two new buildings in connection with the enlargement of the course – the clubhouse and restaurant building and the new maintenance building.

The clubhouse is situated precisely on the topographical crest where the level plateau of the golfing green breaks into a steeply falling slope. At exactly this point, the vista opens out into a view over the lake and the Alps of inner Switzerland. The public footpath that transverses the golf club also runs along this topographical ridge.

Both the architecture and the interior design of the new building aim to combine two distinct atmospheric phenomena of the site into a single effect. This new manifestation is moulded, on the one hand out of the country character of the golfing culture of the Sempachersee course, and on the other hand out of its worldly sophistication. To this end the appearance oscillates between the rural warmth of a timber barn and the clear lines of a Masserati sports car. This is the attempt to embody both the reality of the dualism of the site and its potential within the building itself.

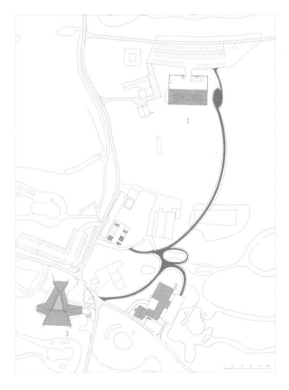

1. maintenance building – new building
2. reception – add-on
3. clubhouse – new building

West view

Veranda clubhouse

Restaurant entrance

Photo: Walter Mair, Christoph Reinhard

Completion Date: 2007

Architect: Smolenicky & Partner Architektur, Simon Krähenbühl, Dirk–Oliver Haid, Juan–Carlos Smolenicky–Munoz

Southwest

BSV College for Further Education

The new class building of the Viège/Visp College of Further Education achieves a transformation in terms of context and enables the linking of the neighbourhood's schools, the creation of a training campus, and the integration of the future workshops and gyms. Associated with the new building, the former school playground becomes the benchmark public space of the campus.

The new building's composition of volumes takes its cue from that of the schools in the area. The typology maker reference to that of the building with its central distribution hall, yet radicalises it into a plan featuring three strata, the central layer serving both as distributive and group-work space. The transparency of the lightweight partitions allows this space to benefit from natural light. The use of materials within the building is confined to the bare load-bearing concrete and to the aluminium combined with the coloured glass of the lightweight partitions. The materiality of the exterior confirms the volumetric character – the mirror-finish stainless steel frames of the glazing and the bare aluminium cladding applied to the section cut away from the base quadrilateral. The fragmentation of the reflections created by the bevelling of the façades generates a new context.

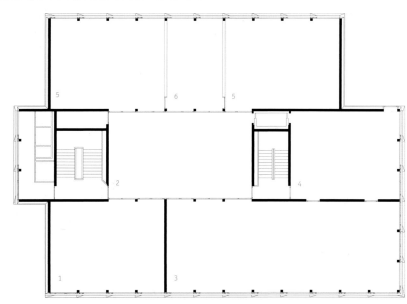

1. entrance
2. foyer
3. refectory
4. kitchen
5. classroom
6. preparatory room

East

Stairs

Foyer level 2

Photo: Hannes Henz

Completion Date: 2009

Architect: Bonnard Woeffray Architectes

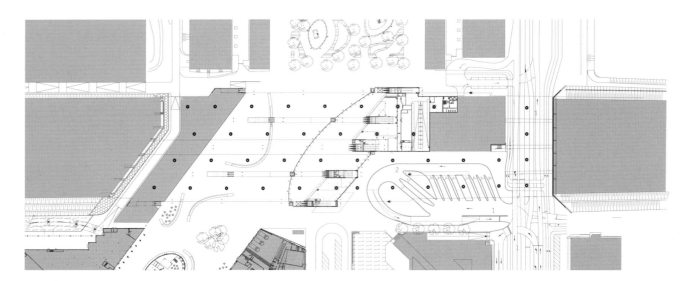

Station Amsterdam Bijlmer ArenA

The station is designed to provide a high level of social security both during the day and at night. Long voids are cut into the platforms to break down the overshadowed sections of the 100-metre-wide area below the viaducts. These voids improve the sense of safety through visual contact and improved transparency between the platform and ground–level areas.

To avoid a dark 100-metre-long tunnel, the concrete structures were spaced apart. Each twenty-metre span was supported at each end on just one column via an integrated cantilevered saddle. Arrays of columns were then aligned on an axis with the boulevard to maximise visual connectivity from east to west. The base–element of the roof structure is a "V" shaped continuous hollow steel boom with steel arms cantilevered on either side to support all the roof glazing. The combined assembly is supported on a series of tubular "A" frames with only a single deep longitudinal stabiliser near the south end. Beyond their last supports these booms cantilever up to eighteen metres, thereby enhancing the sense of linearity and direction. The timber lined elements straddle each track–bed, and are open at ridge level to assist natural ventilation, and allow areas for pressure release in respect of 200k/h trains.

Photo: Jan Schouten

Completion Date: 2007

Architect: Grimshaw Architects

Vuykpark, Capelle a/d IJssel

For the site of the former shipyard "Vuyk" in Capelle aan den IJssel, MIII designed a restaurant. The design of MIII was inspired by the history of this site, a shipyard where craftsmanship was at a highly competitive level. Marine lining, carpentrance, and wood constructions were starting point for the design in which lopside and vigour refer at navigation (shipping).

The outside, visible construction hints at the old craftsmanship of the ship's carpenter. The idea was to envelop the building, so to speak, in a wooden coat. Characteristic of these designs is the sharp contrast between the often introvert exterior and the open and transparant interior. A smooth wooden sheet around its outline makes a connection with the carpentrance of the past. The open–front coping has several advantages above a closed one. Most prominent is the feature that the wind can freely blow alongside the wooden front parts and by doing so, dehydrate these parts in a natural way. Thus, the backside can be ventilated.

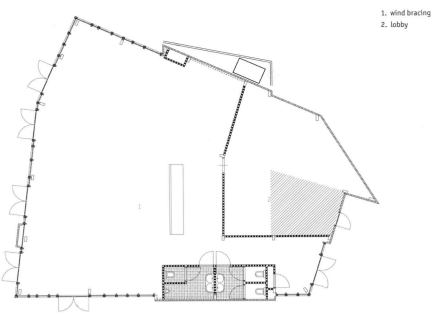

1. wind bracing
2. lobby

Photo: John Lewis Marshall

Architect: MIII architecten

Front

Booster Station–South

Booster Station–South in Amsterdam is primarily a utility building which contains a technical plant and a pumping–engine for sluicing out sewage. The hidden technology of the sewage–system of the Dutch capital emerges in the public realm as an intriguing object. The location in the public realm asks for a careful design that will appeal to the public now as well as in the future, all the more because Booster is located next to a busy traffic junction where different types of transport intersect.

The programme for the pumping–station consists of a high and a low voltage space, an overhead crane, three pumps, a bypass and an entrance. The Booster Station–South can be seen as a metaphorical reference to a streamlined engine. The clinging, aerodynamic skin forms an envelope for the building's technical programme. It also emphasises the relation between form and function the building reveals. The constant stream of passengers by car, metro, train or bicycle perceive the Booster Station as a futuristic sculpture. With its cladding of stainless steel panels, it reflects the movements, shapes and colours of the environment. At night the illuminated seams in the steal skin make the building look like a mesh model.

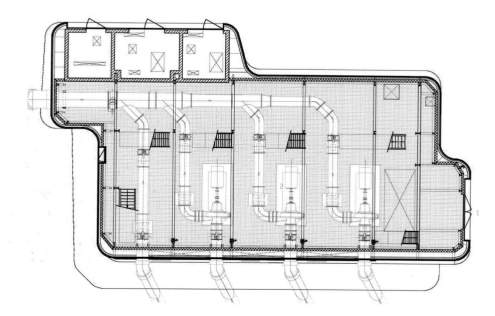

1. entrance
2. pumps
3. stairs

Interior

Detail

Photo: Digidaan

Industrial

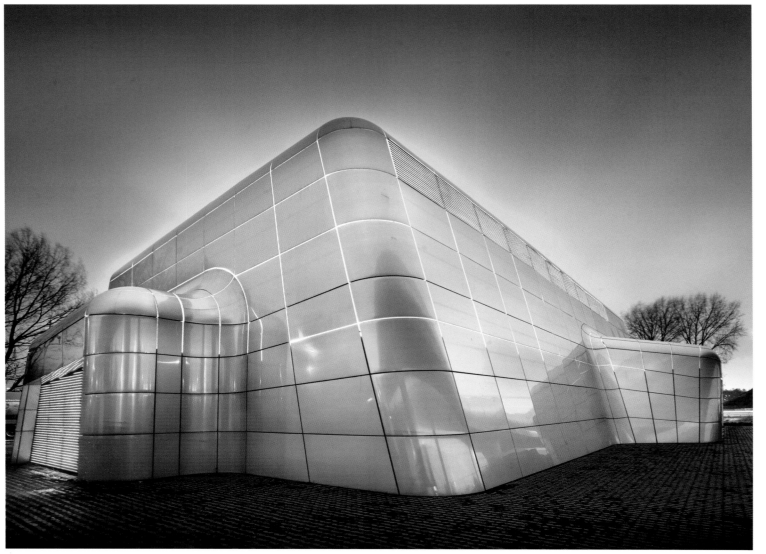

Evening side

Architect: Maarten van Bremen, Jaap van Dijk, Folkert van Hagen, Adam Visser, Jasper Hermans

Completion Date: 2006

School Piter Jelles

The building's shape metaphorically reflects the process of peeling a fruit. A transparent unity of theory and practice makes the fruit, the pupils are the seed. Like half–peeled paring spiralling around the fruit, the façade partially opens up towards its surroundings. The façade is transparent where contact with the outside world is encouraged and alternately open and closed where pupils are working independently.

As a token of appreciation and respect, pupils (and teachers) enter the building via a red carpet covering the stairs leading up to the building's main entrance.

The core of the building is home to practical subjects: mechanics and construction (ground level), kitchen and bakery (first level), electronics (second floor) and the building's technical facility room (third floor). It was a conscious decision to keep technical installations, such as pipes visible for pupils, in order to reveal the complexity of and to stimulate curiosity for the functioning of the building. Located around this core are the shops on the ground floor, with classrooms for theoretical lessons and offices above.

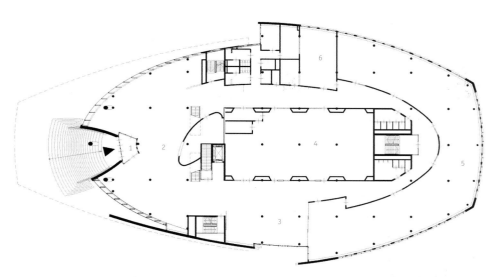

1. entrance
2. main lobby
3. restaurant
4. kitchen
5. classroom
6. administration

Photo: Bjorn Utpott

Completion Date: 2008

Architect: RAU

Exterior

Woonhuis VdB, Prinsenbeek

Located in the outskirts of the city of Breda, on the edge of the urban and rural zone, this house is provided with great views. The clients preferred a maximum volume on this plot and asked the Dutch architects Grosfeld van der Velde to turn this desire into reality. They designed a house with a square floor plan of 15 x 15 metres, stacked up over three levels. The ground floor is raised above the surrounding land so that daylight can enter the half-sunken basement. By lifting the ground floor, the view from the living area of the natural environment is astonishing.

Exterior view

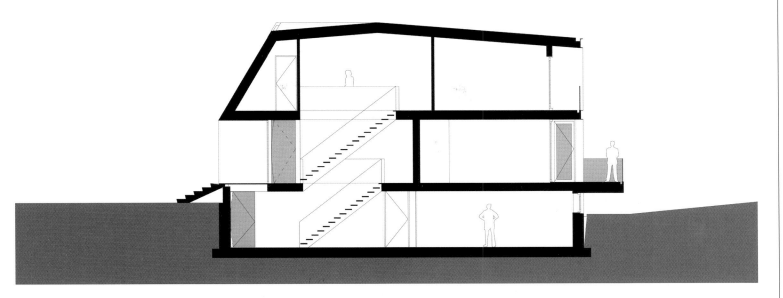

Staircase

Glass door

Living room

Garden façade, northeast

Villa BH

The villa is positioned on a rectangular plot of 35 x 50metres that is enclosed at three sides with similar plots and freestanding houses. On the back (Northeast) of the plot there's an old embankment with several tall trees. From the living programme; the kitchen, dining area and living are all orientated on this green scenery. Here the villa has a glass façade over twenty metres long.

Villa BH is inhabited by a couple of more than sixty years old. To optimise the accessibility of the house, the entire programme is situated on the ground floor around a patio. The specific form of the patio widens and narrows the interior space, making it a variety of areas. The façade of the patio is completely from glass panels, giving the villa great perspectives in its interior but also towards the context. The ceiling of the living area has an extra height in the shape of a sloped roof. The physical appearance of this area is very unique and highly qualitative.

The villa is designed as environmental friendly with extra insulated façades, roofs and floors. The roof is covered with sedum that regulates the distribution of the rainwater gently. On the flat roof are twenty solar panels for electricity. A heat pump warms the floors in the winter and cools them in the summer with natural temperature differences retrieved deep in the ground. As an extra heating there are two fireplaces for wood, one in the living and the other in the TV-room.

Entrance façade, southwest

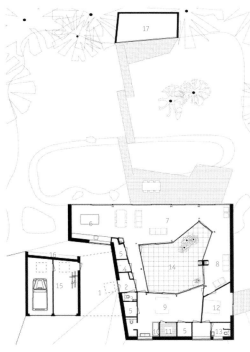

1. carport
2. entrance
3. toilet
4. installation room heat pump
5. closet
6. kitchen
7. living
8. TV room
9. main bedroom
10. bath
11. sauna
12. guestroom
13. guest bathroom
14. patio
15. garage
16. wood storage for fireplaces
17. garden house (still to be realised)

Detail

Interior of the main bedroom with the view on the patio

Photo: Sylvia Alonso

Completion Date: 2010

Architect: WHIM architecture

Exterior view by day

Merry–Go–Round

Although ideas about recreation and the design of the landscape have changed over the years, the typology of the holiday cottage has hardly altered at all. Ever since the recreational outing of several days or more came into vogue in the 1960s, we have seen the same mini–version of the standard home.

Whereas the confined space of a boat or caravan has led to clever design solutions, the country cottage has never developed an identity of its own. The design of the Merry–Go–Round gives new meaning to the holiday cottage by taking the traditional floor plan with its rooms opening onto a central hallway and turning it inside out. The rooms are replaced by eight open alcoves in which furniture, colour, light, material, lines of sight and views of the outdoor surroundings are bundled into one compact, fixed interior. The alcoves are connected by a corridor that runs all around the perimeter of the dwelling and opens onto the landscape. By adjusting the façade, which is composed of shutters, the vacationing residents of the Merry–Go–Round can determine the view and their privacy themselves.

Exterior by night

Sofas

Corridor

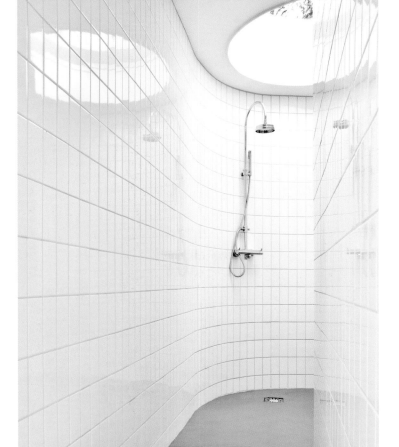

Toilet

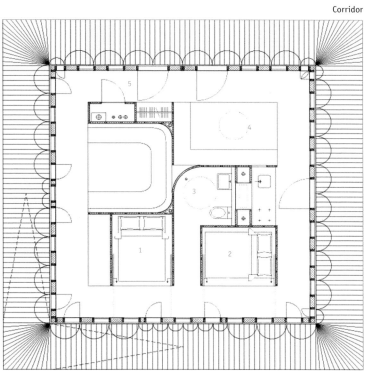

1. bedroom
2. bedroom
3. bathroom
4. living room
5. kitchen

Photo: Bureau Ira Koers

Completion Date: 2009

Architect: Bureau Ira Koers (www.irakoers.nl)

Main entrance

WWF Netherlands Head Office

RAU transformed a former 1950s agricultural laboratory into the first CO_2-neutral and (almost entirely) self-sustaining office in the Netherlands. By breaking through the rigidity of the existing structure and adding an organic blob at the centre, the rejuvenated building got a friendly and inviting appearance. Natural materials have replaced bare concrete; what used to be grey and confronting is now in harmony with the surrounding natural reserve. RAU's intervention not only give a the building a new face, but fundamentally changed the user experience. Natural ventilation and the use of natural materials offer a balanced and healthy indoor environment.

Energy and Environment
The use of renewable energy is not the only environment-friendly aspect of the building. Energy and construction materials were saved by keeping the concrete skeleton of the former laboratory. All used wood is FSC-certified. The doormat is made of old car tires, and the flooring is made from recycled carpets. All used materials are child labour free. Bats have access to an especially prepared area of the basement and birds can nest in the façade.

Flexibility and Efficient Use of Space
The building is divided into two zones. All public functions such as the reception, the call centre, a shop and meeting rooms are grouped around the central staircase in the blob. Glass walls emphasise the open atmosphere in this part of the building.

The non-public functions are accommodated in the two wings of the complex. A smaller-scale floor plan creates a more calm environment, allowing employees to focus on their work without distraction. The first floor of the complex has a flexible layout so that it can partly or entirely be let to third parties.

General view

1. entrance
2. main lobby
3. call centre
4. office space
5. restaurant
6. messenger room
7. storage and archives
8. info centre

Main stair

Stairway

Exterior

Photo: Hans Lebbe, Kusters Fotografie, RAU

Completion Date: 2006

Architect: RAU

Façade

The 4th Gymnasium

The façade has two effects that intensify the character of the building. The plinth is made of flat, coloured aluminium panels and continuously follows through into the façade of the courtyard; as a foretoken of the colour explosion in the court. The wooden façade has been developed more spatially and in depth and gives the building plasticity. This expressive modular built façade is hard to distinguish from a traditional façade because of a number of innovations, which prevents the monotonous picture of piled up units. By choosing a relative deep outside façade, it was possible to bring on relief. Under the frame, the façade withdraws twenty centimetres through which the image of two piled up arcades is created. And the seams between the modules are hidden; the wooden front parts are built from narrow planks, which are placed vertically and on small distance from each other. Through the number of artificial seams that arises, the real seams become invisible. At the plinth and the façade of the courtyard, the seams are hidden behind the rhythmically placed coloured aluminium boards of different widths. These creative solutions give the gymnasium a permanent and nevertheless dynamic charisma.

Inner court

Inner court & façade

Façade

Photo: John Lewis Marshall.com

Cultural

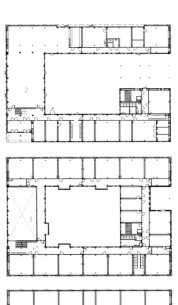

1. section A–A
2. ground floor
3. first floor
4. second floor

Auditorium

Completion Date: 2008

Architect: HVDN Architecten

General view

Het Kasteel

Its location adjacent to the railway lines necessitates a high level of sound insulation and it is this that defines the external expression of the "Kasteel". The building is enveloped in a glazed skin that stands free from the apartment block behind. In order to give the skin a tactile quality, the panels are angled slightly to each other; this artifice lends the building the appearance of a gigantic crystal.

The "Kasteel" consists of a forty-five-metre-high tower standing on a four to five-storey base. It is surrounded by water and pedestrians and cyclists access the internal courtyard via a bridge. The car parking, storage spaces and some of the ground floor dwellings' living spaces are positioned underneath the courtyard's half-open wooden deck. The dwellings vary in size: those on the ground floor include a living space just above the water level while those above contain either a balcony or a terrace. The interaction between the apartment block's recessed elevation and the glazed panels of the building's skin ensures the entrance building acts as an icon for the Science Park.

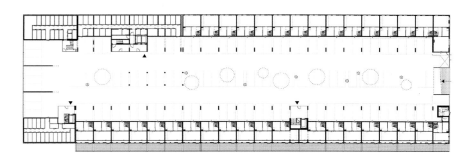

Courtyard on the roof

Details

Interior

Exterior

Photo: Luuk Kramer, John Lewis Marshall

Residential

Completion Date: 2008

Architect: HVDN Architecten

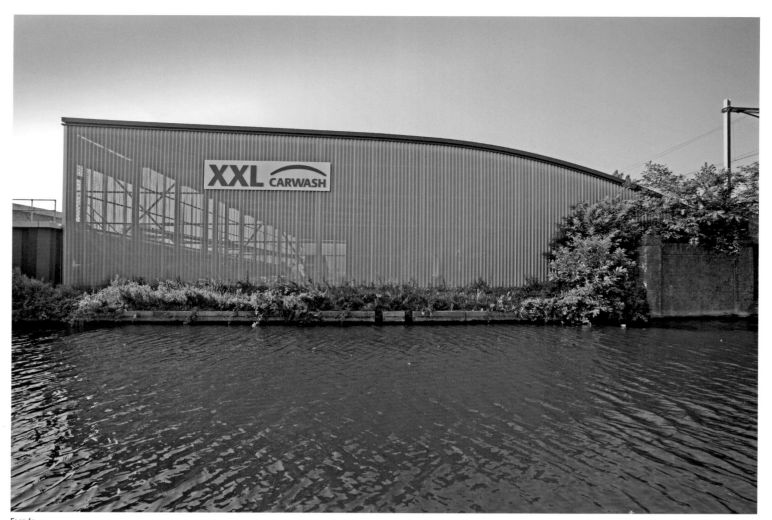

Façade

Waldorpstraat

The building is more than 165 metres in length and its total surface area of more than 5,500 square metres is divided among the ground floor and the entresols. One of the units accommodates a wholesaler in paint accessories. Another houses an innovative, environment-friendly carwash, no less than fifty metres long, in which ten cars can be washed at the same time and waiting times are short. After the wash, customers can vacuum-clean their cars at one of the 38 indoor vacuuming points. Because the carwash is bounded by a side wall of perforated steel, there is always a light, sight and climate relationship with the outside world.

With its fixed grid pattern, the building has been fully designed according to the principles of industrial, flexible and sectional building, and it is easy to extend or to add extra floor surface on the inside. Because it is partly sunken in the railway embankment, the building is equipped with a curving roof that does not disrupt the view of the engine drivers and train passengers. At the front, the building is eight metres high, and at the rear it is only four. As the train occasionally spreads sparks and dust, the roof of the building is coated with sedum vegetation, which also offers a pleasant view to the residents of the neighbouring apartment block.

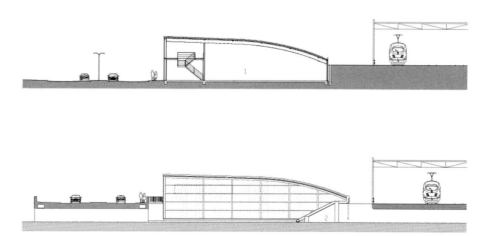

1. elevation wall
2. stairs

Main entrance

Bird's-eye view

Interior

441

Solar

Solar was initially intended as two separate buildings and later transformed into a single development in which the two halves of one building are connected by a full-height glazed atrium that facilitates all vertical and horizontal traffic movement.

The sturdy building was conceived as a rectangular concrete block in a strict grid pattern contrasted by a free-form shape of wire mesh. The grid pattern was then filled with window frames over the longitudinal direction of the building facing the adjacent square on one side and the street on the other. The image presented by the elevations on the cross direction with their brickwork infill reflects the area's nineteenth century roots. At the top, deflecting and refracting the sunlight, the wire mesh draped around the tough concrete edges and corners like a veil.

The interior remains loyal to the industrial character of both the area and the building in displaying stout metal constructions in the atrium and allowing the technique of the building to be in view in much of the office space. The harshness of it all is mediated by warm wood tones and smooth white surfaces.

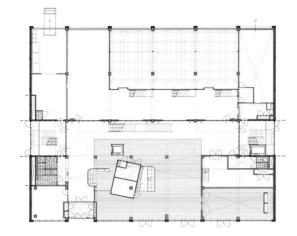

General view

Freely-shaped wire mesh

Wire mesh construction

Detail

Atrium and connection between the two buildings

Shaken Office

Yushi Uehara search form that shines soul and energy, builds with user's dynamism, the Super Functionalism with the combination of subtle differences, and pursues the concept that innovate utilitarian aspects. Obviously, the intention to this "Super Functionalism" urged to stacked-up boxes of diverse dimensions, the minimalist floor plans with single cores, with which he created the workspaces with varied dimensions. He reached even to a building system. A light-body concrete on steel plates prefabricated timber sub construction façade are sealed by a sheet of black corrugated steel plates that shield the rain frills where façade panels are screwed on finely perforated, folded steel plates that let only the half of openings open. The monolith overshadows over these sensual openings. Lightness creates large impression: that is the rhetoric.

Photo: Jim Ernst

Completion Date: 2009

Architect: Yushi Uehara

Exterior view

Agora Theatre

The Agora Theatre is an extremely colourful, determinedly upbeat place. The building is part of the masterplan for Lelystad, which aims to revitalise the pragmatic, sober town centre. The theatre responds to the ongoing mission of reviving and recovering the post–war Dutch new towns by focusing on the archetypal function of a theatre: that of creating a world of artifice and enchantment. Both inside and outside walls are faceted to reconstruct the kaleidoscopic experience of the world of the stage, where you can never be sure of what is real and what is not. In the Agora Theatre drama and performance are not restricted to the stage and to the evening, but are extended to the urban experience and to daytime.

Inside, the colourfulness of the outside increases in intensity. A handrail executed as a snaking pink ribbon cascades down the main staircase, winds itself all around the void at the centre of the large, open foyer space on the first floor and then extends up the wall towards the roof, optically changing colours all the while from violet, crimson and cherry to almost white.

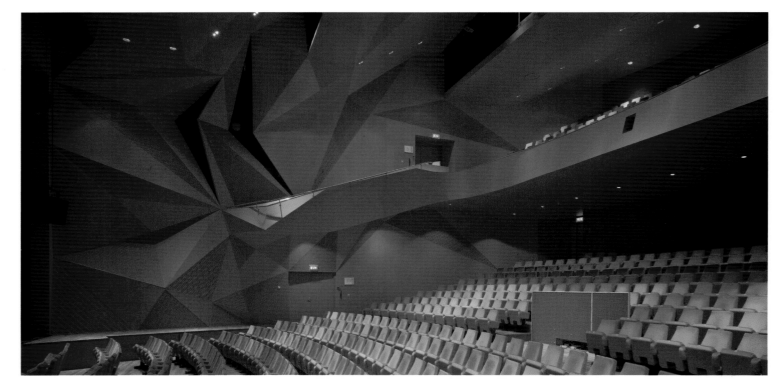

Stage main hall

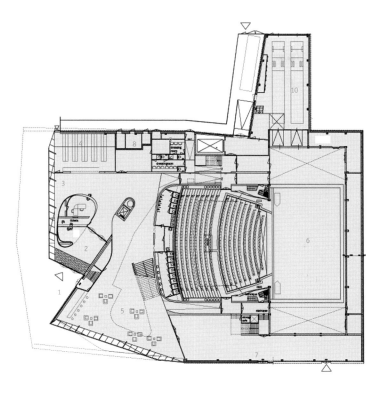

Ground floor plan
1. entrance
2. ticket desk
3. reception counter
4. cloakroom
5. foyer
6. stage main hall
7. restaurant
8. machinery
9. dressing rooms
10. loading bay

Foyer with skylight

Photo: Christian Richters

Completion Date: 2007

Architect: UNStudio, Amsterdam

Façade

General view

Betty Blue

As unambiguous as this shopping machine is lying here on its doorstep, waiting for visitors, as ambiguous it is in relation to its shape and colour, it is sometimes straight and other times round, from the one side purple and from the other side blue. In the shelter of this enormous lifted and stretched drop of water, an inner square with almost exotic conditions has been shaped. It is as if a whole life of its own has been able to develop itself inside this inner space, in which façade openings, bill boards, lampposts, wastebaskets, bicycle sheds and road markings have gone through a joint and balanced growth.

That exclusivity does not necessarily mean an extraordinary budget. In the task the designers set themselves by making something with a modular, and therefore efficient building system is specific and thus unique. Where modular systems usually result in all too predictable shapes, the designers managed, within the regime of recurring façade elements, to put up a system of façade openings with such variation that a seemingly much bigger variety of windows, shop windows and entrance doors can be made.

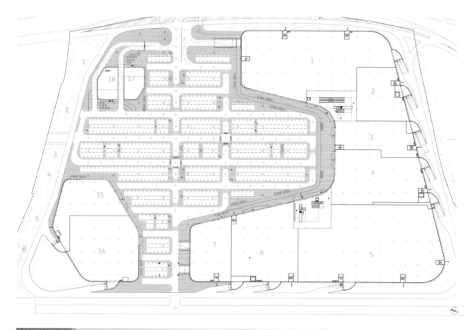

1. supermarket
2. home electronics
3. dieren
4. 5. home electronics
6. speelgoed
7. PDV
8. outdoor
9. woonwarenhuis
10. 11. 13. PDV
12. Sport
14. fitness
15. disco
16. 17. fast food

Entrance

Bird's-eye view

Night view

Interior

Completion Date: 2008

Photo: Van Pol beheer, Arjen Schmitz, Hans Pattist, Hennie Retera

Architect: NIO architecten

Exterior glass façade

The New Martini Hospital

Flexibility is currently one of the most important factors in an ever–mutating healthcare environment where rapid developments in medical technology make it difficult to predict the future. That is why it is important to design a hospital now that will last for the next forty years and can easily adapt itself to an unknown future. It is for this reason that the concepts of the IFD (Industrial Flexible Demountable) programme spearheaded the design of The New Martini Hospital in Groningen, the Netherlands.

It is always difficult to predict what functionality must be accommodated for in a hospital building with a set lifespan of forty years. For this reason the designers chose a uniform building block which, in a general sense, complies with the demands of safety, natural daylight, structure, services and floor planning. The design brief was tested on a number of important frequently occurring departments such as general nursing and outpatient clinic. A uniform building block therefore acquired a useful aspect in that it could be functionally totally interchangeable in the design phase as well as later on once the building is being used. A nursing department can be converted to an outpatient clinic or offices.

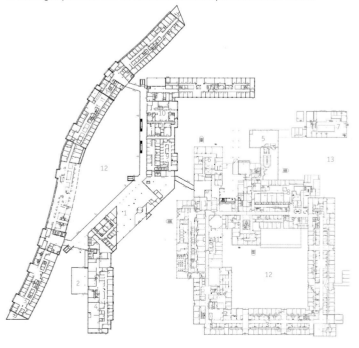

1. main entrance
2. ambulance entrance
3. outpatient clinic
4. emergency
5. personnel's restaurant
6. conference Centre
7. technical services
8. rentable floor area
9. phlebotomy
10. endoscopy
11. teaching and training
12. inner courtyard
13. delivery
14. lift core

Exterior details

Passage

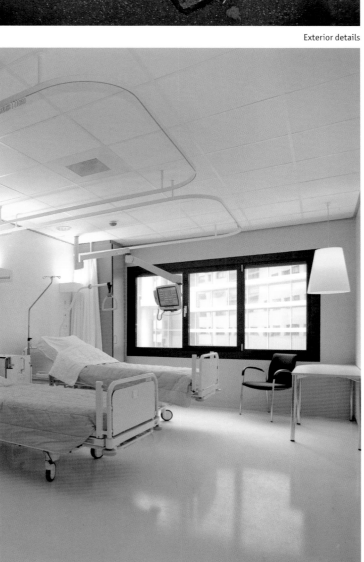

Treatment room

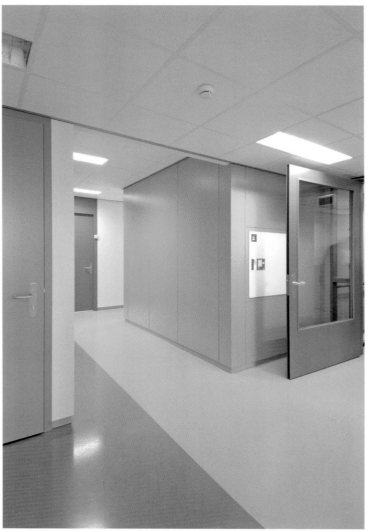

Colourful corridor

Photo: Mr. Rob Hoekstr and Mr. Derk Jan de Vries

Hospital

Architect: Mr. Burger / SEED architects (before Burger Grunstra architecten adviseurs)

Completion Date: 2007

Tea House on Bunker

The project involves the reprogramming of a historical and derelict building through renovation and addition. The original bunker is part of an intricate water management system that enabled the inundation of land situated in a classic, Dutch polder landscape.

Stables and polo fields now surround the building and the new addition is intended as a large space with facilities to support a meeting space or business retreat. The existing 1936 bunker remains intact except for a portion of the concrete roof where the new structure connects whilst the new addition is like an umbrella, an addition that could be removed and does not damage or permanently influence the historic structure. The metallic addition appears to have grown out of the still visible concrete façades of the bunker, cantilevering out towards the sports fields with its large single window. In fact the space is designed with steel structures within its two main walls which act as one-storey-high beams. These beams are balanced off centre on two columns that land directly in front of the existing bunker. Stability is achieved by using the massive concrete shell of the bunker as a counterweight.

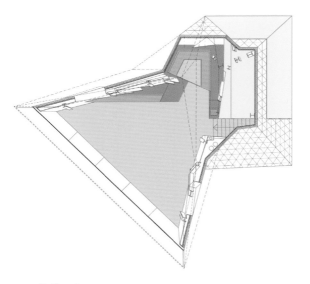

First floor plan

Photo: Christian Richters

Complex

Completion Date: 2006

Architect: UNStudio, Amsterdam

Night view

School 'tij49

Even though the time frame from conception to completion was less than six months, the client stipulated that this should not manifest itself in the building's appearance.

The proposal involves a three-storey building with a wide, double-loaded central corridor. By compartmentalising the building vertically to comply with the fire regulations, the stairwells and voids form part of this central space. The three entrances are located in the building's long elevation facing the schoolyard.

To harmonise the stacked prefabricated elements into a convincing building, the horizontal bands in the façade are strongly articulated. The cantilevered strips also function as effective sun screens and shelter for the entrances. They are finished with a sprayed rubber layer, white on the outside and with a different brightly coloured soffit per floor. The colouring corresponds with the school's internal colour scheme. By illuminating the bands at night, the building acts as a beacon in the neighbourhood.

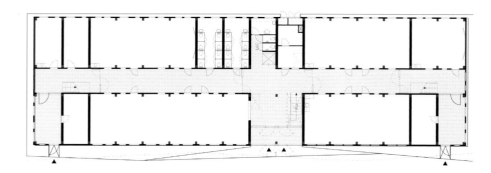

1. entrance
2. stairs
3. washing room

Wall with pattern

Details

Photo: Luuk Kramer, Jan Derwig

Completion Date: 2007

Architect: HVDN Architecten

View of the warehouse cargo unloading area

Warehouse – Refrigerators & Office Building

The issue in the architectural composition was to provide, in morphological terms, for the co–existence and unification of two main functions (office building and warehouse – preservation refrigerators) so that the structure was a uniform one. This objective was achieved by including the following morphological elements: The office building's sides were covered in Etalbond panels and passive metallic systems (blinds) because of the unsuitable orientation. The warehouse – refrigerators' sides were covered in aluminium panels and, in morphological terms, an attempt was made to include the functional areas of the warehouse, loading – unloading bay with their special requirements into the overall scheme. Metal frames in the warehouse were repeated, spaced at thirty-metre intervals, covering blank spaces and assisting in integration with the office building. The metallic decorative elements (in the form of netting) and partial covering with inclined panels demarcate the entrance area in the form of a niche.

The partition walls between offices are panels covered in plasterboard. The floors are covered in granite tiles. The suspended ceilings are made of mineral fibre tiles. All facilities including lighting and air–conditioning for the building are hidden behind the suspended ceiling.

1. warehouse cargo unloading area
2. office building facility entrance
3. main building
4. warehouse loading area

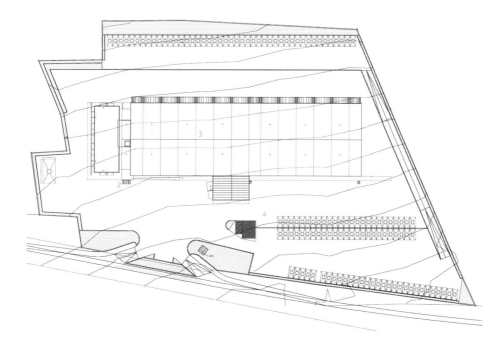

General view of the entire complex: warehouse, cold storage, and office facilities

Warehouse unloading area

View of the office building facility entrance

View of the office building facility entrance

Reception area on the ground floor of the office building facility

Photo: Psaros Vlassis

Industrial

Completion Date: 2005

Architect: Yanniotis Yannos, Yannioti Vasiliki Nilent Paul;
Civil Engineer: Karoukis Panagiotis–Polixronopoulos Kostas
Mechanical Engineer: Klissiounis Dimitris, Yanniotis Constantinos; Owner: Mevgal S.A. Construction: Terna S.A.

A view of the stairwell leading to the swimming pool from the main yard

Two Detached Holiday Residences in Paros Island

The compositional objective

Two residences to be integrated, in terms of volume and shape, into a single building but retaining their difference. In morphological terms, the composition had to refer to traditional Cycladic architecture in other words small sized one or two–floor volumes blending into the natural terrain, arrayed around courtyards, and a strong presence for the colour white.

Choices made

Uniformity in terms of volume was achieved by an intermediate semi–outdoor area which led from the parking area to a well–proportioned inner courtyard that allowed access to the residences and the pool area. The detached houses were laid out horizontally with one section extending to a second floor, and the roofs were flat in the style of local Cycladic architecture. Each was different because of the layout of the guest houses, one being located around the inner courtyard and the other just beside the pool and its grounds. All walls and ceilings were white. The floors were the same colour laid with squared–off artificial stone tiles in a light grey colour. In addition to natural light, lighting is provided with sconces or standard lamps.

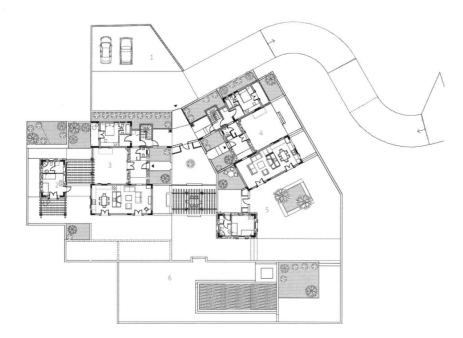

1. garage
2. gate house
3. room1 (dinner room and bedroom)
4. room2 (dinner room and bedroom)
5. garden
6. swimming pool

View of the residence from the nearby road

View of the guest house entrance and courtyard of the residence from the semihypaethral area

Living room

Architect: Yanniotis Yannos, Yanniotis & Associates; Civil Engineer: Retzepis Ioannis; Mechanical Engineer: Klissouris Dimitris, Yanniotis Constantinos; Lighting Design: Simon Simos, Lighting Design SARL Construction Firm: Structura Aete; Owner: R.E.

Completion Date: 2009

Photo: Psaros Vlassis

Residential

Bird's—eye view

Office Building in the Centre of Athens

The building is situated in the old centre of Athens on a main street. It has a total surface of 1,634 square metres on six floors with two basements for electromechanical equipment and parking area. The building makes use of all the depth of the site and the interference of two patios, and two gardens bring natural light and air to all the offices. All the façades to the patios are enclosed by glass partitions which give a visual connection between all the offices. The curtain wall of the main façade is divided in horizontal strips which recess into the building and project over the street providing a fluid border between the urban and private space. At the same time they offer a play of shadows during the day and a play of light at night.

On the ground floor the urban space penetrates into the private. Only a small part of the ground is covered for the building entrance, and the rest, the arcade, the two patios and a terrace are open to the city. Through the open patios on the ground floor, the urban space penetrates also into the building. The patios are planted with Mediterranean plants offering a garden to the city and a different value to the urban space.

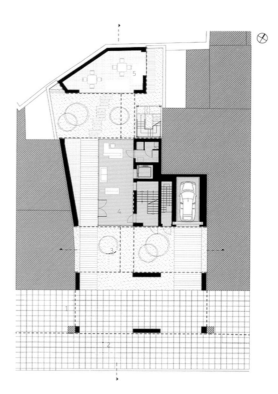

1. arcade
2. pavement
3. garden
4. entrance
5. outdoor sitting area

Main view

Details of façade

Entrance road

Entrance

Photo: Charalambos Louizidis

Completion Date: 2008

Architect: Alexandra Kalliri and Associates Architects

Dot Envelope

The existing site is listed as an industrial historical area with buildings of an old butchery complex, which included the water–tower and old butcher hall. Demand of National heritage was to rebuild the tower as it was originally and to integrate the main façade portal of old hall in front of the planned new shopping mall.

The client's permission and expected plan was prefabricated concrete hall of 46x42x7 metres. After detailed calculation the budget for covering all elevations was at 60,000 EUR. The pattern was based on different stepped elevations in order to soften basic cube shell.

The surface which could fit into the budget for the façade used of basic metal sheets which painted in bronze structured colour. After cost evaluation only 20% of the concrete shell could be covered with the metal sheets. So the sheets were perforated with holes in different sizes. Furthermore, the cut metal circles from the sheets were used and arranged on the rest of the façade surface. The new shopping mall has parking facilities and customer approach on three sides of the building. Therefore it was important to cover three sides with final decorative finishing with the budget of one side only.

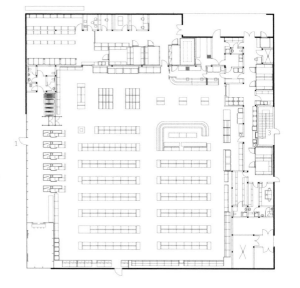
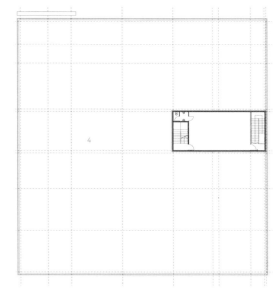

1. entrance
2. washing room
3. stairs
4. roof

Photo: Tomaž Gregoric

Completion Date: 2008

Architect: OFIS Arhitekti

650 apartments, Ljubljana

To make planning and construction simple and to allow for the use of such prefabricated elements as bathrooms, windows and façade panels, the buildings were designed in module form. Each building is divided into four identical modules, each with its own vertical communications core. There are forty-two apartments in each module, varying from small thirty-square-metre studios to 1.5–bedroom sixty-square-metre apartments on four identical floors, and larger duplex apartments from 85 to 105 square metres on the top two floors. The module is repeated four times with slight variations at the far ends of the building.

The façade is designed in two layers, the inner façade and outdoor space being formed by items such as glazed loggias, balconies, terraces and verandas. The second skin is constructed with pre–formed wooden panels, glass and metal rails. The structure of the apartments is such that each apartment gets at least one balcony and loggia that connects outdoor and indoor spaces. Like the modules, the façade layer is also repeated four times, but given the different geometry of the elements and the repetition passes virtually unnoticed.

There are two parking levels beneath the site. The landscape provides a contrast to the geometrical façade through the use of gently curving rails and other features. It breaks up the sightlines through the complex and creates a difference between public and private spaces.

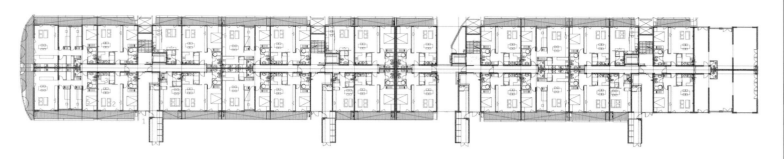

1. entrance
2. living room
3. kitchen
4. washing room
5. bedroom

Photo: Tomaž Gregoric

Architect: OFIS Arhitekti

Completion Date: 2006

Residential

Lace Apartments

The Lace Apartments are located in Nova Gorica in the west of Slovenia, on the Slovene–Italian border. Situated ninety-two metres above sea level, the town is said to be the hottest town in summer, while in winter it suffers from very strong winds. The climate, vegetation and way of life of Nova Gorica are very Mediterranean, with a strong emphasis on outdoor living, making external shady areas an important feature of the town's architecture.

The client of this project requested rich external spaces with different characters. The client was also very specific about the apartments' size and typology, which needed to be simple and repeated. Because of the fixed urban plot, the building had to be an orthogonal block of forty-eight by sixteen metres and five levels. The architects studied the external spaces of the area's existing house and proposed balconies and terraces, which can both be opened and covered with a roof or pergola, and loggias that are closed from the side and fully or partly glazed, with different type of fences – transparent with glass or metal, full or of varying heights. This second skin of terraces gives each apartment a different character and allows the buyer to choose a space that responds to his/her lifestyle.

Though the façade's colour pattern is inspired by the area's typical colour elements, such as the valley's soil and the wine and brick roof tops, the locals soon nicknamed the building "pyjamas", as it reminded them of a pattern on a man's nightwear.

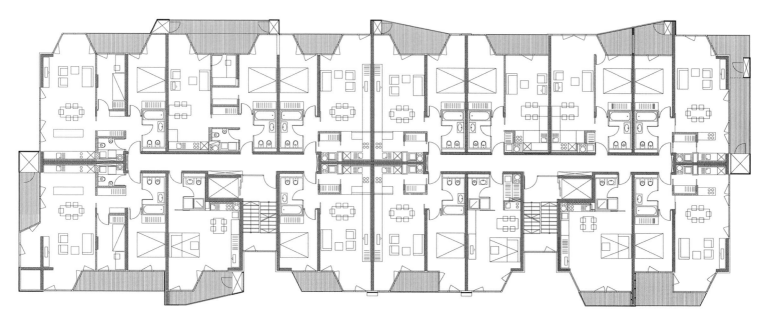

Photo: Tomaž Gregoric

Residential

Completion Date: 2008

Architect: OFIS Arhitekti

Tetris Apartments

The building stands on the edge of the "650 Apartments" development which was finished a year ago. By urban regulation the block is sixty-five metres long, in width fifteen metres and three floors high. Since the orientation of the building is towards the busy highway, the apartment opening together with balconies is shifted as thirty degrees window–wings towards the quieter and south orientated side. Long after the elevations were planned, many people associated them to Tetris game, and so the building got its name.

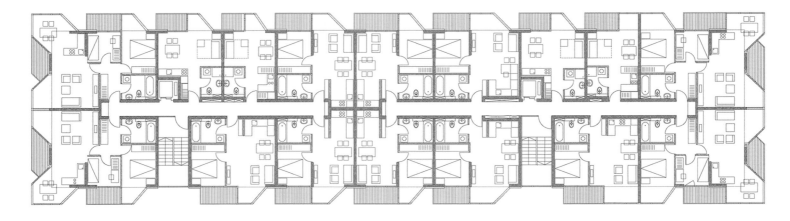

Photo: Tomaž Gregoric

Residential

Completion Date: 2007

Architect: OFIS Arhitekti

Hayrack Apartments

The site is the edge of Alpine town Cerklje (near the Ljubljana Airport) with beautiful views to surrounding fields and mountains. On the site there is a beautifully protected 300 year old lime-tree. The plan of the building therefore is L-shaped and embraces a green area around the tree. And mountain views are opening from this courtyard, therefore most of apartments have beautiful views.

The landscape and villages in the area remained unspoiled with many examples of traditional architecture such as old farms, barns and hayracks. The concept of the façade is taken from the hayrack system, wooden beams follow traditional details and patterns. Traditionally farmers store grass and corn on beams, and on the housing one can store flowers or other balcony decoration.

The balcony layer runs all around the block. The wooden ornamental construction elements in front of the balconies and loggias are designed in the same sense as traditional hayracks, wooden objects in function of storing and drying the grass. They provide first entrance temperature zone to the main living and sleeping areas and also create shading for the balconies. Additional aluminum shading panels are placed on the outer sides of the winter loggias and balconies. The service and communication spaces are reduced to minimum thus the daylight is provided on the shafts. The monthly basic energetic and service costs are very low, so they are also economic for the habitants since the apartments are social type.

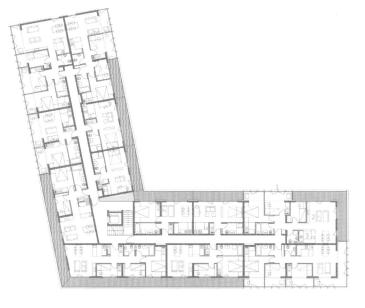

1. entrance
2. living room
3. kitchen

Photo: Tomaž Gregoric

Completion Date: 2007

Architect: OFIS Arhitekti

Social Housing on the Coast

This project located on the Adriatic coast in the south-western tip of Slovenia is the winner of a competition organised by the Slovenia Housing Fund, a government-run programme which provides low-cost apartments for young families. The winning points of this project were economic, rational and functional issues, but more importantly, the ratio between gross versus saleable surface area and the flexibility of floor plans.

The residential blocks are built on a hill with a view of Izola Bay on the one side and the surrounding hills on the other. Each block sits on a sixty by twenty-eight metres plot. The brief required thirty apartments of different sizes and structures, ranging from studio flats to three-bedroom apartments. There are no structural elements inside the small apartments in order to provide plenty of flexibility and the possibility of reorganising the space.

Considering the Mediterranean climate, each apartment has a veranda, partly connected to the interior, which provides an outdoor space for the tenants as well as shading and natural ventilation inside thanks to perforated side panels, which allow the summer breeze to ventilate the space. Semi-transparent textile shades block direct sunlight and help accumulate an "air buffer" zone. In the summer the hot air is naturally ventilated through the ten-centimetre holes in the side panels, while in the winter the warm air provides additional heating for the apartments.

Photo: Tomaž Gregoric

Residential

Completion Date: 2006

Architect: OFIS Arhitekti

Shopping Roof Apartments

The initial task from the client was to build a new shopping mall on the plot of the existing one. Furthermore, the new project proposed use of the shopping roof for additional volume as new apartments.

The stepped volume of the building follows the silhouette of surrounding landscape. On top of the shopping mall apartments are set in the form of stepped L–volume. From the west where strong wind and snow arrives, the façade is opened only towards enclosed balconies and its material is grey slate–it is designed as a vertical roof. L–shape volume encloses inner communal garden that is the roof of the shopping mall. The front and courtyard façade is warm and open, made of wooden verticals with different rhythm.

The organisation of the housing and the envelope of the apartments open towards mountain views and the sun. Therefore the front, wooden façade is mostly transparent with panoramic windows. From side windows views also open to the mountains. Local larch is used and slates in diagonal pattern are traditional materials used for roof and façade. Play of transparency formed by wooden verticals that form balcony fences, façade panels or mask characterizes the north and south part of the building. On the east and west, pitched rhomboid–textured roof interpolates into vertical surfaces that protect apartments from snow and wind. Shopping mall façade is combination of steel and glass panels.

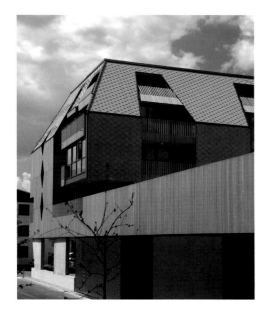

Photo: Tomaž Gregorič

Commercial

Architect: OFIS Arhitekti

Completion Date: 2007

Office, Store & Shop Concrete Container

The building dimensions are 35 x 22.5metres and 11.5metres in height. Furthermore, contract included executive Construction Company for entire industrial zone with their system of prefabricated concrete system with ready–made openings on each elevation.

The project task was to merge a programme inside the given volume and redefine the existing elevations. The existing sections had to remain the same. A client's company produce and merchandise safety equipment and devices which had to be stored in the 2/3 of the volume.

The elevation cuts break the functional façade grid and reinstate flowing concrete elements in between translucent screens. Offices are made up with transparent double–glazed façade, storage spaces with semi–translucent polycarbonate elements, and two openings on the back are used as loading dock doors.

The roof is ready–made functional pitched system that is incorporated into façade boards in a way that the exterior seems a rectangular block.

Materials of exterior are prefabricated concrete, glass, metal and polycarbonate plates. Interior is functional, flexible and simple. Storage has industrial durable reinforced floor, and wall finishing is concrete. Offices and shop are combination of concrete and wood.

The result is façade playfulness that shines through and provides a navigation system for the zoning of the building. Intriguing chequerboard goes way beyond the usual industrial park (non)aesthetic.

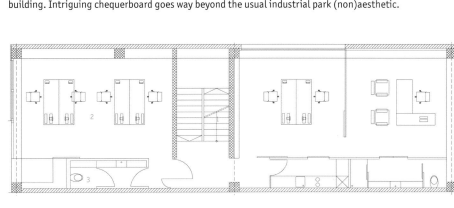

level–1
1. stairs
2. office
3. washing room

Photo: Tomaz Gregoric

Completion Date: 2009

Architect: OFIS Arhitekti

Side view

Hotel Sotelia

Wellness Hotel Sotelia fills the gap between two existing hotels, neither of them hiding their different architectural origins. The new hotel is not trying to summarise samples from nearby structures but rather clearly distances itself from the built environment and connects, instead, with its natural surroundings.

In design process primary concern was to avoid immense building mass, like the one suggested in the client's brief, which would have blocked the last remaining view of the forest. The volume is broken up into small units arranged in landscape–hugging tiers. As a result, the four–storey 150–room building appears much lower and smaller than this description would suggest.

The specific shape of the hotel was dictated by the folds in the landscape. The unique structure offers passers–by some strong spatial experiences: from the front, the building is perceived as a two–dimensional set composed of parallel planes placed one behind the other; a walk around the hotel reveals entirely different views of the timber façade, from a plane vertical wooden slats to a rhythmic arrangement of balconies and wooden terraces.

Atrium

Lobby bar

Entrance

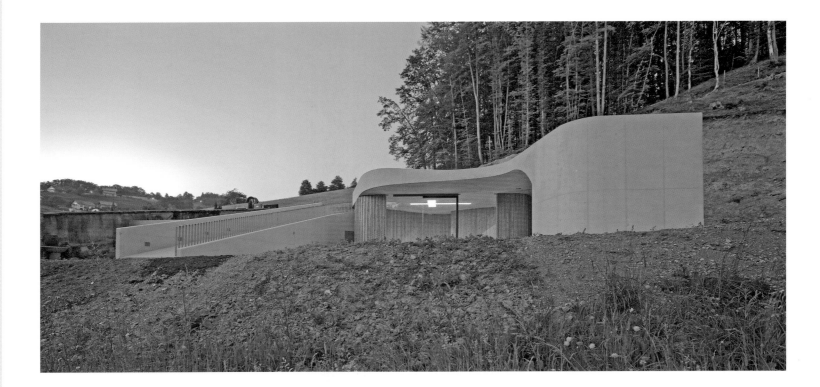

Farewell Chapel

A farewell chapel is located in a village close to Ljubljana. The site plot is next to the existing graveyard. The chapel is cut into the rising landscape. The shape is following the lines of the landscape trajectories around the graveyard. Three curved walls are embracing and dividing the programmes. External curve is dividing the surrounding hill from chapel plateau, and also reinstates the main supporting wall. Services such as storages, wardrobe restrooms and kitchenette are on the inner side along the wall. Internal curve is embracing the main farewell space. It is partly glazed and it is opening towards outside plateau for summer gatherings. Roof is following its own curvature and forming an external porch. The cross as catholic sign is featured as laying feature positioned on the rooftop above the main farewell space. It also functions as a luminous dynamic element across the space during the daytime and lighting spark at a night time.

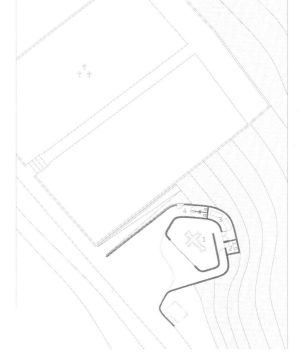

1. main space
2. kitchen
3. storage
4. washing room

Architect: OFIS Arhitekti; Project Leaders: Rok Oman, Spela Videcnik
Project Team: Andrej Gregoric, Janez Martincic, Magdalena Lacka, Katja Aljaz, Martina Lipicer

Completion Date: 2009

Photo: Tomaz Gregoric

Cultural

Universidade Agostinho Neto

Located on the outskirts of Luanda, Angola, the master plan for a 2,000-hectare campus for 17,000 students consists of a core of academic buildings with research and residential buildings to the south and north respectively. Phase I, currently under construction, includes four classroom buildings housing faculties of chemistry, mathematics, physics and computer sciences and the central library and plaza. A refectory, student union and conference centre are also included.

The guiding principle of the master plan is to create a low-maintenance sustainable urbanism. Development is concentrated on the semi-arid rolling site, leaving as much of the existing vegetation and river washes as possible untouched. The ring road is conceived as a pure circle, distorted into an ellipse to fit between the washes. Within the ellipse, which differentiates natural landscape from man-made pedestrian streets, quadrangles pinwheel from the central plaza. The orientation of the man-made grid is approximately nineteen degrees east of the north/south axis, a compromise between the ideal solar orientation and the need to be perpendicular to the prevailing southwest breezes. Landscaping within the site channels the wind to maximise natural ventilation and cooling.

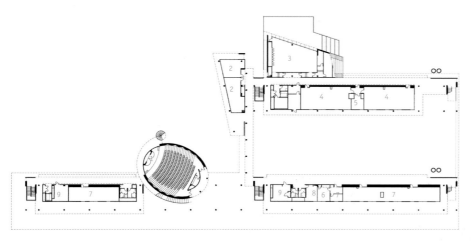

1. auditorium
2. seminar
3. assembly
4. teaching lab
5. lab support
6. department head office
7. office
8. receiving
9. mechanical

Architect: Ken Soch, Marius Ronnett

Completion Date: 2010

Photo: Provided by Architect

Educational

Main entrance, night view – a source of pride for the nation it represents

Tripoli Convention Hall

Tripoli Convention Hall signifies the spirit of its homeland and claims to establish a physical relation with the global community. As an outcome of intensive urban and architectural movement in Libya, new innovative and prestigious buildings in Tripoli started to signify the power and contemporary style.

Open to the world cultures and where diverse languages meet up, the Convention Hall is a strong element of high representation and welcomes presidents of the world in the texture of the natural environment and as a source of pride for the nation it represents. Surrounded by the woods, the rectangular two-storey "block" is nestled in a metal envelop that opens up to the external landscape with a wide portico that defines the main entrance.

A semi-transparent perimeter "shield" of designed bronze mesh application flows around the building, protecting the inner glass walls; an eight-metre corridor encircles all three sides; the main building is flanked by a four-metre-wide reflection pool and another four-metre is left as a semi-open shady circulation area. The metal mesh walls carry incise patterns that are inspired by the trees that surround the site, permitting controlled daylight to diffuse into the central space.

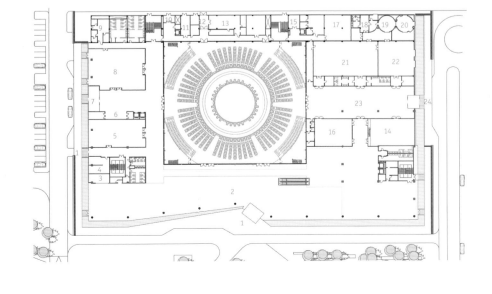

1. presidential entrance
2. main foyer
3. store
4. security office
5. minister lounge
6. front office/cloak room
7. minister entrance
8. minister lounge
9. cold storage
10. staff entrance
11. technical area
12. service entrance
13. service kitchen
14. press hall
15. cold storage
16. meeting room
17. storage
18. VIP security
19. VIP lounge
20. VIP suite
21. president lounge
22. president salon
23. VIP meeting room
24. VIP entrance

Semi–open shady circulation area

Controlled daylight to diffuse into the central space

Completion Date: 2010

Architect: Tabanlioglu Architects

Meeting room with transitivity

Elandra Beach Houses

The project is a collection of fifteen stylish beach houses set in a pristine bushland setting. The site itself is just back from the beach and has stunning views of Port Hacking and Hastings Beach. What is unique about this development is that each house has been designed as if it were a stand–alone luxury designer home. The houses were designed for a sophisticated style–conscious market, for the person who would live in a luxury contemporary apartment in the city. The idea was to provide holiday housing for the sophisticated inner city dweller.

Stage 1 consists of a type called the "cross–over house". In this house, the top floor, which contains the living areas, is oriented east/west at and the lower level bedrooms run north/south. This allows the house to sit into the slope with minimal impact on the landscape. The top floor maximises exposure to the northern sun, whilst the lower level is directed toward the beach. These houses were designed specifically with environmental issues in mind, and have been orientated to maximise passive solar design. Design for water conservation is always important — all the plumbing relies on recycled water.

Lounge

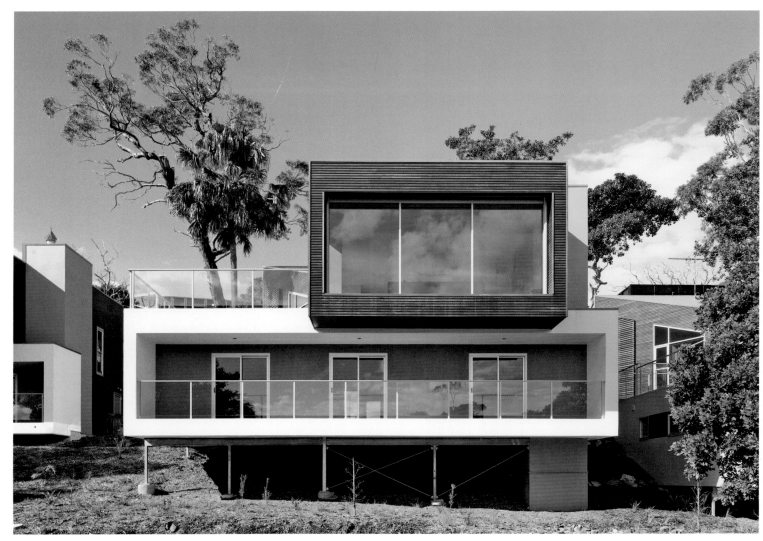

Front view

Side with trees

Front side

Interior full view

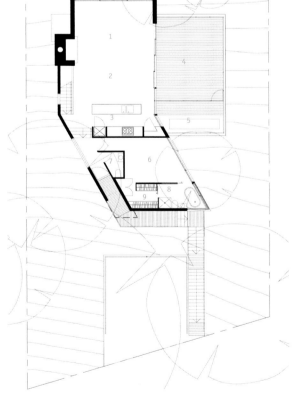

1. living
2. dining
3. kitchen
4. terrace
5. plunge pool
6. bed
7. WC
8. ensuite
9. robe

Photo: Brett Boardman

Completion Date: 2007

Architect: Tony Owen Partners

Night view

University of Queensland Rural Clinical School

The principles of functionalism and rationalism are manifested in the UQ RSC project, which in turn, reflect to the programme. Reductive detailing, robust material selection and expressive volumes pay homage to these principles. These aspirations, not often associated with medical training facilities, offer an alternative to the cold institutional paradigm of past. The building's plan form is simple and rational, largely driven by the limitation of the site and programme. Entrance into the building itself is via a centrally located, double volume, addressing the two programmes contained within the building–training and administration.

The contemporary use of materials and the large expanses of glass brought the building in line with the expectations of a modern institutional building while delivering a warm, tactile and inspirational internal volume within, in which to learn. The east and west façades are formed up, textured in natural, white concrete walls. The walls have a series of perforations which increase in density and size across the façade to emphasise the entrance. The north and south façades are clad in full–height, structurally glazed curtain wall. Winter sun is allowed to penetrate the building while allowing views to the north over the suburban district and south over the hospital grounds.

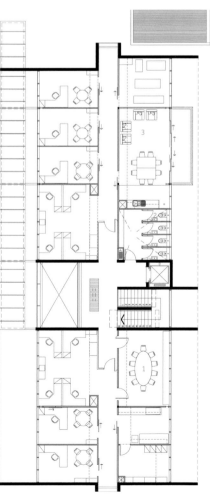

1. meeting room
2. washing room
3. lecture room

General view

Photo: Scott Burrows

Educational

Stairway

Outside of the wall

Completion Date: 2008

Architect: Arkhefield (www.arkhefield.com.au)

General view

Adelaide Central Bus Station

The Adelaide Central Bus Station is the culmination of four years of master planning and design. This new station is a quantum leap in quality from the old bus station and provides travellers with modern facilities, and sets the standard for terminal design in Australia. The design strove to provide an architectural landmark offering an immediate sense of place and orientation to the traveller, and an environment that is light, airy, welcoming with a certain sensory impact.

The bus station's distinctive Mandarin Orange palette references its location, in the environs of Adelaide's lively Chinatown. The strong colour also reinforces the pedestrian access to the terminal from Grote Street.

A series of aluminium grids make up part of the bus station façades – these create a contemporary imagery that is drawn from its transportation–based uses–bus station and car parking. These curved and folded aluminium arcs are perforated, creating visual interest and emphasising the best features of both old and new transport facilities. The curved canopies on the street frontages project out from the line of the glazing, offering a degree of protection for pedestrians and continuing the notion of the verandah. In addition to the bus station the project provides 550 car parks over five levels and thirty-nine residential units. The bus station will be home to fifteen coaches, and approximately 300,000 people per year will pass through its doors on both interstate and intrastate travel.

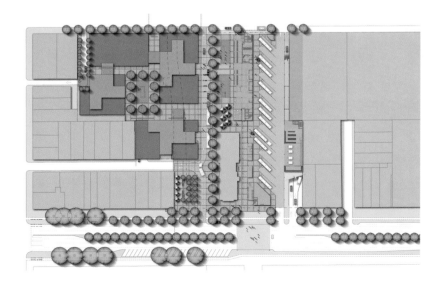

1. bus station plaza
2. west central plaza

Front view

Entrance

Reception

Photo: Drew Lenman

Completion Date: 2007

Architect: Woodhead + Denton Corker Marshall

Entrance area

Southern Cross Station

The commission for the redevelopment of Melbourne's Southern Cross Station (previously known as Spencer Street Station) arose out of the need for an upgraded terminus to accommodate the anticipated rise in demand for public rail services in the future. The brief required a fully-integrated transport interchange, which would also provide essential public transport upgrades as well as pedestrian connections between Melbourne's Central Business District (CBD) and the developing Docklands area. This increased connectivity would encourage regeneration and improve commercial growth locally.

While the design approach endeavoured to create a visually inspiring structure, the key generators for the station were always practical performance, ease of passenger circulation and an improved working environment for staff. The newly refurbished Southern Cross Station provides fifteen million users per annum with fully sheltered, high-quality ticketing, baggage-handling, waiting and retail services, all equipped with comfortable seating, lighting and passenger information display systems. Internally it is a vast hall, with uninterrupted vistas in every direction so that the interconnection of different streets surrounding the station can be easily understood. Pods of accommodation beneath the roof, house administrative functions as well as providing a defined retail space below. By their nature, stations must work across many different levels to enable passengers to access the various train lines. At Southern Cross Station, the ground plane itself changes, with Bourke and Collins Street rising in parallel to either side of the building. The concourses rise in response to the street plan so that level change with the station is almost imperceptible.

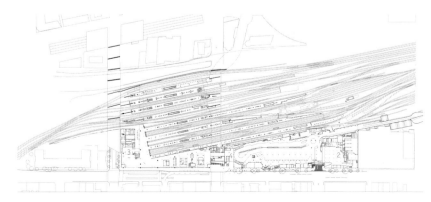

1. terminal areas
2. control centre
3. lounge area
4. activity space

Aerial view

Escalator

Photo: Shannon McGrath

Completion Date: 2006

Architect: Grimshaw Architects

View of main lodge

Southern Ocean Lodge

Southern Ocean Lodge, perched on a forty–metre–high cliff with panoramic views over the wild Southern Ocean. The Lodge houses twenty-one spacious guest suites and restaurant/bar/lounge, primarily for international visitors seeking a unique Australian experience.

The architecture has a close relationship with the dramatic site. The Main Lodge is tucked back into the cliff top, with large sweeping window walls capturing the expansive views of the ocean, rugged coastal cliffs and pristine bush. A strong sculptural element is the 100–metre–long curving Kangaroo Island Limestone wall, which weaves from a covered entrance, through the largely untouched bush and into the Main Lodge/restaurant. It provides a textured backdrop for the refined details of the guest areas with recesses accommodating desks, seating and reception facilities for guests and staff.

Guest suites cascade down the slope from the Main Lodge, with access from a breezeway ramp. Roofs follow the slope of the land, but with a gentle upward, wave–like curve every fourth suite. The curves define the rainwater collection system with gutters extending out to galvanised iron rainwater tanks. Such tanks are ubiquitous iconic structures in dry rural Australia, and here they emphasise the sustainability principles of the project, with all rainwater collected for use within the Lodge.

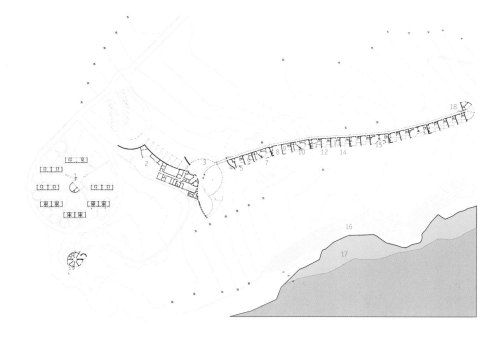

1. staff village
2. service yard
3. reception
4. guests office
5. disabled
6. departure lounge
7. family suite
8. deluxe
9. standard
10. family suite
11. deluxe
12. standard
13. standard
14. standard
15. premium suite
16. rocky cliffs
17. beach
18. sub premium
19. spa retreat

View of main lodge and suites stepping down the slope

Entrance to the Lodge

The Great Room

Little Creatures Brewery

Little Creatures Brewery is a production brewery and multi–facetted hospitality venue located alongside the picturesque Fishing Boat Harbour in Fremantle Western Australia. In 2008 Little Creatures commenced a significant expansion and now occupies five different interlinked buildings comprising a mixture of nealy built and substantially converted existing buildings.

The completed facility now boasts a large purpose–made brewery operating twenty-four hours a day, six different bars, outdoor harbourside dining, a Bocce court, live music venues and even a gallery. The total capacity allows for up to 1,200 patrons interspersed around the brewing and fermenting tanks of a busy working industrial space.

The architectural expression consistently reflects the industrial nature of the brewing environment. All brewery processes, from the grain delivery to the chilled serving tanks in the main bar take precedent in planning and functionality and remain open, visible and accessible. The hospitality and associated services have all literally been fitted around the available remaining space.

The architecture makes few concessions to decorative interior spaces normally associated with hospitality venues. The customers are actually immersed in an active working industrial environment, which is reflected in the built form, the open kitchen, hard–edge finishes and furniture.

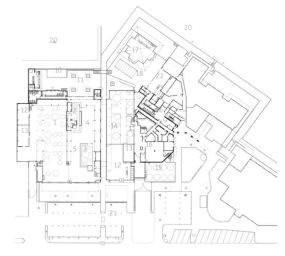

1. storage tanks
2. main kitchen
3. beer serving tanks
4. restaurant
5. bar
6. front verandah
7. male WC's
8. female WC's
9. courtyard kitchen
10. bocce court
11. rear courtyard
12. retail bar
13. boiler
14. brewhouse
15. storage tanks
16. services
17. deck bar
18. rear deck
19. boardwalk
20. harbour
21. carpark
22. burger kitchen
23. mezzanine
24. brewhouse mezzanine
25. music room
26. loft
27. deck
28. verandah

Front elevation

Overview of the exterior

Photo: Jody D'Arcy

Brewhouse bar

Sofas in the brewhouse

Completion Date: 2009

Architect: Paul Burnham Architect Pty Ltd

Anglesea House

The Northern addition replaces an old timber deck that previously divided the two storeys and radically reduced sunlight to the living area on the lower level, making the space beneath damp, dark and disconnected from the rest of the house. The trafficable roof of this addition is now extruded down to the earth, creating a three-metre-thick deck and grounding the entire house to the site, while extending the top floor living spaces out into the treetops.

The glazing to the new northern box addition has been located in such a way as to allow winter sun to penetrate deep within its interior, warming the concrete slab provided for thermal mass and block out the high summer sun. Besides, carefully located, timber boxes appear on the southern and eastern edges of the existing structure. The former is a glass roofed & walled shower. Its transparent material, pushing the privacy boundary to create a shower experience immersed in gum trees and sky – something that cannot be easily achieved in the city – reminds the user of the natural beauty of their coastal environment. To the eastern side of the house, other newly introduced structures nestle under the existing carport providing much needed external storage space and a children's bunk retreat.

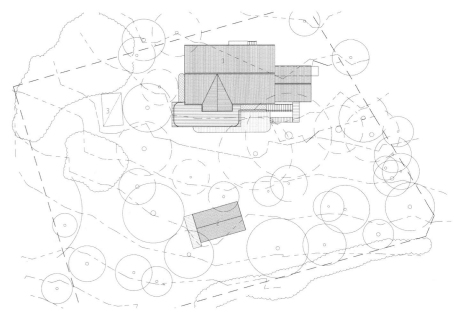

1. Existing house
2. Boat Shed
3. Trampoline

Photo: Peter Bennetts

Residential

Completion Date: 2009

Architect: AMA Team, Andrew Maynard, Mark Austin, Matthew McClurg

Open room

Essex Street House

It is a residential alteration and extension to an existing double-fronted weatherboard house. The brief required two bathrooms, a bedroom, living area, kitchen and increased connection with outside areas.

The context is typical of inner suburban Melbourne. The site is double-fronted with a deeper than usual block running east-west. The initial brief asked for an extension along the full width of the existing house. The response to the brief was that any addition should run along a southern boundary to maximise solar access to new and existing spaces and to bring external space into the middle of the living areas.

The original house has been restored to its simple four-room square plan. The new structure sits lightly beside it like a loyal companion. Rather than build a hard-edged or strongly defined object, the new structure has a blurred or vague edge. The recycled grey iron bark portal frames are of a larger, non-domestic scale. They were envisaged as an old relic of a pre-industrial age, an old, wise element to a new and vibrant addition. Within the robust portals is the delicate layered box. The use of screening and the glazed garage doors creates a soft edge that allows the internal spaces to spill into the outdoor spaces. Within this structure are the small, colourful boxes of the bedroom and kitchen. These objects separate functions and act as a bridge between the original house and the extension.

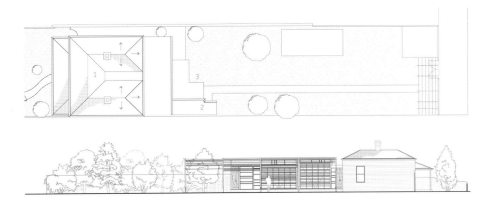

1. custom orb roofing
2. clear polycarbonate roof sheeting
3. bathroom & laundry & WC

Bathroom

Outside view

Photo: External photography by Peter Bennetts
Internal photography by Dan Mahon

Residential

Completion Date: 2006

Architect: Andrew Maynard Architects

Interior

Front exterior

Beresford Hotel

Thomas Jacobsen, has had a hand in crafting every aspect of the heritage hotel's transformation: from the new architecture's sweeping curves finished in bespoke green Spanish tiles to the sculpted olive oil vessels in the 130-seat bistro.

Phase one of The Beresford hotel, now completed, is the ground floor public bar wrapped in tile and Tasmanian oak, the bluestone-clad bistro and a spacious garden where films can be projected under the stars. Upstairs is a 1,000-square-metre ballroom, a live music venue and function room that will open soon. Glamorous balconies lined with custom-made stainless steel tiles and faced with rusted steel panels lend the new external elements a tough elegance.

Little expense has been spared on this beautifully-finished project which Jacobsen calls "New Deco" for the way it takes traditional values and craftsmanship and give them a funky twist that is undoubtedly of our time. Even the hidden elements to the design have integrity. In the front bar, for instance, the lighting concealed behind new polished stucco deco cornices is neon rather than the usual fluoro to ensure just the right light colour tone. There are sixty individual pieces of neon subtly intalled into the back bar alone.

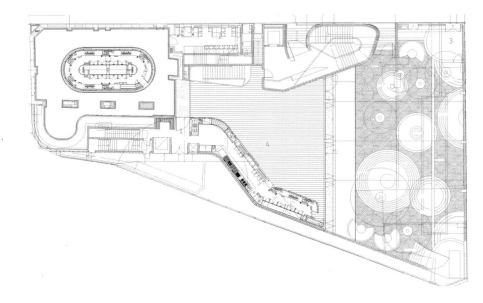

1. staff access
2. gaming
3. fire service
4. kitchen

External with courtyard

Exterior at night

Restaurant

Photo: Ross Honeysett

Completion Date: 2008

Architect: Thomas Jacobsen

The Village at Yeronga

The Village at Yeronga is the master planned and integrated retirement village development located in the inner city Brisbane suburb of Yeronga on a 28,000-square-metre site previously occupied for light industrial building use. The first two stages of the village have now been completed comprising 91 independent living apartments and associated community facilities. On completion of all stages this medium density project will house 240 independent living apartments, 60 assisted living apartments and a 110-bed full aged care nursing home facility. This integrated retirement project is designed to respond to the Australian Government's "Ageing in Place" policy which encourages developments to cater for all three levels of care (i.e. independent, assisted and aged care) within the one facility.

The buildings were constructed predominantly in precast concrete which was chosen for its long-term low maintenance properties. The building uses different panel colours to assist the elderly residents to find their way within the project, such as the strong ochre colour which is used to accentuate the building entrance points.

The feature of the building is undoubtedly the resort-style communal facilities provided within the development. These facilities include a fully-equipped commercial kitchen and restaurant for residents and their visitors, cinema, club lounge and bar, library, lobby lounge and café, indoor swimming pool, gymnasium, beauty salon and wellness centre, billiards room, medical centre and administration. These facilities also assist the residents in building valuable social networks within the retirement village community.

Entrance of the village

Panorama of the village

Buildings

Interior details

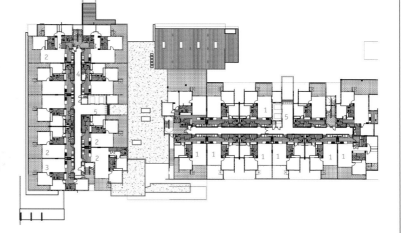

1. bedroom
2. bedroom
3. bedroom
4. corridor
5. lobby

Lobby

Photo: Scott Burrows (Aperture Photography)

Residential

Completion Date: 2009

Architect: Arkhefield (www.arkhefield.com.au)

Berry Sports and Recreation Hall

Set on sixty hectares of rolling countryside in Berry, three hours' ride south of Sydney in Australia, the site was originally an experimental dairy farm and has made way for a magical and innovative multipurpose hall for basketball, netball, rock climbing, dance and theatre.

Reminiscent of a modern farm shed, the building comprises two long sides of precast concrete panels, each pierced by 500 shards of glass in amoeba–like windows, allowing natural light to flood the halls in the day and interior lights to shine through at night, illuminating the building and making it "disappear" into the night sky.

The building also features environmentally sustainable design (ESD), with a dozen wind turbines combining with panels of louvers to create a natural ventilation system which cools the structure in summer and creates an insulation blanket in winter. Roof water is tracked back from the 3.5-metre cantilevered composite roof via a steel beam to provide water for irrigation tanks.

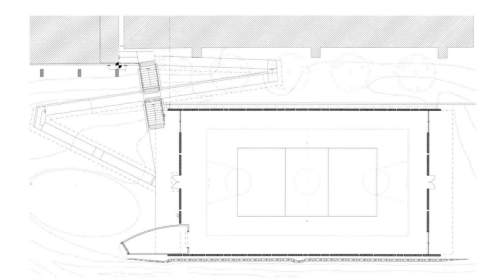

Photo: Nic Bailey

Completion Date: 2008

Architect: Allen Jack & Cottier